NURTURING YOUR AUTISTIC YOUNG PERSON

A Parent's Handbook to Supporting Newly Diagnosed Teens and Pre-Teens

Cathy Wassell

Foreword by Emily Burke
Illustrated by Eliza Fricker

Jessica Kingsley Publishers
London and Philadelphia

First published in Great Britain in 2023 by Jessica Kingsley Publishers
An imprint of Hodder & Stoughton Ltd
An Hachette UK Company

6

A CIP catalogue record for this title is available from the
British Library and the Library of Congress

ISBN 978 1 83997 111 2
eISBN 978 1 83997 112 9

Printed and bound in Great Britain by Clays Ltd

Jessica Kingsley Publishers' policy is to use papers that are natural,
renewable and recyclable products and made from wood grown in sus-
tainable forests. The logging and manufacturing processes are expected to
conform to the environmental regulations of the country of origin.

Jessica Kingsley Publishers
Carmelite House
50 Victoria Embankment
London EC4Y 0DZ

www.jkp.com

Contents

PART 3: DIAGNOSIS AND BEYOND

Foreword

Nurturing Your Autistic Young Person is a book which is very much needed. In some ways, I suppose, the reason that this book exists is because people like me need it to.

Let me introduce myself. My name is Emily. I'm 20 years old, and a trustee of the Autistic Girls Network. When Cathy, the CEO, reached out to me to invite me to be a trustee, I didn't hesitate. I recognised in myself Cathy's passion and determination to improve awareness, mental health, and education for autistic girls, so I jumped at the opportunity to join the charity.

You see, my journey up until now hasn't been an easy one.

I discovered that I was autistic when I was 16. Unfortunately, the road to diagnosis wasn't easy. Although my younger childhood years passed by fairly smoothly, when I reached 13, something inside of me broke. The death of my grandad, the difficult school environment, and the pressure of keeping up the pretence (aka, 'autistic masking') got too much. I began to experience debilitating panic attacks, which stopped me from going to lessons, socialising with my friends, and enjoying my life. Suddenly all the issues I had been hiding for years seemed to be on display for everyone to see.

The years that followed were hard. My panic attacks developed into an anxiety disorder, then OCD, before finally difficulties with self-harm and depression consumed me. I couldn't understand why I found everything so much harder than other people my age, and why I felt so different. I decided that the world wasn't made for me, so I attempted to end my life aged 16 and was admitted to an adolescent psychiatric unit. When I asked to leave, I was sectioned under the Mental Health Act.

The number of professionals I saw during this time was countless, and the number that picked up on my autism was zero. I don't blame them. I blame the lack of education, awareness, and understanding of autism. But the memory of my doctor on the unit saying to me 'I don't think you're autistic, I think you just have high social anxiety' is a memory now hard-wired into my brain, and one which drives me to want to make a difference for others. I was having obvious autistic meltdowns daily on the unit, and because I was so distressed, my autistic masking was poor, yet it still wasn't recognised. It was almost like professionals looked at me, saw I had friends, liked socialising, got good grades, and was chatty, and decided that I couldn't possibly be autistic.

I wish that they had been able to recognise what a distressed autistic person looked like, instead of labelling me with a personality disorder and telling me that my meltdowns were just me being hysterical. I wish that they had been able to understand why I was so distressed, instead of just looking at the behaviour that they could see. I wish that they had been able to see past the stereotypes surrounding autism, and considered for a moment that I could be autistic.

When I eventually got my diagnosis six months after I left the unit, the relief I felt was indescribable. Everything started to make sense. But I was also angry at the system which had allowed me to reach rock bottom without helping me. I felt let down. I began to understand that if it wasn't for me being autistic, and if it wasn't for the fact nobody around me had recognised that and implemented the support I needed, that I wouldn't have found myself detained on the psychiatric ward, and I wouldn't have had to go through the traumatic experiences that I did. And that made me feel both angry and deeply sad.

Unfortunately, I am not alone in my experiences. So many autistic people go unrecognised and unsupported and end up with severe mental health problems. So many are not given support which they are able to engage with, because their needs aren't met. So many are retraumatised by encounters with professionals and their experiences within the mental health system. Even for those diagnosed earlier, there is the risk of being made to feel like an outcast because of the diagnosis, or of being forced into traumatising therapies like applied behavioural analysis.

This is why we desperately need change, and soon. Because autistic children deserve to grow up feeling included, supported, and secure in their autistic identity.

When I began to feel that, everything changed for me. I began to see that I had a future. I was given the opportunity to learn about myself, understand my brain, and start to make adaptations to my life which made it easier to navigate.

I needed a healthy way to direct my anger at my experiences into something useful. So, I joined my local CAMHS young people's council, to be able to have influence in shaping services. I then stood for election as a public governor for my NHS mental health and learning disability trust. I am now in my fourth year as governor. I started university to study mental health nursing, and I qualify later this year. I became a trustee for the Autistic Girls Network, of course. I started to write blogs, give talks, and work alongside organisations to create change.

Autistic Girls Network is part of the change we need to see. Cathy's book is also part of that change. If every parent and every professional could read this book, autism understanding would come a long way. And this is so important, because at the heart of this are young autistic people all over the world who are continually being failed by the people who are meant to protect them. And that has to change.

Emily Burke
www.authenticallyemily.uk
www.instagram.com/itsemilykaty
www.twitter.com/ItsEmilyKaty

Introduction

This book is for parents of older children and young people who may be autistic, or have just been diagnosed, or who are struggling with their autistic identity. It won't tell you everything you need to know, because your child is totally unique, and their strengths and challenges are not the same as another child's strengths and challenges. But it will help you and your child to navigate the difficult journey to diagnosis, support, and finding a place in society. I've been through it myself, with two autistic teens, but again, my experiences will not be exactly the same as yours as both of my children are unique too, and in fact as different from each other as they could possibly be. But we all have enough in common to take this journey together, and to weather the often bumpy ride over the more pathologised model of autism.

We have been through quite a few diagnoses in our household in the last few years, but the first was autism, during a very difficult time. The effects of that time have essentially changed the trajectory of my life, and are the reason I turned Autistic Girls Network into a registered charity which supports and campaigns for autistic girls and their families, and for earlier diagnosis of internalised presentations of autism which are harder to spot and less likely to be diagnosed. In early 2020 I took over the running of what was then the FIGS group (Fighting Inequality for Girls on the Spectrum) from a lovely lady who had experienced great difficulty in getting her daughter diagnosed and supported. We grew rapidly, changed our name, and decided that becoming a charity was the best way to continue our campaigning work as well as supporting families and autistic girls themselves. We are just getting started on our journey as a new charity but hope that the girls' groups we are launching will be the first of many around the UK. For lots of autistic young people, especially those diagnosed later, finding others who experience the world the same way is vital in healing the trauma they've been through as an unrecognised autistic in a world that's arranged around the needs and wants of those who aren't autistic. That's why groups will be our first funding ask – as many as we can in areas where there isn't already a good group. Many of the families in our Facebook group have similarly difficult histories, and many have spent years trying to get recognition that their child is autistic. If this is you, you're not alone.

Our knowledge of autism is based on stereotypes and now hopelessly outdated judgements which show us that the 'classic' autistic person is a young, white male who likes trains, a la Sheldon Cooper from *The Big Bang Theory*. While I have an undeniable soft spot for Sheldon, getting stuck in such a narrow definition of autism created by middle-aged white men 60 years ago has not helped us. What it has meant is that the whole diagnostic system has grown up around this stereotype, and consequently those who don't fit it – such as many girls, non-binary or Black and Brown people – get missed. When the diagnostic criteria are stacked against you, it's hard to get a diagnosis. Four times as many boys are diagnosed. Four times as many boys as girls used to feature in research on autism. And so it goes round in a circle. But things are changing. More professionals are aware of this gap and are trying to close it.

Greta Thunberg, probably the most famous autistic person on the planet, believes that her autism helps her look at the world and see what others cannot, or perhaps will not, see. 'To get out of this climate crisis, we need a different mindset from the one that got us into it.' Thunberg is equally forthright about the unhappiness she experienced as a child. 'For many years, people – especially children – were very mean to me. I was never invited to parties or celebrations. I was always left out. I spent most of my time socialising with my family – and my dogs.'[1]

Difference does not mean deficit. The world is becoming more aware, but not always – yet – more understanding. As an ally to your autistic child or young person and the autistic adult they will soon become, you can spread understanding to your friends and family, to their school. You can make your child's world an easier place for them to navigate, and one more accommodating to autistic people.

---

[1]   McKie, R. (2020) 'Greta Thunberg: "Only people like me dare ask tough questions on climate"'. *The Guardian*, 11 October. Accessed on 30 May 2022 at www.theguardian.com/environment/2020/oct/11/greta-thunberg-people-like-me-ask-difficult-climate-questions

Late Diagnosis

If you're reading this because your child has acquired or looks likely to acquire a late diagnosis of autism, you're likely to follow quite a different pathway to families whose children are recognised as autistic when they are in their early years. I'm using the term recognise quite deliberately there – the word diagnosis implies illness and autism is not an illness. When autism is recognised early, it would be an exaggeration to say that a well-oiled machine slips into place, but there is a process of support depending on the needs of the child. For example, speech and language therapy or some kind of play therapy might start, and if in school, there might be an education plan drawn up (whatever that looks like in your area). Those children who are recognised at an early age tend to have more obviously autistic traits, hence the recognition.

But many in the charity I run, Autistic Girls Network, navigated their child's toddlerhood and early school years with none of those aha moments. They didn't distinguish meltdowns as anything more than toddler tantrums, their child was verbal to the point of exhaustion, and there were no rows of lined up cars. Looking back now though, their parents will be able to remember a particular event or behaviour and say 'Oh so THAT'S why!' We might look back now and remember lined-up Barbie dolls (and yes, there were cars and trains in the house so it wasn't for lack of transport vehicles!) but that was just how she wanted to play (and indeed lining up cars and trains should never be seen as problematic but just another way to play – let's move away from society's prescriptive 'right' way to play). We also remember children who spoke early, who were quite precocious in the depth of their vocabulary, who made us laugh lots and sometimes made us cry. We remember night terrors and some difficulty sleeping. We remember beds heaving with cuddly toys.

When autism isn't recognised until late childhood or adolescence, the child is disadvantaged twice. First, they don't get onto a pathway of support. They may well have been waiting a long time on a waiting list, but they pretty much get their diagnosis, maybe get signposted to a few autism sites, and that's it. No more support unless school insists, or it's part of an education and health plan (whatever that looks like in your area). Second, the efforts of masking their autism for all that time may well mean they now have mental health issues. Sadly, in general, state support for child and adolescent mental ill health is rather poor, with long waiting lists and often severe budget restraints, which means gatekeeping and a triage system of deciding tiered support is necessary. Even if the referral to mental health services is accepted, lots of families in Autistic Girls Network have experienced one of the following difficulties: the mental health service considers that anxiety and even depression are part of autism and therefore decline to treat it; or the mental health service accepts the referral to treat the mental ill health, but the therapy it offers is not appropriate or adjusted for an autistic person, and the service staff and therapists themselves don't appear to have a good understanding of autism.

Autistic Girls Network is campaigning for earlier recognition of autism – and it's no coincidence that other neurodivergent conditions like attention deficit hyperactivity disorder (ADHD), dyslexia, and dyspraxia are also woefully underdiagnosed in primary school. Join us and help spread the word. But until things change, it's best to be forewarned that your late-diagnosed child is going to need you to advocate for them. And to do that, you need to be as clued up on autism as you can possibly be. You came to the right place. Read on to learn what you need to support your child to become their very best, happy, au-some autistic selves.

HOW TO READ THIS BOOK

This book is meant to be the kind of book I'd have liked to get my hands on when we first considered autism – though we were in crisis at the time. It's not necessarily meant to be read all in one sitting – although feel free to do that! – but to be dipped in and out of, and be referred back to when your family is in a different stage of your adventure. If you're only just beginning on this road, you might not recognise everything that's in here. Some things will be new, some might sound a little scary, some will involve long words you've never heard of before. It's OK for it all to be new. It was new for all of us at some point. It's OK if it's too much to take in all at once. It will still be here to come back to.

The more you talk to other neurodivergent families, the more stories in this book will seem familiar. And don't we all want that validation that we have things in common with others? We have many things in common but we are all different – all of us part of the diversity of human life. Wouldn't the world be a kinder, better place if we all accepted our differences as much as our similarities?

The book jumps straight in looking at different possible aspects of being autistic, and while they definitely won't all apply to your child, you might find some in there that you'd never considered before and say 'Oh THAT's the reason X did this!' Hindsight gives us all kinds of useful answers. You might find, as we did, that sensory areas give you the biggest surprise. If your child is a champion masker, there are all kinds of surprises that might be awaiting you as they start to drop the mask at home – but they're good surprises, and they bring good results. You might find, as we did, that you begin to suspect other co-occurring conditions like ADHD and want to get them investigated. There's nothing quite like watching your child enjoy reading a book for the first time after they're finally diagnosed with dyslexia and you can make the simple adjustment of dyslexia-friendly text. We look at tips for home and school, myths, dos and don'ts. We look at how to get your wider family and friends to understand. And finally we look at diagnosis – though many of you might have passed this stage, for your child at least. All done in a positive framework of building support and confidence for the future.

So dive in, and remember, we can't change what has already happened, but going forwards we can try our hardest to make a calm, safe space for our autistic young person.

PART 1

WHAT IS AUTISM?

Chapter 1

Is There a Typical Autistic Person?

Short answer? No.

Like all of us wonderful humans, autistic people are hugely varied.

Greta Thunberg believes that her autism helps her look at the world and see what others cannot, or perhaps will not, see. 'People like me, who don't follow social codes – we are not stuck in this social game of avoiding important issues... We dare to ask difficult questions. It helps us see through the static while everyone else seems to be content to role-play.'[1]

She wasn't diagnosed until the age of 11, after she had become depressed about climate change and stopped eating. She seems to have had difficulty with social connections from a young age, as she talks about other children being mean to her and not being invited to parties. Her experience is a very clear pointer that it's the environment around a neurodivergent person which needs to do the changing, rather than the person themselves.

Difference does not mean deficit. As the name suggests, autism is a spectrum 'condition' which means that there will be wide variations. There's all kinds of language used by professionals which has changed

1   McKie, R. (2020) 'Greta Thunberg: "Only people like me dare ask tough questions on climate"'. *The Guardian*, 11 October. Accessed on 30 May 2022 at www.theguardian.com/environment/2020/oct/11/greta-thunberg-people-like-me-ask-difficult-climate-questions

over the years, from Asperger's to low functioning and high functioning (and we're going to look at why these aren't well-liked terms), but the official diagnosis now is ASD – autism spectrum disorder. Your child may have other diagnoses too, and there is a whole neurodiverse family of conditions including ADHD, dyslexia, dyspraxia, dysgraphia, dyscalculia, Tourette's, etc., which have a tendency to stick around each other, and can make identifying autistic traits a challenge sometimes. If your child is autistic but also has ADHD, dyspraxia, and obsessive compulsive disorder (OCD), which 'condition' is causing the trait? Ultimately, it doesn't matter, because your child is unique and the way they do things is their way.

AUTISTIC STRENGTHS

One of the main features you are likely to notice about your autistic child as they grow older is that they have a strong sense of social justice. They like equality. They feel strongly about the little guy. Far from being incapable of empathy, a myth that seems to have grown legs about autistic people, they feel deeply about injustice. This is something that benefits our whole society. And just as Greta Thunberg is defending the biodiversity of our ecosystems and the calamities brought about by climate change, so others defend the diversity of our human ecosystem. Whether it's skin colour, religion, sexuality, neurotype, or ethnicity, we are all made stronger by diversity. Neurodiversity is all around us, and yet the default and accepted 'right' neurotype is the neurotypical one – someone without autism, ADHD, dyspraxia, dyslexia, etc. What if we challenge that there is a 'right' way of doing things? What if we challenge social norms that say we must look people in the eye when we talk to them, or that we must show automatic respect to elders? We're all different, so why is there a default perfect human, and why are these so often white, cis, straight, not disabled, and male? Let's challenge that notion and show that everyone has value. Some areas of business value ideas outside the norm, coining the phrase 'thinking outside the box'. The box is normality. I'm asking you to reframe your thinking around 'normality'.

Now it's certainly another myth that all autistic people are great at maths and science. In fact they are just as likely to be deeply creative, but what those two things have in common is that society 'allows' them to be different. We expect artists and scientists to be a bit wacky. We expect, indeed we actively want, a different kind of thinking from them, thinking divergent from the norm. That's their strength, so why have we fallen prey to this idea that to be autistic is a negative thing? Certainly, autism is a spectrum, and there are some autistic people who also have learning disabilities, and other conditions, some of which impair them very much. Equally there are millions of autistic adults around the world still undiagnosed and leading employed, (what society would call) productive, and fulfilled lives.

The world is set up to accommodate neurotypical people. We assume that tasks 'should' be easy or difficult. We assume everyone's brain processes things the same way, when in fact even among neurotypical people that's not true at all. As the neurodivergent parent of neurodivergent children, I encourage you to question these assumptions. It's the same with cultural differences. When I graduated from university, I got a job with the Japanese government teaching English in a high school. I was on a programme with hundreds of other English teachers from the UK, the US, Canada, Ireland, Australia, and New Zealand. I stayed in Japan for three years, and during that time I underwent a huge change in the way I thought about the 'right' way to do things. We're all brought up that the accepted way we do things in our culture is 'right'. For example, in the UK (and most other Western cultures), for breakfast we eat things like cereal, toast, or bacon and eggs. But in Japan 30 years ago, a traditional Japanese breakfast was rice, fish, and miso soup, sometimes with a raw egg poured over. In the area where I was based there were around 100 assistant English teachers (AETs), and when we first arrived in Japan we had a huge orientation in Tokyo with all the other AETs who were going to be scattered all over Japan, which was in the Keio Plaza, a grand, posh, skyscraper hotel where you could select a Western breakfast. Once we split into our areas, we had a more local orientation, at a small hotel where they could only provide a Japanese breakfast, and you should have heard the complaints! I'm now ashamed to say that very few breakfasts were eaten. And yet if I had repeated that experience the next year or even more so the year after, I would have happily eaten it. There's nothing like living in a different culture to disabuse you of the notion that there is only one way of doing things. To this day, as in Japan I often take off my shoes when I enter a house (which seems a much better idea to me than tracking all the dirt and germs you've picked up on the bottom of your shoes around your house). By the beginning of my third year, when the new intake of AETs came, I could already spot those who were going to struggle most with the cultural differences, those who held most tightly onto the notion that their culture's way was the 'right' way and all other ways were wrong. Almost without fail they were Americans, perhaps formed by a culture which told them they were the world's superpower and elite... perhaps things have changed now.

Once you let go of this notion that there is only one 'right' way of doing things, and loosen your grip on some of the social niceties we can't really justify, it becomes a lot easier to reframe your thinking into a mindset which is going to create an environment which nurtures, not repels, your autistic child.

You can accept how your autistic child is, just as they are, while still acknowledging there may be things they struggle with, or things they'd like to do but can't. After all, if you as their parent can't accept them exactly as they are, how can they learn to accept and be confident in themselves? That doesn't mean we can't strive to improve ourselves – we should all want to do that, whatever our shape, size, colour, sexuality, or neurotype!

Chapter 2

Useful Subjects to Know About for a Happy Autistic Life

COMMON PHYSICAL TRAITS

First let's take a look at some of the possible physical traits that may present in your autistic child. As you're going to read me saying again and again – everyone is different, and your child may not experience all of these, or even any of them, but they are possibilities.

Hyperacusis and Misophonia

Both of these conditions relate to hearing and both could be described as acute hearing sensitivity, often bundled up with an auditory processing difference which makes it difficult for the person to filter sounds. Having hyperacusis means it may be physically painful to hear some sounds. Having misophonia means that some everyday noises may be unbearable, such as snoring, the sound of someone eating, a boiling kettle, the noise of plug sockets or light switches (yes, I know you may not be able to hear them, but you need to believe your child if they say they can). A person may be affected mildly or severely, but if the latter this can be very debilitating.

How this can affect a child or young person at home:

- Your child may be able to hear far more noise than you

can – and also be unable to filter out the noises our brains usually register as useless or harmless. This is not only painful but exhausting. Wearing ear defenders or ear plugs will help.

- Your child is not being rude when they say they are unable to sit at the dinner table – imagine if you had a giant chewing noisily directly into your ear, and consider if you would still have much of an appetite? This is just one of the reasons society's rule of eating at the table doesn't always work well in neurodivergent households.
- Your child may find it difficult to get to sleep because their brain keeps bringing them household noises – snoring, dishwashers, heating timer switches, noise on the street. A variation on a white noise machine can sometimes help, for example an app with the sound of rain playing, and some people find night ear plugs help.

How this can affect a child or young person at school:

- The child may find it very difficult to focus on the teacher's voice because it is one of many sounds their brain cannot filter – people talking in other classrooms, classmates whispering, florescent lights, birdsong, cars on the road outside, a PE lesson. Audio processing problems can co-exist anyway so the teacher should also use methods other than just verbal ones to help and check understanding.
- Lessons which are chaotic and loud will be extremely hard for these children, as will being shouted at, packed corridors, and busy dining rooms. Autistic children need awareness and understanding that just being in that environment is making them work much harder than their neurotypical peers. And they need a calming and silent space to retreat to, both at school and when they get home at the end of the day.

Hyperosmia

Hyperosmia relates to our sense of smell, and it can be heightened to the point some smells become extremely unpleasant. It can cause physical reactions like nausea and vomiting, and – as will become a common thread in this book – if your child tells you they are experiencing it, please believe them. It's hard to imagine if you don't experience it too, but it's real. Hyperosmia is another reason why eating at a restaurant or in the school dining hall can be difficult – so many smells at once mean some are bound to be less pleasant. There are fairly easy adjustments that can be made though – it just needs the team around your child to understand autism. Once you understand that a strong smell can make that child vomit, you're liable to be more understanding about changing arrangements so that they don't need to experience that, and the older your child gets the more they will get to know their limits and be able to advocate for themselves.

This sense can be used to good effect too though, such as using a smell your child finds calming as part of their 'chill out' routine. Aromatherapy rollers – if in a fragrance they like – can be good for this. It also opens up career possibilities – what perfume brand wouldn't want someone with such an enhanced sense of smell?

CASE STUDY

Beth, age 11 in the US[1]

Beth went with her parents to look at an alternative school provision. It provided education for only 30 students and was based in an old, rambling industrial building where they concentrated on subjects like art, photography, and music. Beth already knew two girls who went there. She and her family spent half an hour being shown round by the school director, and she didn't say a word. Her mum knew something was wrong. As soon as they left, Beth told her that each room had its own overpowering, horrible smell. She couldn't go there, and they ruled it out as provision immediately.

---

1 Pseudonyms have been used in case studies throughout the book.

Beth's mum couldn't smell anything out of the ordinary, but she knew her daughter's senses were much more acute than hers and accepted what Beth said. It would have been a disaster as a provision for that reason alone.

Temperature Regulation

Some autistic children and adults can be either hypersensitive or hyposensitive to temperature – meaning they can either feel heat or cold intensely or barely feel it at all. It's all part of the sensory make up that's unique to them, and the better you understand it, the better you can support them.

Society, when you really think about it, is a little obsessed about the 'right' clothes for the season, and how whether someone wears them or not is being polite. We must take hat or coat off when we come inside, we must take off our jackets for the dinner table, we mustn't wear coats or sweaters in the summer... the list is endless. But, in general, your autistic child doesn't subscribe to those social rules, and since the rules don't actually make sense, you'll be hard pushed to make them.

How Can You Help?

Throw the social rulebook out of the window (as long as it's safe to do so). If they wear a coat all through the hot summer, it might open them to teasing but it won't harm them. Likewise, if they can't bear to wear anything but short trousers all through the winter, respect that decision as long as their legs aren't turning blue! If you're not autistic with the same sensory differences, you can't feel what they are feeling but you can honour it. And you can encourage grandparents and extended family and friends to do the same.

Light Sensitivity

Another area where autistic people can have highly responsive senses is their reaction to light. If you are light sensitive too, you'll get it. If you aren't, listen to your child and advocate for them at school when they say things are too bright.

What are the signs that your child or young person is particularly sensitive to light? Do they often turn off the light or keep the curtains drawn? Do they squint outside in photos (if they will allow you to take a photo of course)? Do they prefer to be inside when it's bright outside? Do they gravitate to darker spaces? At school, this might translate to coming into the school building at break or lunchtimes too (though obviously there can also be social reasons for this happening).

How Can You Help?

First address the natural/unnatural light situation. This will be more difficult at school of course, but at home you can install blinds, make sure there's no fluorescent light, and use lamps rather than overhead lighting. Natural light, away from windows, can work best as long as it's not too bright. Reactive or tinted lenses can help if your child or young person wears glasses. Remember that other light and reflective surfaces can also cause discomfort such as light shining on a reflective kitchen worktop, an interactive whiteboard, or a computer monitor.

Sleep

There are definite co-associations between neurodivergence and sleep problems, and there are various reasons for this. If you're reading this book as the parent of a later diagnosed (or pre-diagnosed) child or young person, you might feel rather sleep-deprived by now. Solidarity sister (or brother)! I feel your pain. So let's look at the reason WHY sleep eludes your child, before we figure out what to do about it.

There may be reasons within the body that they have difficulty sleeping, such as:

- A sleep disorder. These include delayed sleep wake disorder (DSWD) which is the most common of the circadian rhythm sleep disorders (CRSDs).[2] Those with DSWD have a naturally delayed urge to sleep, falling asleep – and therefore waking up – much later than is generally considered socially acceptable.

---

2   Nesbitt, A. (2018) 'Delayed sleep-wake phase disorder'. *Journal of Thoracic Disease*, *10*(1). S103–S111. doi: 10.21037/jtd.2018.01.11.

- A lack of melatonin, which is the 'sleep hormone' in our bodies. It's produced in our brain and helps us regulate night and day because, in most people, more is produced at night time. It helps to regulate our circadian rhythm, perhaps better known as our body clock. If not enough is being produced or distributed, it's not surprising that we have difficulty getting to sleep.
- A food sensitivity – especially since studies have shown that autistic people tend to be prone to gut issues.
- Sensory issues – they may feel too hot or cold, the bedcovers may feel too soft or too scratchy, the house may be too quiet or too noisy (those with misophonia may be able to hear even the hum of light switches and electrical sockets).
- Anxiety – they may become more anxious in the evening (this is common), and worried that they are going to be separated from you. After a busy day, the transition to sleep can be difficult.

How Can You Help?

- Naturally, all of the classic 'wind down' routines touted for all children can help – hot milk, no screens for an hour before bed, lavender spray on the pillow, etc. – but they probably won't be enough. (And if your child or young person has strong sensory needs regarding smell, make sure you get to know them and choose a smell they find relaxing.)
- In terms of physical help, melatonin in capsule form has been proven to be successful in assisting sleep.[3] It isn't without critics, but it has helped lots of families, including my own. The drawback is that, in the UK, it can't be prescribed by a GP but needs to be prescribed by CAMHS (Children and Adolescent Mental Health Services; throughout the

---

3   Sletten, T.L., *et al.* (2018) 'Efficacy of melatonin with behavioural sleep-wake scheduling for delayed sleep-wake phase disorder: A double-blind, randomised clinical trial'. *PLoS Medicine Journal*, 15(6): e1002587.

book CAMHS is used as an acronym for whatever children's mental health services are local to you), a paediatrician or a sleep specialist. In the US it is more readily available.

- Weighted blankets may also help to reduce anxiety in the evening – guidelines say children shouldn't sleep through the night with them on – and compression sheets, which are like a stretchy sheet tethered under the mattress, can help sensory seekers feel more comfortable in bed. Some children and young people will feel safer in a cocoon-like atmosphere, so sleeping with a bed tent over them, or even sleeping on the floor between the bed and the window (yes I know you spent good money on that bed!) might help. It's going to be trial and error here I'm afraid, because different children have different needs and sensitivities, but you'll find what works.

- White noise machines can help, although see if you can check out the different sounds before you buy as some of them can be quite alarming (I don't find thunder storms soothing for example). The 'galaxy projection' machines which project stars and planets onto the ceiling can also benefit some children and young people including my own.

- If it makes a difference to your child in terms of going to sleep or waking up early in the months of long daylight, blackout blinds or curtains might help – but you'll need to know your child because some don't like not having any light coming in, even keeping their curtains partly open at night.

- For children and young people who are on the alert at every little sound, night time ear plugs can help.

- If smell can help to make your child's bedroom a more pleasant place to be then take advantage of that and use a spray or diffuser to make the room smell of their favoured smell (with the proviso that these methods should of course to be checked that they are safe for your family).

- For those who seek vestibular movement (they love swinging and rollercoasters!), going for a drive or having an energetic half an hour on a swing or climbing wall may help their body settle down for sleep, especially if it's part of a routine.

- Do make sure you are allowing enough transition time between your child doing whatever they do in the evening and you asking them to go to bed. Transitions are tricky and this might be the trickiest one of the day because you are (usually) asking them to go from doing something they enjoy, with you easily available, to lying in a bedroom on their own. Even when your child is a typically rebellious teen by day, this may still be an unhappy transition.

- Before you start the bedtime routine, make sure you or your child has prepared all they can for the next day, because worrying about tomorrow might make up some of the pre-sleep anxiety.

- Many authors might tell you to take away all screens, but though this might be desirable it's not necessarily the right thing for all autistic young people, who often self-regulate using their phone.

NON-VERBAL COMMUNICATION

That's the physical aspects covered, now let's look at communication which doesn't involve speaking, and how this communication might be affected by autistic traits.

Alexithymia

Alexithymia is a standalone condition commonly (but not solely) co-occurring with autism and ADHD. It could be defined as a difficulty in recognising and articulating emotions and feelings. Alexithymia is also thought to cause difficulties in what's called emotional face recognition – being able to tell how someone else is feeling by their facial expression. And unsurprisingly it's associated with a difficulty in emotional regulation, since how can we act on our feelings when we can't accurately identify what they are? Please note though that alexithymia doesn't mean that someone doesn't feel emotion – they may feel all too much at times.

There are differing issues in dealing with the effects of alexithymia. First, that it's scary to not be able to identify your array of emotions. You may be able to identify the really strong emotions like anger or fear, but not the rest, and that means you can easily misidentify other emotions as those. You may be able to feel that your heart is beating very fast but not be able to identify that you're anxious, and so it feels like you're having a heart attack. I don't advocate much in the way of 'intervention', but helping your child to identify emotions is an important life skill.

Second, if you can't identify your emotions you also can't fix anything that's wrong, or stop yourself from being overloaded. It's really important that autistic children learn to self-regulate, ideally before hormones push emotions into overdrive, so that they can identify if something is wrong and what would be a good way to balance it. That might be to take themselves somewhere quiet to decompress, it might mean using some items from their sensory toolkit, it might mean being with their mum – the 'fix' will be different for each person.

And third, not being able to identify what others are feeling by the facial expressions we use commonly in society puts someone at a disadvantage and causes frequent misunderstandings. This doesn't mean that the person doesn't feel empathy – in fact some autistic people feel empathy very deeply indeed – but instead means that although they can for example identify that another person is feeling upset, they can't identify what exactly they are feeling and therefore how to help them.

Alexithymia is also a spectrum condition, and I was rather surprised to find out that one in ten people fall in this spectrum. In 2022 there are over 7,875,000,000 people in the world so that means almost 800 million people are alexithymic, though most will never be diagnosed and will perhaps just be viewed as not 'emotionally intelligent'. That suggests teaching children to recognise their emotions in primary school is a good idea – all children and not just those already identified as autistic, because some will not have been recognised yet, and those who are alexithymic but not autistic may never be recognised. Recognising and regulating our emotions well will help to give all of us better life outcomes. If we are alexithymic with poor interoception, which is the feeling of everything going on in your body, we may well not realise we are becoming overloaded until it's too late, so being able to recognise the signals that your body is becoming stressed is really important.

There is a clear link between alexithymia and interoception. Our emotions often come hand in hand with physical feelings, for example a physical manifestation of anxiety might be what we call 'butterflies in our stomach' (rather alarming to a literal-minded autistic child on first hearing – no actual butterflies involved!), but while we can feel something in our stomach, if alexithymia stops us identifying anxiety and poor interoception means we can't distinguish between 'butterflies' and some other stomach feeling, it can be very disconcerting. Those with alexithymia often know others can identify these feelings better than them, leading them to believe there is something wrong with them.

The better we understand, the better we can support, and I have found that an understanding of alexithymia and interoception (which will be covered more in Chapter 3) in particular have really helped inform support for my own children.

Facial Expressions

We've just talked about having difficulty interpreting facial expressions on others, but another autistic trait is not to really be aware of your own facial expressions. That along with slower processing times can sometimes lead to misunderstandings, especially in situations where facial expressions might be scrutinised such as in the doctor's office or hospital or in an emergency with the police. In an ideal world, health, emergency, and education professionals would all have a good enough understanding of autism to be able to know that they shouldn't make assumptions about facial expression based on their neurotypical thinking. Sadly that's not always the case and either you or your young person may need to educate them.

Face Blindness

Something like one in 50 people are face blind, including very well-known people like Brad Pitt and Oliver Sacks.[4] But many who were born with it remain undiagnosed (it can be better recognised if it occurs after a brain injury), and don't understand that they are not experiencing the world in the same way as others until they are older. Some research suggests that 40–45% of autistic people have some degree of face blindness.[5] That can range from having difficulty recognising specific aspects of unfamiliar faces to even being unable to recognise your own children in the most extreme cases.

My husband is face blind (the medical term for face blindness is prosopagnosia). He can't recognise the faces of people unless he is very familiar with them. He uses other characteristics such as hair, clothes, and glasses, or focuses particularly on eyes or noses if they have something special about them. For example, at the age of 51 while he has never met Queen Elizabeth II he has obviously seen her picture very many times. But he doesn't recognise the Queen by looking at her face. He recognises her by looking at her hair, her glasses, her clothes, or hearing her voice.

Growing up, he didn't realise he was face blind, he thought he just had difficulty remembering people. When you're growing up, you assume your normal is THE normal, and it's only as you mature that you start to feel different. This can make you come across as aloof and disinterested, even arrogant, but he is none of these. The first time he realised he might be face blind was during an organised quiz night. He was great at many of the questions (except sport!) but when presented with a large piece of paper covered in images of various celebrities, he had no idea who any of them were.

There have been some embarrassing incidents. He ended up on

---

4   Philby, C. (2018) 'One in 50 of us is face blind – and many don't even realise'. *The Guardian*, 29 January. Accessed on 2 May 2022 at www.theguardian.com/society/shortcuts/2018/jan/29/one-in-50-of-us-is-face-blind-and-many-dont -even-realise

5   Robison, J.E. (2013) 'How much Asperger's is really face or emotion blindness?' *Psychology Today*, 24 March. Accessed on 2 May 2022 at www.psychologytoday.com/gb/blog/my-life-aspergers/201303/how-much-aspergers -is-really-face-or-emotion-blindness

a course with the husband of one of my friends, who he had met a few times at children's birthday parties. Of course, the guy recognised him and chatted but my husband had no idea who he was. Parents' evenings at our children's secondary schools have always been difficult when he can't recognise the teacher from the last time they met. In work meetings, he recognises people he works with all the time but remembering clients' faces or people he doesn't often meet is hard. With in-person meetings he tries to subtly draw a map of everyone in the room with their name. Virtual meetings are much easier because their name is right there on Teams or Zoom!

Making mistakes at work is a source of anxiety for many but face blind people like my husband are already working much harder just to do everyday things. Introducing new joiners at work and giving them a tour to introduce them to people is a particularly tricky task because he can't recognise most of the faces. He has to draw a plan of where people would be and memorise it. He feels anxiety about failing because to not remember your colleagues is not socially acceptable and so he's worried at being found out. If any of his colleagues are reading, here's why!

If you'd like to read more about face blindness in children, have a look here: https://lab.faceblind.org/dpkids/dpkids.html

Your child or young person may not realise that they are face blind yet. If they are, some of these observations might have made you consider the possibility. But I hope it heartens you to know that despite all this, my husband did well at school, graduated from Oxford University, qualified as an accountant and has been gainfully employed almost ever since. He has found the strategies that work for him.

Aphantasia

Aphantasia is the inability to visualise things in your mind (the opposite is hyperphantasia which is the ability to richly visualise things in your mind). It may well be related to prosopagnosia, or face blindness, and it seems to be relatively common for autistic people, though you certainly don't need to be autistic to be aphantasic.

What Does This Mean?

If I asked you to picture a night club, presuming you'd ever been to one you'd likely be able to picture a scene from a night club in your head. It might not have many details other than flashing lights and people dancing, and the scene might not last very long, but you'd be able to do it – unless you were aphantasic.

Why Does This Make a Difference?

It's not just people asking you to think of something, it's also memories. Some aphantasic people can scrape a visual image together about something they feel very strong emotions about – perhaps their wedding day or a special holiday, particularly if they've looked at lots of photos of the event. Others still can't make that visual connection, and that has wider implications: they may not be able to visualise their children or – obviously much less important – picture how furniture in a room was laid out before you rearranged it.

Remember – and it's the same for all these experiences – your normal is your normal. Just as my husband didn't realise everyone else could recognise faces much better than him for a long time, so someone might not realise they are aphantasic if it never becomes obvious that other people can do something they cannot. They probably feel 'othered' though, just like undiagnosed neurodivergent people.

Eye Contact

Eye contact is one of those situations which can look very different in different cultures. For example, in Japan it's very rude to enter a house with your outside shoes on. In other countries it may not be. In most Western countries at least, it's considered polite to look at someone when they are talking to you. It's supposed to be respectful, and show that you are paying attention and are being honest. But is that the case in all cultures? Actually, no.

> In many cultures... including Hispanic, Asian, Middle Eastern, and Native American, eye contact is thought to be disrespectful or rude, and lack of eye contact does not mean that a person is not paying

attention. Women may especially avoid eye contact with men because it can be taken as a sign of sexual interest.[6]

It's certainly not the case in autistic culture. Let's lose the idea that there's only one right way to do things. There isn't. Not anywhere. So in autistic culture, eye contact is problematic, and for some it's physically painful. In a school, I'd like to make all staff aware that for autistic people, making eye contact with you doesn't necessarily mean that they are listening to you. In fact, it may mean they are concentrating on masking and are absolutely unable to focus on what you're saying. It may be hurting them. They may be looking at the top of your nose instead of your eyes (bet you can't tell!). So for neurodivergent children (it's much the same with ADHD), schools need to lose the notion that eye contact equals paying attention.

This means that some generic school behavioural policies which require sitting still and eye contact, for example, are not appropriate for you child. Chapter 10 discusses SLANT and other behaviour management strategies and offers advice about requesting reasonable adjustments.

And if you as a parent have told your children 'Look me in the eye while I'm talking to you!' in the past, apologise, forgive yourself because you didn't know and move forward determined to stop anyone saying it to them now.

VERBAL COMMUNICATION

Now we're going to take a look at some of the ways that verbal communication can look different in your autistic young person.

Echolalia

Echolalia is essentially repeating sounds, words, and phrases you have heard. This isn't going to be the last time I say this while writing this

---

6   Willingham, E. (2012) 'Low eye contact is not just an autism thing'. *Forbes*, 16 October. Accessed on 30 May 2022 at www.forbes.com/sites/emilywillingham/2012/10/16/low-eye-contact-is-not-just-an-autism-thing

book, but there is a wide spectrum of echolalia possible. For some, it might actually be difficult to spot that it's being used at all, because let's face it we all use set phrases or perhaps repeat marketing phrases we've heard, either as part of everyday speech or as humour. For others, there is a lot more repetition and it will be more obvious that echolalia is happening.

Echolalia can be a form of stimming, a comfort and stress-reliever, or it can be a helpful method of learning. For some, it's not controllable and can be inconvenient and frustrating if they feel they have to say words or phrases when they don't want to, such as when the subject of conversation is already over. But it isn't anything to be worried about or try to change for that person themselves – it's other people's perception of them which needs changing.

Situational Mutism

If your child sometimes (or indeed often) doesn't speak in stressful situations, you may have heard the phrase selective mutism used, but I don't like that phrase, which implies that the person is choosing not to speak. In fact, selective mutism can be completely out of the person's control – a stress response or even a survival mechanism in the body. Once you accept that your child or young person is not deliberately choosing not to speak, it makes it much easier to advocate for them. Now you just need to convince the school of that. Language matters, so don't allow the use of the phrase 'selective mutism', to enforce the idea that this is not something your child or young person is controlling. It's your job to make sure everyone accepts that there will be times your child or young person will feel safe to talk, and times when they won't. When these times are depends on how safe they feel in a space or with a professional. The more trusted people they have the better, but that trust needs to be earned, not forced. The most important thing is that everyone involved with them needs to know not to keep encouraging them to talk, but to accept that they can't. It's not their fault.

It's also important to talk to your child or young person about their situational mutism. They may not understand why they are feeling this way, and it can be scary. Chat with them when they are relaxed with you, and let them know that it's absolutely OK to feel this way and not to talk if they don't feel safe. You may want to use a 'social story' if they are young (only a properly formulated one – more on these later) and share it with those involved with them so that they all understand. They can then all be on the same page and behave in a consistent way with them when they are situationally mute and possibly distressed. It isn't your child who needs to change – those around them must make reasonable adjustments to accommodate what is a coping strategy for them. Gradually, as they feel safer and everyone around them understands what is stressful for them and works to improve their environment, they may be able to talk more, but the less pressure and the more acceptance the better.

It should also be noted that situational mutism is one of the 'flag' signs for a more internalised presentation of autism which can be more common in those raised as girls. So as a teacher, if a young person in your class is situationally mute, this is a sign not only of anxiety but that a closer look needs to be taken into the possibility of neurodivergence.

Being Non-Speaking

If your child or young person wasn't recognised as autistic in their early years, it's likely that they will be speaking. But even autistic adults who regularly speak can be non-speaking at times of overwhelm, anxiety, stress, or exhaustion, and this is nothing to worry about. There are other very valid methods of communication, but it's equally important to be accepting of the need for silent space.

And as allies, you need to be equally validating and accepting of autistic people who are non-speaking where you have the chance to do so. Reading or watching the wonderful *The Reason I Jump*[7] will illustrate why much better than I ever could. And if you'd like to read some of the writings of non- or seldom-speaking autistic adults, there is a great resource to jump off from on NeuroClastic.[8]

Tone of Voice

There are two different points to bear in mind regarding tone of voice, and both revolve around the 'double empathy' theory by Dr Damian Milton which highlights that we shouldn't make assumptions about

---

7   *The Reason I Jump* by non-speaking autistic 13 year old Naoki Higashida, translated into English by Keiko Yoshida and her husband English author David Mitchell (2014), was made into a widely-acclaimed movie released in 2021.

8   https://neuroclastic.com/category/culture-identity/nonspeaker

how someone else is experiencing the world.[9] First, you shouldn't assume from your autistic child or young person's tone of voice that they are being rude. And second, you shouldn't assume that they can unpick some unspoken social rule of etiquette from your tone of voice.

Be aware, if you, or friends or family, or teachers and school staff, are neurotypical, you're likely to expect certain things from someone's tone of voice and interpret it in a way which will not be the same as your autistic child or young person. In fact, if their tone sounds rude to you, it's very possible that they have no idea how it sounds and are certainly not trying to be rude or give any other impression. It can be difficult for some autistic people, children and adults alike, to control the tone, pitch, or volume of their voice. It's also possible they can't convey emotion in their tone, or extract it from someone else's. It makes sense therefore not to jump to any conclusions about hidden meaning, when likely there is none.

Literal Thinking and Direct Language

As a generalisation (because what else can we do in a book that's about all late-recognised autistic children and young people?), your autistic child or young person will be quite literal in their thinking and will prefer that you and indeed everyone in their social and educational circle uses direct language. Unfortunately, English is full of a LOT of indirect and idiomatic language, which doesn't make sense if you rely only on the meaning of the words used – it needs a further level of social understanding. Your child might well find this pointless and stupid, to put it bluntly, and you have to admit they have a point!

Naturally, they will come to understand and use some of the well-used phrases, although even those might need some explanation early on – think of it like learning a foreign language. But equally, meet them half way and try to avoid the kind of misleading language which can

---

9   The double empathy theory considers the problem that autistic people are considered not to be good at communication because they don't understand neurotypical society, but in fact neurotypical people don't understand autistic people either. There is misunderstanding and miscommunication on both sides. We're going to look at this more later on.

be difficult to understand for a brain that interprets literally, or which is open to too much misinterpretation.

Examples of the kind of language to avoid or explain – think about what these sound like if you don't know the idiomatic meaning:

- Draw the curtains.
- Run the bath.
- Wind your neck in.
- Be careful or you'll break your neck.
- If the wind changes your face will stay like that.
- You're so yummy I could eat you up.
- You've got ants in your pants.
- It's like pulling teeth.
- You've shot yourself in the foot.
- It'll blow your head off.
- The bulb has gone.
- You're on fire today.
- If you eat any more you'll pop.
- You need to make your bed.
- Take x to the toilet for me.
- Don't talk in class (think about it!).
- Just jump in the shower.
- You're driving me up the wall.
- What are you doing? (speaking on the phone).

Also take care that you are not framing instructions as questions. If, as a teacher, you say 'Do you want to just bring your chair over to my desk?' then don't be surprised if the child says no, which is a perfectly legitimate answer to that question. More legitimate in fact than the action which you actually want the child to take. Think about the language you are using.

In addition, you and others around your young person need to expect them to speak literally. I came across a particularly sad example of this the other day. A belief held among some mental health professionals is that if someone tells you they are thinking of attempting suicide, they won't actually do it. Mental health professionals may even say this to the person. But if this person is autistic, this is a strange, baffling, and frankly dangerous interpretation. It's a very neurotypical interpretation perhaps. But it needs to stop.

FUNCTIONAL SKILLS

Next, let's take a look at areas of difference that might be possible in your young person's wide-ranging functional skills.

Executive Function

The part of the brain which deals with executive function – the prefrontal region – is one of the last areas to develop in children. This is why children and young people are impulsive, can't always put together a plan of action and don't always evaluate their behaviour. For some autistic (and other neurodivergent) people, the development of their executive function is delayed or may always stay incompletely developed to some extent. Research shows that this area of the brain can still be developing in your 20s, and that's research that hasn't paid any attention to neurodiversity. Basically don't be surprised when your teen still doesn't listen to you and goes ahead and does what they wanted to do!

This part of the brain, the prefrontal region, also covers self-regulation, and there's still an awful lot to learn about this. All the processing needed to plan actions, inhibit them, and monitor and evaluate them afterwards starts here, and is affected by executive function issues. So how can we help?

Does your child laugh at awkward and seemingly inappropriate moments? Likely an anxiety reaction they can't inhibit.

Do they have difficulty with a string of commands? Well, we all do to a certain extent – a string of commands is brain overload and not a good way of asking someone to do something. We can all – especially in school – change the way we are asking, and it will benefit everyone, not just neurodivergent people. But someone with poor executive function may simply not be able to process more than a couple of commands at once (and that's not even taking into account that your autistic young person may be demand-avoidant).

For example, you might say to them, 'Can you take this upstairs for me [where do they put it?], and while you're there, empty the bin in the bathroom [into what – the floor?] and put it into the outside bin'. First, that's more commands than they may be able to process. Second, you haven't been clear enough. They may be confused at the first command and you may find the object placed at the top of the stairs, whereas to you it was obvious that this particular object had a specific place to go. Executive function difficulties may well have made them freeze at that point and not even hear the remaining part of the sentence, and now they are both confused and worried that you'll be cross.

Executive function can also undoubtedly be affected by tiredness and stress, so if autistic people are subject to sensory stress, or exhausted mentally and physically from masking, they may well have some executive functioning difficulties.

People with ADHD and dyspraxia also experience executive functioning difficulties, and of course lots of autistic people have at least one of these conditions too.

Time Blindness

As you can probably imagine, time blindness is when a person becomes unaware of the passage of time. We all have this happen to us to some extent when we become engrossed in a topic, film, etc., and we don't realise how quickly time has passed, but in general we know how to measure and more importantly manage time as part of our executive function. When we live in a society so full of deadlines, time management becomes an important skill to have, especially once you reach the world of work, but also in school. Imagine you are studying for ten different GCSEs (British national exams). You need to not only divide your time between these ten subjects (and life outside of school of course) but allocate the right percentage of time to coursework and revision, judge which subjects need more of your time and set yourself a revision timetable in order to prepare for exams on a particular day. This is actually quite extensive time management we expect from our youngsters.

As you probably already know, autistic people have a wonderful propensity for hyperfocus. It allows them to absorb masses of information on a topic, but also means time blindness can be more likely. Many amazing neurodivergent people have utilised their hyperfocus to gain success in their respective fields, but likewise they may be somewhat maverick in their social niceties!

An additional reason for being late to meetings, appointments, etc. can be that you are unable to accurately estimate how long a task will take. If you estimate it will take ten minutes to clean your kitchen, and start to do it before you need to leave the house, but it actually takes 30 minutes, you are going to be late.

So how can we help limit the effects of time blindness? For a start, it will help to have visible clocks around in key places, preferably whichever ones are easiest for your child or young person to read (likely to be digital – and remember ticking clocks can be a sensory nightmare). Technology can also be used to send reminders and set alarms, as long as it's in a way the person has control. There's no point setting it all up for them to be reminded to shower at 7 am if they have no intention of ever doing that! But it's very possible, if you have access to them, to get Amazon Alexa or Google Home doing the work for you in every room of the house.

More detailed and structured planning can also help – break bigger tasks down so that accurate time estimates and a realistic appraisal of where to fit that task into the day can be made. Plan in contingency time too, so that you're planning to be early.

Lastly, work on the basis of one of my very favourite mottos – done is better than perfect.

Object Permanence

This is another of those traits you won't see in any diagnostic manuals, but anecdotally it happens a lot in autism and ADHD – in the latter it's often called 'out of sight, out of mind'. Object permanence is actually the name of a baby developmental milestone – when the baby realises that objects and people are still there even if they can't see them. The meaning we are discussing here is different – the autistic person knows that the object still exists when they can't see it. But they either don't know where it is, or it's in plain sight but as it has been there so long they just don't notice it anymore.

I'm going to hazard a guess that your child's room might be very untidy. That they put something down and it doesn't move again – those clothes they took off, dropped onto the floor, and spent days just stepping over. That they resist putting things away. And part of the reason for that (other than executive function difficulties, which is a very real barrier to room organisation) might be their perception of object permanence. If you go in and tidy things away into boxes, your child may well have no idea where they are, and may actually soon forget they are there at all. While having everything spread around the room makes it look as if there has been an explosion, in sight is in mind (unless, as I just mentioned, it has been in sight so long it has become just another piece of furniture, like the floordrobe).

How Can You Help?

- Use see-through containers, labels, and pictures. This tends to be more known about in ADHD circles, so check out some ADHD bloggers for good ideas.
- Avoid closed drawers.
- See-through containers can be visually cluttered, so you might want to have a curtain you can draw over them for visitors, but you DON'T want them put away in a cupboard – remember, out of sight, out of mind.
- Don't say 'Just look for it' – once the object is gone from consciousness, it's gone and the idea of looking for it is gone too.
- Put specific objects together – a general box of bits and pieces is destined to never be looked at ever again.
- Items of clothing that have been in the washing basket a while have probably also been forgotten about – introduce

them again and suggest (depending on how old your child or young person is) very specific organisation of clothes.

• Don't move your child or young person's stuff without them knowing – they will be rightly upset with you.

A last note – it's not just objects who suffer this fate. The same can happen with friends you don't see for a long time, TV programmes you don't watch, etc. If your working memory is not so stretchy, your brain chucks stuff out you don't need (technical term there!).

Hyperlexia

If a person is hyperlexic, they tend to be very interested in letters and/ or numbers, and were likely early proficient readers. In some cases, children have taught themselves to read and adults have been taken by surprise when they read something aloud. Hyperlexic children may have a large and precocious vocabulary, probably considered very cute among the adults around them. (Just a note though that this tendency is not wedded to hyperlexia – my daughter had a huge vocabulary as a toddler but is actually dyslexic.)

Such early, extensive reading means that sometimes children are reading words they don't yet understand, with decoding skills stretching ahead of comprehension skills. It can also mean that children are not happy when they start school and are unchallenged by what's happening in class, especially when doing any group or class reading. A hyperlexic person's mental reading speed is likely to be faster than their spoken reading speed, so reading as a class can be tiresome and frustrating. (And speaking as an adult, there's nothing worse in a presentation than someone reading from the slides when I read them as soon as the slide went up. ADHD impatience may also be weighing in there...)

SOCIAL SKILLS

Next let's shine a light on another area where your young person may feel different to their peers – the sometimes scary social arena.

As social interaction is one of the diagnostic criteria, there is often a lot of emphasis put on it.

Empathy

I often read that autistic people don't have empathy. This has been repeated in countless psychology courses – even the ones that teach future clinical psychologists who will diagnose autism – but it's actually one of the biggest and most damaging myths there is about autism.

In a poll for autistic people on Twitter, 949 people replied to the question 'Do you generally care what happens to other people in your life?' Only 1% said no.[10] In another piece of research from Autistic Not Weird, with responses from 11,500 autistic people or their families, almost 60% said autistic people felt intense empathy[11] – this can be the issue, that (some) autistic people feel so deeply that it can be overwhelming. So don't rely on books (oh the irony!) to tell you how autistic people feel, or by their facial expressions which may be different to neurotypical ones – listen to what autistic people are saying.

Let me tell you a story of something that happened long before I knew our children were autistic. My son was around four and my daughter was about six months old. We were at home, snuggled on the sofa watching *Beauty and the Beast* for the first time. Near the end, I had to take my daughter upstairs quickly to change her nappy. I was only gone for a couple of minutes, but by the time I came back my son was lying on the floor crying his eyes out as if his heart would break. What had happened? The beast had turned into the prince, but my son thought he had died. He couldn't be consoled. Now I look back and realise this was one of the occasions where my son had such huge amounts of empathy it was almost unbearable for him. At the time, I just thought he was 'sensitive', and indeed lots of autistic children get

---

10 Memmott, A. (2020) 'So, what might autistic people think? The Polls'. Ann's Autism Blog. Accessed on 2 May 2022 at https://annsautism.blogspot.com/2020/09/so-what-might-autistic-people-think.html

11 Bonnello, C. (2018) '11,521 people answered this autism survey. Warning: the results may challenge you'. Autistic Not Weird. Accessed on 2 May 2022 at https://autisticnotweird.com/2018survey

this label. Yet how on earth can they be both sensitive and lacking in empathy? It doesn't make sense!

By the way, it's probably not a coincidence that it's the beast he was worried about. Many autistic people have a huge empathy for animals especially, and let's face it animals are a lot less complicated than some people! My son is at university now and he still calls not really to speak to me but to FaceTime the dogs. I know my place.

The autistic academic Damien Milton came up with the double empathy theory and there is a great explanation of it on the Frontiers for Young Minds website.[12]

Basically, the theory goes like this. Lots of research has shown that autistic people have trouble understanding neurotypical communication. What tends to not be researched so much is that neurotypical people also have trouble understanding autistic communication. In actual fact there is two-way misunderstanding – both sides need to make an effort to metaphorically put themselves in someone else's shoes. The double empathy theory highlights a lot of the problems with research about autistic people – it's very one-sided and historically has had almost no input from autistic people themselves.

Socialising

The medical model of autism tells us that autistic people lack social skills. What they actually mean is that they lack neurotypical social skills. In fact, put a group of autistic friends together in a room and you'll soon see that their social skills are not lacking, they are just distinct from and different to their neurotypical counterparts.

Our society is hugely complicated, full of unspoken rules and rigidity. Just as neurotypical people don't tend to understand neurodivergent society, autistic people can have difficulty navigating the stormy waters of neurotypical society, which values verbal communication and conformity. Neurodivergent people, to generalise, aren't big on conformity.

Our historically negative view of autism has conditioned all of us to believe that autistic people are not capable of forming deep friendships, but that's most definitely not the case.

---

12   https://kids.frontiersin.org/articles/10.3389/frym.2021.554875

So when we think about teaching social skills, I suggest that we actually teach self-awareness to autistic kids, and awareness of other neurologies to everyone else. What I suggest we DON'T do is try to change autistic children into neurotypical ones. That will not be a happy path. When I say teach self-awareness, I mean that we need to teach how what someone says or does makes someone else feel – but that works in both directions. Neurotypical people can be just as blind to the effects of their words as neurodivergent ones.

If your child has social skills taught to them by, for example, a speech and language therapist, make sure they are not being taught to conform to a neurotypical sense of 'right' communication. To be honest, I am wary of any therapy or lesson that calls itself 'social skills', because it's unlikely that it has truly been created with your autistic child or young person's best interests at heart from a neurodivergent point of view. Another thing to watch out for is ABA (applied behavioural analysis), or PBS (positive behaviour support), which is what it tends to be called in the UK. Making eye contact is definitely something that an ABA practitioner would teach, but it's just teaching the student that their own autistic way of communication is wrong (it's not!) and to mask their own tendencies, raising the possibility of mental health problems down the line.

If your child has a special interest that they could talk for hours about, it's good for the other person to know about that, and show an interest. But it's also important for the child to know that the other person is not quite so enthusiastic and there will come a point when they have overshared. Both parties can – theoretically – then communicate with each other with kindness and understanding. Likewise, there needs to be understanding about making eye contact, and about interrupting. It helps to have an understanding of working memory too – if you have a very short working memory then a) you can easily forget your train of thought if people interrupt you, and b) you may have to interrupt someone to stand any chance of remembering what you wanted to say!

Can I also say that online socialising (whether through Roblox or Instagram or any other means) shouldn't count as 'screentime', especially if screentime is being rationed. For your autistic child or young person, this is an authentic, important way of socialising and it should be given the same priority as you would give to having a friend round to play at your house face to face.

It boils down to awareness, and being led by your child. Help them to find a neurodiverse bunch of peers, and good, understanding friendships are more likely to be made. But don't try to force friendships on a child. You may find they are comfortable with their own company much more than you'd expect.

IDENTITY

Now we're going to look at what might be most important for your young person's wellbeing as time goes on – identity.

Gender Diversity

Gender diversity is a catch-all term to capture those who identify their gender as different to the one they were assigned at birth – transgender, non-binary, and gender-queer. People who identify as the same gender they were assigned at birth are termed cisgender or cis. There's a confirmed link between autism and gender diversity, in fact gender diverse people are between three and six times more likely to be autistic, a figure that's undoubtedly higher when you consider so many autistic adults are as-yet undiagnosed.[13]

Gender diversity doesn't equal gender dysphoria though. The latter is a condition diagnosed when the reality of not 'matching' the gender you were assigned at birth becomes a cause of distress and trauma. It's mostly those gender diverse people with gender dysphoria that there is data for, because it's this population who have featured in a few academic studies. A recent study at the University of Cambridge had a large sample size of over half a million people in the UK, and the

---

13   Warrier, V., *et al.* (2020) 'Elevated rates of autism, other neurodevelopmental and psychiatric diagnoses, and autistic traits in transgender and gender-diverse individuals'. *Nature Communications*, *11*(1), 3959. doi:10.1038/s41467-020-17794-1

findings were significant – only 5% of the cis participants were autistic, whereas 24% of the gender diverse participants identified as such.[14]

Why Are Gender Diverse People More Likely to Be Autistic?

Or vice versa... We don't know. But it seems part of a common autistic profile to not be bound by social conventions, and what could be more conventional than society's ideas and rules around gender? It isn't surprising to me that neurodivergent people in general feel more comfortable in gender fluidity than their neurotypical peers, who are more bound by society's rules.

How Can You Help?

Being gender diverse puts someone in a minority, and being autistic they are already in a minority – this can cause stress. So being absolutely calm, accepting, and non-judgemental is key. If you need outside help with gender dysphoria, make sure that help is adapted for an autistic mind, otherwise it may be the opposite of helpful. And as always, be their rock, and love them.

Non-Conformity: Attitude to Adults or Leaders

We've already touched upon non-conformity to society a little, but as you'll see, your autistic child or young person is likely to care little for society's rules if they don't make sense to them. This is unsurprising when you consider so many social 'rules' which don't appear to take neurodivergent people into account at all. This doesn't mean that all neurodivergent people are going to be feisty, outspoken rebels (though I certainly hope some will!), but it does mean they will probably need a social rule to make sense before they blindly obey it. And this may mean that they question it, which can come across as 'sassy'. One thing to reframe the sassiness a bit – your child doesn't naturally follow the societal rules that elder/parent/teacher = automatic respect. In their eyes, we are all equal. So for them, an adult talking in

---

14   Warrier, V., *et al.* (2020).

a demanding, entitled, autocratic way is just as 'sassy' as their replies sometimes seem to you. Once you realise this it becomes easier for you to understand – though I know that it's harder to reframe for others who might overhear.

So how can you help other people to understand, other than of course explaining what's above? Ask them to be aware of this aspect of your child or young person's autism profile when they are interacting together. If the child pushes back, ask them to really think through what they are asking. Does it actually make sense through an autistic lens? Is there really a reason why that's a better method/way to behave than another way? Or is it just a blind assumption that this is the 'right' way to do things in our society? Always remember that neurodivergent–neurotypical communication is a two-way street. Both neurotypes experience the world in different ways, but we all need to make allowances for the other viewpoint. How your child or young person reacts to an authority figure touting society's viewpoint in their face is going to depend on their individual personality. Some will fawn and mask, and do everything they can to please that person despite it being harmful to themselves to do so. Others will take the opposite option in the fight/flight/freeze/fawn reaction, and will fight it for all it's worth. This isn't always acceptable. But school must understand that a child cannot constantly conform to ideals which make no sense to them, and indeed can actively harm them. Understanding is key.

Passionate Interests

It was hard to write this section. While passionate interests (more often called special interests, or in medical terms repetitive and restrictive behaviours!) are very much a part of 'classic' autism, they can be much harder to spot in those raised as girls. Many parents wouldn't have said their daughter had a passionate interest until well after they finally got their autism diagnosis.

So what is a passionate interest in terms of autism? It's your child's favourite topics or hobbies that they love to do or talk about the most, and it can vary widely. A stereotypical one is trains (think of Sheldon in *The Big Bang Theory* for more stereotypes) but in fact it could be literally anything: Reborn Dolls, Pokémon, supercars, feminism. You name it, someone somewhere loves it. These interests may become quite fixated, and presuming your child is verbal, they may like to talk on their favourite subjects extensively!

How Do Passionate Interests Help Your Child?

- Passionate interests are something they can control in a world which is sometimes baffling, frustrating, and upsetting.
- Your child can become an expert in this subject – often knowing more than anyone else in the family – which not only helps them order their confusing world but increases self-esteem.

The hyperfocus needed to concentrate on their specialised subject (Mastermind, anyone?) is going to be useful at other times in their lives. My son has managed to weave one of his passionate interests (specifically Mandalorian battle armour cosplay costumes from Star Wars) into his university degree studies. We can speculate that it was their hyperfocus that allowed Steve Jobs to achieve great things at Apple and Bill Gates to do the same at Microsoft. Historically there are likely to be all kinds of great achievements which took place due to hyperfocus – Michelangelo's Sistine Chapel and Alan Turing's Enigma Machine for example. I'm not saying your child needs to invent something world-changing, let's face it most of us don't, but it's good to reframe the medical model of deficit and see hyperfocus as something positive.

Love of Animals

Many autistic people (and of course many people of all neurotypes) love animals. But there are examples where even when someone finds social interaction hard, they can more easily build a relationship with a cat, dog, or horse (for example). I guess animals don't expect so much from us – just food, a home, and love. They don't expect us to partake in complicated social scripts or make eye contact (although my own cocker spaniels with their sorrowful puppy dog eyes might beg to differ!). For this reason, pets are generally popular in autistic households, although that's not always the case and if your child is going to be upset by the dog barking, or the dog is going to be upset by unpredictable behaviour, pet ownership is not for you.

There are now quite a few social enterprises providing therapy dogs. I have no experience of these so I can't make any recommendations, but do your homework – some cost as much as a new car. A properly trained therapy dog can be wonderful, but make sure you know what you're getting. Equine therapy is also becoming equally popular, and I know many girls particularly who are really helped by this, but it's not for everyone – the smell and the stable environment, plus needing to touch and groom the horse, can be too much for some sensory needs. Worth a try if you think your child or young person will like it though – there are charities who offer equine therapy, and I have even seen it written into Education Health and Care Plans (EHCPs)/ Individualised Education Programs (IEPs).

There's also the 'good' sensory aspect of having animals – they generally love to be stroked! My children love our spaniels, but after one of them has just been groomed she is called 'sensory pup' because her fur is extra soft and stroke-able. Let's be clear though, they are cocker spaniels so they live for human contact and attention... they're not short of cuddles even with ungroomed fur! When choosing a pet to bring into your household, that is something to be considered – will the animal like to be cuddled and stroked? There's no right way or wrong way, and there's no perfect animal for all, just the perfect one for your family.

Sense of Social Justice

Having a highly developed sense of social justice is not a part of the diagnostic criteria for autism. But it probably should be.

We've partly covered this when talking about your child or young person's attitude to authority, but we're going to take a quick look at a typical autistic person's (if there is one) sense of social justice regarding others – justice for the whole human race if you like. As has already been mentioned, everyone is equal. It follows therefore that all parts of the human race should be equal – all colours, all genders, all sexualities, all abilities, all neurotypes, all levels of financial wealth. You'll find that many of the activists who fight for all these causes and for climate change are neurodivergent. Greta Thunberg's passionate interest is climate change – she has changed the world, and hopes to change it much more, because of this, but she's also passionate about other kinds of social justice. Her hyperfocus on her passionate interest may ultimately save the planet.

The same little get-out clause needs to appear: 'not all autistic people'. But you wouldn't expect all neurotypical people to act the same way either would you?

How Can You Help?
As parents we have a duty to nurture these aspirations. If our nine-year-old says they're going to save the world, instead of giving a

knowing smile, think of Greta and tell them you KNOW they will. Whatever your own personal opinion, support your young person's championing of LGBTQIA+ rights. Help them fight disability or racial discrimination. Get behind them protesting about corporations that cause pollution or don't pay their taxes. People who feel strongly about social issues and don't get distracted by other issues are exactly who this world needs.

COPING STRATEGIES

Now let's take a look at some autistic traits which tend to occur because they are strategies a young person has learned to cope in a neurotypical world.

Masking

Many parents end up in the Autistic Girls Network Facebook group because they have spent a long time trying to get education or medical professionals to 'see' their girls. As a generalisation, a more internalised presentation of autism tends to be common in girls (and some boys, and non-binary children and young people). Because they are not presenting in a more recognisable external way, these children and young people are often not spotted, even if the parents have been trying to tell professionals for quite some time that they need assessment. This is because they (usually unconsciously) camouflage and mask their autism in order to fit in with the social group they belong to. Until they can't anymore. Let's get two things clear though, there isn't a 'boy' autism and a 'girl' autism. Just different ways that people behave which can make autistic traits harder to spot. And masking, as it's commonly known, is not something that autistic girls are particularly doing on purpose – it's not something else they can be blamed for. It's a reaction to stop themselves from being stigmatised. Although they and you as parents are frequently told they need to be more resilient, actually they are being far more resilient than their peers already just by being in school.

Unfortunately, 'camouflaging' autistic traits (hiding or compensating for them in order to fit in with their peers) has been shown to correlate highly with the severity of their mental health issues. Masking is associated with depression, suicidal thoughts, stress, and anxiety, and that anxiety can cause autistic people to be unable to do everyday tasks they might usually manage easily. That's what shows up in studies, but of course it's not the masking itself which is causing the depression, it's a society which stigmatises difference so much that even a child subconsciously realises they need to protect themselves.

Masking isn't coping. Masking is not necessarily a choice or a conscious decision.

Masking doesn't mean they are 'fine in school'. It means the opposite in fact.

And if pupils, especially those brought up as girls, who are trained to be socially aware more than boys, present with great distress or social anxiety but seem otherwise 'fine in school' this should ring bells about autism or ADHD.

When a child or young person is camouflaging, it's difficult to spot unless you know the kind of thing you are looking for. And therein lies the problem: the vast majority of GPs, SENCOs (special educational needs co-ordinators, or special education coordinators in the US), head teachers, teachers, educational psychologists, speech and language therapists, clinical psychologists, and even CAMHS staff do not recognise masking. In Autistic Girls Network we've had diagnoses refused because the child or young person:

- can look you in the eye (they are masking)
- has empathy (autistic people do have empathy)
- has friends
- talks a lot
- is too sociable.

There's a lot more to autism than not being able to do those things. A good masker will be able to keep up friendships – at primary school at least – but they will pay a heavy toll for it later. And camouflaging autistic traits has been associated in some research studies with more severe psychological impact. Women tend to need more of a social network than men, and so it's not a surprise that this camouflaging tends to happen more with women than men (but men and non-binary people do it too). If a woman has difficulty in fitting into social situations (neurotypical situations), it's more likely to lead to mental health issues, and the difficulty may well lead to reduced social support, which will also impact mental health. A person in this situation, undiagnosed, is likely to have a low sense of self-worth because they perceive that they don't 'fit', that they are 'weird'. In fact, they haven't connected with their autistic tribe to see that they are not alone, and when they understand this they might feel a lot better.

Examples of masking and camouflaging:

- Joining in with (or just listening to) conversations in their peer group they have no interest in, e.g. about boys or football/soccer.
- Practising facial expressions in a mirror.
- Avoiding excessive talking about their own special or passionate interests.
- Avoiding stimming and repetitive behaviour.
- Making eye contact – often very brief or looking at eyebrows or bridge of nose instead.

Although special interests are mentioned in that list, this can actually be a confusing part of an autism diagnosis for those raised as girls, since diagnostic questioning has been very much built up around the assumption that autistics are males. Males might tend to be interested in trains or cars, but in general autistic girls tend to have the same kind of interests as their neurotypical peers, just more intensely. The classics are bands (and at the moment K-pop!), horses, Harry Potter. Again, this makes them difficult to spot.

CASE STUDY
Mia, age 13 in the UK
Mia wasn't diagnosed until she was 13. Mia had always been quiet and well-behaved at school, and teachers had never flagged any problems, though her parents had queried her spelling capability quite a few times. She is fairly invisible in class and almost never puts her hand up. She has occasionally got into trouble for talking with her friends, though in private she tells her mum it wasn't her

fault and she is indignant at the social injustice. She hates teachers shouting. She is mortified by detention and the sudden imposition of it. She finds homework very difficult to do (at home). She doesn't have a high opinion of her academic abilities and that is the impression teachers give at parents' evenings too. Until her 13th year, nobody had ever suggested she might be autistic, but in that year she began to really struggle. She had been a super masker – until she couldn't be any more.

Her parents reported to school that she was very anxious, not sleeping well, and had some OCD rituals developing. She reported stomach pain a lot, and it became obvious she was avoiding PE. Her attendance at school became lower. She began to speak to teachers even less than usual but generally couldn't tell anyone what was wrong. She was unable to use the traffic light system introduced for how she was feeling, or the time out card to leave class, because she became situationally mute. She attempted suicide and self-harmed.

By this point, it should have been a huge flag for autism, but Mia wasn't referred by any professionals – even CAMHS – and it was her parents who paid for a private diagnosis. (She was later diagnosed with dyspraxia, ADHD, and dyslexia too – no professionals had ever picked these up.) This was accepted by school and CAMHS, and some reasonable adjustments were made by school but it was too little too late, and Mia had suffered PTSD (post-traumatic stress disorder) by this point. She was unable to continue going to the school, or even near it (which she needed to as her brother still attended and was taken by her mum). The school also told Mia's parents that she wouldn't get an EHCP, and believing them they didn't apply for another year. Mia now has an EHCP and a place in a tiny independent specialist school which is much more attuned to her needs.

Masking, and maintaining that social facade, is EXHAUSTING. Add that exhaustion to the possible sensory nightmare that is school – flickering lights, so many sweaty smelly bodies too close, noise, cooking and science smells, students moving round the classroom in an unpredictable way in design tech or food tech, etc. – and it's easy in hindsight to see why so many girls (and boys, and non-binary young people who present the same way) either need considerable adjustments or become too anxious to attend their mainstream school.

Eventually, masking may lead to autistic burnout. This is when the autistic person has reached the end of their capacity to mask, to even do anything but the most limited functions. It may be a dark time. And even then, you are expected to go to school, to get the bus, to join in the noisy tramp down the corridors, to engage with teachers and classmates, to move around the school and be aware of what's going on and where you need to be next. Your brain – and your body – have basically just shut down. You can't do it. But you're a masker. You want to fit in, you want to please. Your anxiety rises, your executive function capability takes a nosedive, the smallest things send you over the edge. You need to withdraw, but society expects you to go to school, so you can't. So you burn out, and shut down. You may not know what's wrong, and if you go to the GP he or she almost certainly won't. Rest, and understanding/enforcing your boundaries, is all that's going to help you. But not many adults will accept children and young people enforcing their boundaries. They assume an adult knows better. That's one reason why we tell schools it's SO important to actually LISTEN to the young person and BELIEVE them.

The answer? The best way you can help autistic people? Give them validation. Stop calling them damaged and disordered. Understand their sensory needs. Let them find out how to self-regulate by allowing them to do calming activities like stimming. Make them feel safe and accepted enough to drop the mask.

Stimming

Stimming seems to have turned into a bit of a controversial subject. It can be one of the most obvious traits to show a person is autistic, and one of the traits some behavioural therapy like ABA may try to stop or redirect. But autistic adults will tell you that stimming is a vital way for an autistic person to regulate their emotions.

So what is stimming?

In diagnostic language, it's what is known as restrictive or repetitive behaviours, but I don't like that negative language. For an autistic person, stimming (self-stimulation) is to do something repeatedly which makes you happy, reflects your excitement, or helps calm you. It could be a wide variety of things, but the most well-known is hand-flapping.

Other stims could be things like:

- pacing
- skin chewing
- rocking back and forth
- chewing clothes or gnawing on something
- swinging
- tapping feet
- fidgeting with an object
- staring or zoning out
- singing the same lines over and over
- coughing or clearing your throat
- bouncing and wiggling
- rearranging items
- cracking joints
- whistling or humming
- shaking something
- dancing
- smelling something
- watching or listening to the same thing over and over
- scratching or rubbing skin or hair.

If you look at that list you can see just how many are sensory behaviours, and how important sensory stimuli can be. We'll look into that in much more detail in Chapter 3 (Sensory Stuff).

Sometimes stims can also be harmful, such as head-banging, and these are the only stims which should be redirected. They are likely to be distressed behaviour, so if you change the environment or circumstance which is causing distress, they should stop. There are concerns that stimming interferes with learning, but this concern is misplaced.

In fact, the stimming facilitates learning in that it allows the person to concentrate on something they would otherwise not be able to.

To some extent we all stim. Tell me that you never tap your foot on the floor, or bounce your leg, or bite your nails, or pace the floor, or hum to yourself? For autistic people, the stimming is more intense and more satisfying.

Stimming can be a source of great joy, so unless your child is hurting themselves or someone else, or causing damage, please don't stop them. Some stims, particularly sexual ones, are obviously better done in private. Stimming is a way of having control over sensory stimuli, and there are too many sensory stimulations which are deeply upsetting or painful for some autistic people, and which they have no control over. It can help get rid of any frustration they may be feeling about needing to mask or behave in a neurotypical way, and it's a very important method of self-regulation.

Stress Regulation

In most books this would probably be called emotional regulation, and indeed it is about regulating emotions. But calling it that (or even worse, calling it resilience, which translates to suppressing emotions *shudders*) puts all of the burden onto the autistic person to do something about it. In fact, the need for regulation is often caused by the environment they are having to navigate which is causing them stress.

Autistic and ADHD people tend to have big emotions. What may feel like a minor inconvenience to a neurotypical person can feel like a catastrophe to an autistic person. Big changes and transitions can also cause big emotions. And once in that state it's hard to get out of it (and that's still another change). When still a child or young person, they are figuring out how to identify their emotions. And it's pretty hard to control them if you can't identify them. We're going to talk more about this in Part 2, but I wanted to mention it here because a big build-up of emotions is generally caused by one of two things – a big event, whether happy or sad, or an overload of stress. (And we need to acknowledge that big events, even happy ones, can be stressful too for autistic people, because they signify big change.)

So How Can You Help to Manage Stress?

Following the tips in this book is going to greatly decrease stress because it's a combination of multiple situations rather than just one thing. As an overview and without going into much detail, because that's going to change for every individual, here's how you can help:

- Remove as many demands as you can. That means demands outside the home such as visiting Great Auntie Agatha as well as demands inside the home such as always keeping their bedroom tidy.
- Keep calm.
- Encourage habits that soothe.
- Keep the home environment to low sensory arousal – keep light, noise, and chaos to a minimum.
- Listen to them.
- Understand autism and encourage your close family to do so also.

Impact Catastrophising

I think it has become clear that being autistic in a neurotypical world can lead to a fair amount of anxiety day to day. And when you're already anxious, the possibility that something is going to happen to make your day worse can send your anxiety skyrocketing. Getting stuck on this negative train of thought is catastrophising. It's assuming the worst will happen without, probably, any logical reason to do so. But while this might seem silly to outsiders, it's very real for the autistic person, and should be treated as such, with feelings respected. We're going to talk more about the fight/flight/freeze/fawn instinct, and this is it kicking in, with the primitive part of the brain telling them attack is imminent. It could be about anything – the car crashing, failing exams, the dog dying or things that might seem less serious (but don't feel so at the time). Something happens which triggers a negative thought and these multiply until they are left with the worst case scenario, which is stressful, very upsetting, and also exhausting.

As we've already discussed, if you don't have the ability to really identify these emotions as your body is feeling them (alexithymia), the situation is made even more stressful as how do you KNOW you're not having a heart attack or some other health disaster? If some negative experiences have already taken place the person is going to be even more likely to assume the worst.

How Can You Help?

- First, don't tell them they are being silly, or they are overreacting. Their anxiety is very real to them.
- Make sure they have enough chill out time in their day, every day, and help them to understand when they need more time (which might be days they have had extra 'peopling' time, for example).
- Help them to find the things which help them relax, whatever that might be – walking up and down the garden, listening to music on headphones, swinging in a hammock, rocking on a birthing ball (presuming a pregnant person isn't using it of course!).
- Recognise the signs early on and distract onto a different path if you can – this won't always work and can backfire if you do it too late, so take care.
- Try to surround them with people who understand autism and will communicate in a reciprocal style and keep sudden changes to a minimum.
- Most important of all – remove what's stressing them if it's in your power to do so. And after the event, don't make them feel guilty for what's happened.

Separation Anxiety

Your autistic child or young person feels safe at home. They feel safe with you. They dislike change, which takes away the feeling of safety. Autistic children's sense of their own self can also be more fragile than their neurotypical peers', and can be seen as part of their attachment to their parent, usually but not always their mother, for longer than those peers. So is it surprising if they don't like leaving you? I understand, of course, that there are levels of separation anxiety, and 'clinging to your hair for dear life level' 24 hours of the day is pretty hard to manage.

How Can You Help?

You've (hopefully) built up trust with your child or young person. They need to build that trust with some other key people too, and those people, no matter who or where they are, need to know that trust is not to be misused. If they make promises, they must follow through. If they say your child can phone home if they feel sad, they must let them do so. No promises they have no intention of keeping – that doesn't work. For the teacher, they must understand that building trust is more important than having compliance. If you are very anxious, you need to feel in control, so having people around who you can trust not to take away that control at the drop of a hat becomes very important. That's why trust is particularly important for children with PDA (pathological demand avoidance) as we shall talk about in Chapter 4 (Co-Occurring Conditions).

If this is happening at school, it needs to be dealt with in a nurturing and gentle way. I've read far too many posts in the Autistic Girls Network Facebook group talking about someone's child being forcibly removed from them, screaming, at the school gate. If you stop and think about this I hope you don't need much convincing that this is wrong for ALL children, but particularly for neurodivergent ones. Make school a fun and sensorily comfortable place for that child to be, not one where they associate being forcibly dragged away from the person they most love and trust in the world. Tough, I know, when you're not in charge of the school.

If it's happening at home, when you go out or go to work, you need to work on another person, or preferably a few people they can trust. Those people need to quell their urge to control and make your child or young person comply because they are the adult – remember everyone is equal in this relationship. They may need to come to your house, at least at first, so there aren't too many changes at once. A bit of bribery and a special treat never hurts. No pressure, no removal of privileges, just fun – and not the adult's choice of fun. The aim is always for your child or young person to feel safe with them. It goes without saying that a person who doesn't believe in any of this, who thinks your child is being 'spoilt' or manipulative, is not the right person to be your substitute.

If it's happening at bedtime, it's time to make that bedroom a sensory haven – star projector, fish bubble tube, bed tent, compression sheets – the lot! If that doesn't work though, it's possible you may all be playing musical beds for a while, or that your child or young person may want to sleep on the floor next to your bed. Don't be too surprised if they feel comfortable being a bit squashed – it can feel safe. And don't make them feel bad about it. You are their safe space. Being next to you. And don't worry, it's not forever.

Anxiety

I find myself a little conflicted in this section. As we've seen, being autistic can come hand in hand with being anxious. But, and this is a big but, I firmly believe that it doesn't need to come with the kind of anxiety which involves your child or young person being referred to CAMHS if they have been recognised and are being supported and accommodated. And I do have a bone to pick here… because not only have we as a family been told that anxiety is just part of autism and can't be treated, but so have many, many other people in the Autistic Girls Network group, and probably in autism Facebook groups all over the world. However, anxiety and depression are NOT part of the diagnostic criteria for autism.

There are all kinds of sad statistics in research papers about autistic adults, and I'm not going to delve into them here, because despite me currently writing a section about anxiety, this is a positive book and your child or young person has a very positive future ahead of them. The statistics are for adults who grew up mostly unrecognised as autistic, or recognised at a time when autism was barely understood at all. Now is a very different time, and things are changing very fast. Even ten years ago, we had nowhere near the understanding of neurodivergence we do now, and while there's certainly a lot more learning and understanding to be done, the future is bright.

Naturally, if your child, like mine, has been recognised as autistic late and is already highly anxious and already perhaps under Children's Mental Health Services, you might not be feeling very positive. At the time, it felt like it would never get better, but it did. Hang in there. Keep holding a calm environment, understand their sensory needs and dislikes, prepare for change. Remember, uncertainty = anxiety. It can be a difficult balancing act. We've talked about letting your child or young person have more control, which means more choice, but in times of high anxiety choice can be problematic, especially infinite choice, and being asked to make a decision is just another demand, so avoid open-ended questions.

Low demands + low sensory arousal environment = low anxiety.

If you want to learn more about helping avoid anxiety for your autistic child or young person, I highly recommend reading Dr Luke Beardon's *Avoiding Anxiety in Autistic Children*.

Meltdowns

Everyone has an idea of what a meltdown is. A toddler screaming on the floor because they can't have the packet of sweets they want. But while that might be what people commonly call a meltdown, it isn't what we mean by an autistic meltdown, which is very far from a tantrum.

The first thing to know is that autistic meltdowns, shutdown, and burnout are involuntary, they are not something the person undergoing them can control. Once you know that, it removes some of your messier emotions from the equation. It's not personal. The other important thing to know is that the person having the meltdown can often feel very guilty afterwards at what they may have said or done, even though it was beyond their control. They don't need, or indeed deserve, any blame or punishment on top of this.

Some of you reading this may already have experienced years of meltdowns without really understanding them. Others may only be experiencing meltdowns from your child or young person now, when they can't cope any more with masking their autism and their anxiety is high – anxiety magnifies everything. An analogy that's commonly used here is the coke bottle effect. If the level in the bottle is high, and it gets shaken, it may explode. Substitute anxiety for fizz, and that's what's happening: an overload of upset or change is causing an explosion. If we look at the fight/flight/freeze/fawn theory again, meltdowns are extreme fight/flight reactions.

Everyone is different and I can't tell you what your child or young person's meltdown will look like, but it will be loud, it will be upsetting, it will be absolutely exhausting, it might be hurtful to you but it will not be under their control. It will be the result of multiple things leading to a high level of stress that can't be managed anymore. It won't be only about the one thing which has pushed them over the edge, which may seem trivial to you – it isn't to them, but it's about much more, and at the time, your child or young person is not going to be able to explain or possibly even identify that. Now is not the time to ask. Their coping mechanisms have been overwhelmed, so later, or another day, when things are calm again, it's time to examine the coping mechanisms and perhaps incorporate some new ones.

How Can You Help?

The best way to help is, as we've already discussed, keep everything as low stress as possible so that overwhelm is avoided. But if a meltdown does happen:

- Accept it.
- Stay calm.
- Reassure them.
- Don't tell them they are overreacting.
- Don't try to 'fix' it there and then. Just listen.
- Give them a safe belonging if it will help – a weighted blanket, a teddy, a fidget toy, a favourite smell – keep a toolbox of these things.
- If not already there, try to direct them to a space they can decompress.
- Provide the atmosphere which works for them – it might be silence, a white noise machine, a rain app or rock music blasted loud.

- If they are already used to listening, a meditation app or an audio book might help – but don't introduce these as a new thing now.

Long afterwards, if your child or young person is up for it, try to gently identify the trigger, so that you can help them avoid it next time. If it's something that's frustrating them, help them to understand how to better get what they want. It's possible they don't understand why people aren't 'getting it' (when it's so obvious to them) – they might need to practice a script for asking for whatever it is they need. If it's possible, try to get them to have an understanding of what it feels like when meltdown is looming, so that they can understand what's happening and either do their 'calm down' things, tell you, or at least get to a safe space. The more they can understand their feelings and what's happening in their body, the better.

In the long term, make sure you are preparing for transitions well in advance, and that length of time will differ for each child, and each circumstance, and will be something you establish by trial and error. For some things you might be just preparing a couple of days before, for others it might be longer and too long will cause more problems. Also, make sure you are aware just what your child considers a transition. For example, you probably won't consider driving a different route to school a big deal, but they might.

Change = uncertainty.
Uncertainty = anxiety.
Anxiety = distressed behaviour.

Preparation for change, or indeed for any kind of demand, can be better for some children and young people if it's visual. In our house, it helps to have a big whiteboard where we write our schedule for a week in advance. That way nothing sneaks up on us. Unless in an emergency, nothing else is allowed to sneak into the whiteboard schedule and we eliminate uncertainty, which eliminates anxiety, which eliminates distressed behaviour. Most of the time!

Autistic Shutdown

If meltdowns are when the unconscious brain invokes a fight/flight reaction, autistic shutdown is when your brain is telling you to freeze. Like many reactions in a child or young person who has remained unrecognised as autistic up to now, it has turned inward, and instead of an outward explosion there is an internal shutdown. There's no screaming or pounding on the floor, but there's high stress just the same, and it's just as exhausting.

Some autistic people don't experience meltdowns, or do so very rarely. Instead, when the sensory and executive function overwhelm becomes too high, the autistic person goes into shutdown. They withdraw, they may stop speaking, they may stop eating. In spoon theory, they have no spoons left.

What Is Spoon Theory?

Spoon theory is the theory that there is a finite amount of energy we have for dealing with everyday life. When living with disability or chronic illness, small everyday tasks take up more energy than they would a peer with no disability or chronic illness. Therefore, if you consider the spoon metaphor, you have a limited number of spoons available each day. Doing a task takes up more spoons than it does your peer. Therefore you have fewer spoons left over for 'extra' activities. An example might be if an autistic person went to a conference, where they needed to socialise, this would take up more spoons than it would for a neurotypical person. They might then be unable to do something else because they 'didn't have the spoons'. In fact, if they had been at a conference all day, they might very well not be able to go to dinner and socialise in the evening at all, they might need to stay in their quiet hotel room and decompress. In everyday life, a healthy neurotypical person doesn't need to worry about how many spoons they have left, unless they've done something extraordinary like run a marathon. But a disabled or chronically ill person needs to constantly balance their stock of spoons – if they do this thing, will they be able to do this other thing?

Shutdown is of course at the extreme end of spoon theory – they have no spoons left not just for that day but perhaps for that weekend, or week. Someone in autistic shutdown is functioning on their emergency battery, and only the most basic services are going to take place. It will happen to different people in different ways, but it will involve withdrawal from people and events around them. They may cover their face or head, curl up, or get under furniture. They may experience emotional pain. It can be difficult to move back out of shutdown, and the experience is especially difficult for those who have alexithymia. Those people will also find it harder to predict when they are about to go into shutdown, because they can't identify their emotions. Their brain is protecting them from sensory or emotional overload.

How Can You Help?

- Make sure they are in a safe, calm, quiet place.
- Try not to ask too many questions.
- Try not to talk a lot.
- Make sure they're not too hot or cold.
- If you know they like it, provide touch (e.g. a tight hug), or if they don't like to be touched, make sure you leave them untouched.
- Find out if you can whether they would prefer you to stay or leave them.
- If they want you to stay, do something quiet next to them like reading a book.
- Be patient and let them come out of shutdown gently.

Autistic Burnout

Autistic burnout is a large step further on than meltdown and shutdown. In this case, the person has been operating at high levels of stress and overload for a long period of time, quite possibly masking their autism, and suddenly they can't do it anymore. As they become more overloaded, their autistic traits may be amplified, and it's not, as we've been asked in Autistic Girls Network, that they are becoming 'more autistic', but that they can't mask so well. It's the real them you are starting to see, but it's the real them in crisis. In children and young people, you may be able to predict burnout if they start to have significantly more meltdowns (or start to have them when they've not really had them before), their fight/flight reaction.

Burnout is like screeching to a stop on the road. Normal life can't continue. It may seem like a nervous breakdown. The person may seem depressed, unable to make decisions they can usually make, may forget to eat, may stim more, may speak very little, will almost certainly be completely unwilling and unable to socialise. They will probably be unable to go to school or work, so for young people this can be when anxiety-based school avoidance really takes hold. Everyday tasks can't be processed in the same way as they usually can. Even the smallest demand is too big.

Burnout can often feel shameful, as if you should have been able to cope. But nobody should feel bad or be made to feel bad about being in burnout.

How Can You Help?

- If you notice symptoms of increased emotional or sensory distress, evaluate the environment surrounding that person and if there has been a high-stress event, a big change, or sensory overload. If you can change things in time, you may be able to avoid burnout. It's very unlikely a child or young person, or even an adult who has never gone through burnout before, may be able to predict this themselves.
- Encourage helpful stims (sitting in a rocking chair, pacing, dancing with your arms waving around – whatever feels good).
- Make a calm, soothing, protective den.
- Give them space – physical and social.

How can burnout be avoided in the future?

- Try to recognise symptoms from the last time.
- Build enough chill out time into a regular day.
- Recognise that big social asks will need big social rests.
- Help your child or young person self-regulate and put into place things that help to soothe them.
- Try to organise their environment to be not overloaded – obviously school is the difficult factor here.
- Give them the capacity to say no when needed and set boundaries.
- Put their needs first, over society's demands.

CASE STUDY
Tom, age 16 in the UK

Tom went to mainstream school, and was studying for his GCSEs. His parents had raised the possibility that he was autistic with the school, as his behaviour was quite different at home, but were told he was 'fine in school'. He had friends, he was no trouble in class, he was doing OK academically. But his mental health really started to suffer. He began to self-harm. He attempted suicide. He begged not to go to school, and his attendance dropped drastically, until he told his parents he just couldn't go anymore. He seemed depressed, he didn't leave the house, he wouldn't speak to anyone outside his family. They didn't know it, but he was in autistic burnout. As he gradually rested at home, he came to behave quite differently – his mask dropped and he began to be able to be his true self there. He got an EHCP and a placement in a small nurturing educational provision. He retook a year and got some GCSEs at a pace that was right for him. He's now much happier and much more comfortable with his autistic self.

Self-Harmful Behaviour

There is more than one type of self-harming behaviour. The first could be a stim that's self-harmful, such as banging your head against a wall. As your child or young person is not being recognised as autistic until they are older, we are not going to talk much about that type of self-harm here, except to say that they are often seeking strong proprioception (which we'll be learning all about in the next chapter), and offering an alternative, as well as identifying triggers to avoid the situation, will help. In a young or non-speaking child, they are demonstrating distress that they can't articulate. Remember that you can't teach anything new when they are in distress. The second type could be a 'lifestyle' type of self-harm which includes drugs, alcohol, and risky behaviour. That could of course happen, though it's more generally associated with the impulsivity of ADHD. In fact lots of adults who have only discovered that they are neurodivergent later in life have realised that they effectively self-treated themselves with alcohol. Risky behaviour like this is difficult to manage and very upsetting to witness as a parent. It's likely that you will feel you need some outside help, perhaps from social services, although sadly there is often little help forthcoming. Self-harm is a method of coping, so to avoid it people must be given other ways to cope. There's no quick fix, but building up self-esteem, providing a calm sensory environment and helping to find ways to self-regulate will lessen the need for self-harm. Which leads us to the next type of self-harm, and the one many of us mean when we use that phrase – cutting and otherwise damaging our bodies.

Content warning for self-harm at this point. Skip to page 79 if you don't want to read this section.

Finding out that your child is self-harming is incredibly upsetting as a parent. It's hard not to believe that you've been doing something wrong, that this is somehow your fault. But it's not.

If your child is a teenager, it's probable that some of their classmates self-harm, and that they have talked about it at school. It's also probable that it's not going to be something they're happy talking about with you, and they may go to some lengths to hide it from you, afraid that you'll be upset, angry, or disappointed. If your teenager who has always worn t-shirts and shorts starts to always wear long sleeves and long trousers, this should be a sign something might be wrong. This kind of self-harm on its own, although alarming to parents, is unlikely to get you an appointment with CAMHS. Sadly the threshold to be seen is much higher than that. But multiple apps and websites will tell you to use 'minimisation strategies' by advising techniques like writing on arms with red pen, pressing ice cubes on the skin, or pinging elastic bands against the wrist. Not only has research found these techniques to not be helpful, but one study found that young people were using the elastic band technique as another form of self-harm. It also pointed out that these techniques were not dealing with the core problem, which was why the young people felt the need to self-harm at all. Being advised to use techniques which are perceived as insufficient or not working undermines confidence in those systems which are supposed to provide support. Therapy, and addressing the issues causing the distress, are necessary for mental health to improve sufficiently to stop the self-harm.

How Can You Help?

- I know it's a shock. But try to stay calm and matter of fact when your child or young person opens up about self-harm. The easier you make it, the more likely your child will continue to include you in the conversation, and it's much better to know than for it all to be secret.
- Ask them to tell you if a wound is bad and needs medical attention.
- Talk about it in a non-confrontational way and setting – while in the car often works well, as nobody needs to make eye contact.
- Try to identify why they have started to self-harm, and how you can help to take the stress or distress away.
- Teach your child about keeping the wounds clean and provide antibacterial spray.
- If you think there might be greater danger, do keep sharps and meds locked away.
- Talk about a way they could alert you to how they are feeling and if they need to self-harm, so that you can distract them from it if possible. (With the proviso that 'traffic light systems' don't always work.)
- Discuss (in a calm way) how your child is going to feel about scars or wounds in the summer weather, when we're all less covered up.
- Talk about how to minimise the scars in the future – a future where they won't still be cutting.
- Be patient.
- Celebrate the small wins.
- Tell them you love them, no matter what.

CASE STUDY

Amy, age 14 in the UK

Amy had to stay in the children's ward at her local hospital when she was 14 a few times to wait for CAMHS to discharge her after some difficult mental health struggles. She encountered other teenage girls there for the same reason each time, and they were self-harming. She picked up how to do it, and how it helped to distract from painful emotions, and she started to self-harm. She bought disposable razors and pencil sharpeners, and used a dinner knife to break them and take out the blade as she had heard how to do from friends at school. The first time her mum saw her cuts, she was really upset so Amy made sure to always wear leggings and long sleeves. CAMHS told her mum not to stop her cutting, so while mum got rid of any other blades she found and locked up all the sharps in the house, she let Amy keep one blade. CAMHS told her to distract herself or draw on her arms instead of cutting, but that didn't help. They told her to keep the cuts from getting infected with antiseptic spray, and she did do that. Her family worked very hard to make home easier and Amy gradually stopped cutting as she masked less. Amy hasn't cut herself for over a year now, although sometimes she leaves a blade where she knows her mum will find it. Even without Amy saying, her mum knows that she's feeling bad and needs extra care at that time.

Violent Child Behaviour

What's called 'violent child behaviour' (but I prefer to call 'highly distressed behaviour') does happen in some neurodivergent children and young people, and while you might feel guilty if it happens in your family, it's not your fault. When you ask for help, though, you are going to be made to feel as if it's your fault, because the first help you're likely to receive is to be sent on a parenting course. Opinions on these differ widely, but without attending you may not be able to proceed towards any further forms of help.

Highly distressed behaviour stems from anxiety, and is communicating distress. In simple terms therefore, to change the behaviour you need to remove the distress. That is, of course, very simplistic and not taking into account at all your level of upset and worry about what's happening in your family. But above all don't despair, it can and will get better. A violent meltdown is triggered by the fight/flight reaction – it's involuntary and your child is not to blame, though they will probably feel guilty.

How Can You Help?

- Make sure they know you don't blame them – someone whose brain tells them fight/flight is the only possible reaction is not to blame.
- Keep calm (though I know it will be difficult) and don't show panic – this would make the brain react to even more danger and might make things worse.
- Don't expect rational answers at this stage.
- Don't try to 'fix' things right now.
- Keep other people out of your child's space right now. Make sure other children (and pets if need be) are in a safe place.
- Celebrate small wins and build self-esteem.
- Tell them you love them no matter what.

Long term, you need to find out the triggers of the highly distressed behaviour. Much of the time for an autistic child or young person it's sensory, so it would be very desirable to have a proper sensory OT assessment to find out what they struggle with and what soothes them. These can be expensive though; in the UK they can be difficult (but not impossible) to get on the NHS or as part of the EHCP process. Once you know, you can change their environment considerably which should improve distressed behaviour.

Many of the tips around meltdowns, shutdowns, etc. also apply here around noise and touch and preparing for change. If your child is 'fine at school' but explodes when they come home, don't assume home is where the problem is – the opposite may well be the case. Since you are their safe human and home is their safe space, that's the only place they feel comfortable to explode. So follow the tips throughout this book for improving things at school.

This very distressed behaviour can be hard to live with. Help your own mental health by joining a group, either face to face or online, where people understand. There are multiple possible groups on Facebook. One particularly good one is Newbold Hope – Distressed Behaviour Information & Support.

Fight/Flight/Freeze/Fawn

We've mentioned the fight/flight/freeze mechanism a lot, but most people tend to forget about 'fawning' at the end. For those children and young people who have got to late primary or secondary school before being referred or recognised as autistic, fawning is probably their primary trauma response.

So What Is the Fight, Flight, Freeze, and Fawn Response?

The first three are the most well-known trauma responses. Someone may stand and fight, they may run and hide from the threat, or they may freeze like a deer in the headlights and not know what to do. However there is a further trauma response which is less well-known: to fawn. Fawning is trying to alleviate the threat or conflict by pleasing the person, possibly at any cost. Examples of fawning by an autistic child or young person might be agreeing to do something they don't want to, saying what they know someone wants to hear even though it's not true, or masking their feelings to put up with a situation they don't like. All of these things are EXACTLY what our children and young people who mask are doing at school, whether consciously or unconsciously, and it's why they have been so hard to recognise as autistic up to this point in their lives.

Why Is a Trauma Response Necessary?

It's a legitimate question. What's so bad that these children and young people feel traumatised? Sadly, everyday life in a society created for neurotypical people can be traumatic. Social conventions they don't understand which leave them feeling wrong, sensory trauma, cognitive and processing confusion, loneliness from difficulty finding friends who understand them – it can all add up.

How Do We Know What Trauma Response to Expect?

That's going to depend on the situation, the person, and just how many spoons they have left. But many autistic people who mask sufficiently not to be recognised as autistic for years are going to fawn. Fawning is not a behaviour which challenges, which doesn't bring the child to the notice of professionals. And most of all, what they want is to fit in – not necessarily to be the same as everyone else, but to be accepted.

Why Do We Fawn?

There's a myth that autistic people don't feel empathy – we'll tackle that myth later! In fact, most very much feel empathy, and they don't want to distress other people. So add in the fact they don't want to stand out and they want the threat (of change, whatever it is) to go away and you have the perfect recipe for fawning. This becomes a habit that's difficult to break.

Why Is the Fawn Response Not Ideal?

Apart from the fact that the fawn response conditions someone to value other people's wants, needs, and opinions above their own, it can also leave people vulnerable to predatory instincts and open to manipulation. It causes people to mask their true feelings which leaves them in situations which can damage them and cause trauma.

These are trauma responses, let's not forget, and it's a fact that lots of neurodivergent children and young people, even if it's never diagnosed, eventually live with PTSD caused by (usually mainstream) school. Many girls with parents in the Autistic Girls Network Facebook group do.

CASE STUDY

Bryony, age 11 in Australia

Bryony started her mainstream secondary school six months ago, and while she's trying to fit in and make friends, she's finding it almost intolerable. When she gets home, she can't hold it in anymore and she explodes with a meltdown that exhausts her and makes her feel really guilty. Meltdowns suck. But when teachers ask at school she says she's OK, and she doesn't use her time out card in class because she doesn't want everyone to look at her. She knows the answers people want her to give and she gives them. But inside she's screaming because it's too loud, there are too many people, too many smells, it's all just overwhelming.

Hearing Voices

Hearing voices, or auditory hallucination, is actually much more common than you might think – 5% of us hear voices at times.[15] It can be your brain's way of protecting you from a difficult situation when anxious – these are intrusive thoughts rather than voices. It isn't necessarily something to be worried about, and definitely not, as we tend to think, always associated with psychosis.

Autistic young people can also tend to internalise their thoughts, which can lead to seeming to hear voices. If your child or young person is hearing voices which are saying very negative things or encouraging them to hurt themselves or other people, you need to go to your GP who will refer you for help.

OCD can also internalise and present as hearing voices (or more accurately, hearing *a* voice), and if the voices are threatening you or your family it can be scary and difficult to 'stand up' to them.

---

15   University of Queensland (2015) 'Hallucinations and delusions more common than thought'. *ScienceDaily*, 27 May. Accessed on 2 May 2022 at www.sciencedaily. com/releases/2015/05/150527124725.htm

How Can You Help?

- Be calm, matter of fact and non-judgemental so that your child will talk to you. It's a big step to tell someone.
- Don't dismiss them.
- Tell your child that they, and not the voices, are in control of their body, even if it doesn't always feel like it.
- Reassure your child that you will be strong for them, even when they can't be.
- If they can't say no to the voices/thoughts, ask them to say 'not yet'.
- Think up a positive mantra your child can say if they will entertain this idea.
- Tell your child how to reply to someone who is being nasty – and do the same to the voices/thoughts.
- Distract your child with whatever they like doing.
- Teach your child to recognise when they are starting and remove themselves to start a new activity – their own distraction.
- Use your child's imagination (with some help from yours) to add a silly detail to the voice which makes them less scary.
- Art therapy can help – your child may find it therapeutic to draw what they are experiencing.

If you need more help with your child or young person hearing voices, this is a good site: www.voicecollective.co.uk/about-voices

Don't Assume Manipulation

We've all heard it. We might even have thought it sometimes.

'Don't give into his bad behaviour. He's just trying to get his own way.'

'Take no notice of her drama. She's just manipulating you.'

As if these distressed behaviours are all part of a grand Machiavellian scheme to pull the wool over our eyes. And I haven't forgotten that your child is also a tween or a teen, who also has a natural urge for drama and rebellion. So how can you tell the difference?

When your 18-year-old is trying to get permission to take your car to go shopping, that might well be a bit of teenage manipulation. But when your 12-year-old is crying their eyes out and holding on to fences desperate not to be dragged into school, that's a rather different situation. That's not bad behaviour. That's not manipulation. That's a fight or flight trauma response, and no amount of telling him he can't get away with it will reverse the situation or make it any easier for him to deal with. His brain is protecting him from trauma the only way it knows how, and our reaction should be to find the cause of his trauma and remove it. My controversial belief is that the reason we so often don't do that is because the reason for his trauma is our supposedly inclusive mainstream school system.

When the reason for the trauma is so fundamental, no amount of reward charts or incentivising is going to work. It's why, when school placements have broken down, it's almost impossible to make them work again – because you're asking that child or young person to go back to the source of all their trauma.

People who say 'he's just playing you', even when it's your mother-in-law or your best friend, or the headteacher, don't understand the way autistic people experience the world. They don't understand how the world is set up to be accommodating to neurotypical people only. And when it's your best friend saying that, of course it's even harder. But you know better. You can be compassionate and understanding. You can stop the trauma, not add to it, and you will have a much happier child. Of course, it will be even better when you feel strong enough to educate your mother-in-law and best friend and headteacher too. When we feel safe and loved, we don't need to fight, flight, freeze, or fawn.

Chapter 3

Sensory Stuff

This chapter is going to look at our senses, and it might well introduce you to some you didn't even know you had. Bruce Willis might have starred in a film about an 'extra' sixth sense, but actually we've got three extra ones!

INTEROCEPTION
The eight senses of the human body:

- vision
- smell
- hearing
- touch
- taste
- proprioception (body spatial awareness)
- vestibular (balance)
- interoception (feeling inside the body).

All of these senses can be hypersensitive (over-responsive) or hyposensitive (under-responsive) in autistic people and they contribute massively to autistic people's different ways of experiencing the world. Understanding what we call in my family 'the sensory stuff' is therefore really important if you are going to understand what your child or young person is experiencing, and how to help them navigate a world shaped for another neurotype.

The sensory aspect of being autistic is not all that commonly known, but for some autistic people it can be SUPER important. Many of us know about seams in socks and labels in clothes being irritating. But few know that for some autistic people these things are not just irritating but painful. And there is much much more to sensory sensitivities than seams and labels. But first, let's take a look at why the senses might be so impacted in autistic people. What's different about the senses of an autistic person compared to a neurotypical person? We're going to need to understand how our brains understand the signals being sent by our bodies, and how our senses are linked to our emotions, not just how we feel physically but our personal wellbeing. Let's look first at interoception.

Interoception is not well-known, but it's one of our senses and it's a really important part of understanding some autistic people. That's why, despite it being the eighth and last sense, we are starting with it. It's the sense which alerts us, through receptors in our organs and skin, as to how our body is feeling. It also makes us experience sensations which generally lead us to take an action. For example, our stomach rumbles or we feel what we identify as hungry, and we know we ought to eat some food. Our heart beats very fast or our muscles tense and we know that we're excited or scared. Our mouth is dry and we know that we're thirsty and need to drink. Our bladder feels full and we know that we need to go to the toilet – all important, indeed vital, things for our body to know how to do.

But what happens when our sense of interoception isn't working well? If we can't interpret these signals that our body is sending to our brain properly, and we know that we need something but we don't know what it is?

Some of the things which can be difficult with a poor sense of interoception (your child or young person may have difficulty with one, some, none, or all of these!):

- Knowing when you're hungry.

- Knowing when you're full.
- Knowing when you're thirsty.
- Knowing when you're in pain.
- Knowing if you're in serious pain.
- Knowing where the pain is.
- Knowing when you feel nauseous.
- Knowing when you feel itchy.
- Knowing when you're hot or cold.
- Knowing when you need the toilet.

If your brain isn't getting or correctly interpreting these signals, then there's scope for some serious trouble there. Not realising when you feel itchy might not be too problematic, but only feeling itchy instead of feeling bad pain could potentially be fatal. Everyone is different, and I can't tell you if your autistic child or young person will have any of these issues, but it's something to be aware of. As well as physical sensations, a poor sense of interoception can also mean a difficulty in 'feeling' emotions, such as in the example given about not being able to identify a racing heart and tense muscles so not feeling fear. A child who doesn't feel fear can end up in some sticky situations. Not being able to interpret some bodily sensations can make it difficult to identify those strong emotions (and identifying emotions is also a problem for those with alexithymia, often seen together with interoceptive problems – we'll cover this later).

PROPRIOCEPTION

Proprioception is the other sense most people don't even know they have. Just as signals travel to the brain with interoception from sensors in our organs and skin, so the receptors in our muscles and joints signal to the brain where the different parts of our bodies are. Our proprioceptive sense makes us spatially aware of where our body is in relation to objects around us, both still and moving. It's vitally important to us, and allows us to walk, for example, without thinking about how our feet and legs are moving or consciously controlling them.

I'm using my proprioceptive sense right now while writing this book, typing without looking at my keyboard.

Our brains are constantly sending signals to our bodies, telling us how to move to finish whatever task we've decided we want to do. But for some, the signal is not getting through. Most people, if they closed their eyes and lifted their hand up as far as it could go, would know that they'd raised their arm above their head. But someone with proprioceptive difficulties might not be aware of that without looking. It means it's very difficult for your body to direct your limbs to be in the place you want them to be at the right time, such as when you're playing any kind of ball sports for example.

Proprioception is often called the 'safe sense' by therapists because things we do which stimulate the sense help our brains to carry out activities needing organisational skills.

Activities which stimulate our proprioceptive sense are:

- pulling
- pushing
- stretching
- climbing
- squeezing.

To understand why proprioceptive stimulation is important, we again need to look at how our brain works. We all have a part of our brain called the reticular activating system (RAS), and all nerve pathways in our body are eventually connected to RAS. The important role of RAS for us here is in regulating levels of alertness in our bodies. RAS enables many of us to focus on one thing by dampening down our levels of alertness to other things. For example, we can tune out the background traffic noise while we are talking to a friend outside a cafe. And RAS generally 'wakes up' and 'goes to sleep' when we do. Light touch, pain sensations, and hearing all follow pathways in the body which come close to the RAS, and can be a sign of danger (think of a fire alarm, or burning yourself) which would lead to you feeling alarmed. In contrast, deep touch and proprioceptive actions follow pathways further away from the RAS, so don't cause alarm and can make us feel less anxious. This is what an occupational therapist (OT) means when they say your child needs 'deep proprioceptive input' which could be, for example, carrying heavy shopping bags, strong hugs (only if they like this), using a climbing wall, sitting with a weighted blanket.

VESTIBULAR MOVEMENT

Our vestibular sense is our sense of balance. It's centred around the inner ear and the brain. It detects movement and gravitational pull (pretty impressive, eh!), and it provides information to our brain about the position of our head in space and acceleration and deceleration of movement around us. The vestibular system affects not only posture, balance, movement, and co-ordination, but also things like attention, arousal level, impulsivity, and behaviour. We use this sense all the time unless we're asleep – sitting up, standing, walking, dancing, climbing, shaking our heads. Many of us will have experienced what happens when our vestibular sense system gets overloaded and we get motion sickness. Dizziness with heights is also due to a difference in sensory processing of our sense of balance.

People with sensory processing difficulties revolving around the proprioceptive and vestibular senses may:

- Have trouble co-ordinating motor skills such as running.
- Have difficulty predicting the trajectory of and therefore catching a ball.
- Come across as clumsy.
- Spill stuff as their brain may not signal the right amount of muscle strength to use for an activity.
- Push too hard when writing.
- Pull a window blind too hard.
- Hug you so hard it takes your breath away.
- Have difficulty alternating between looking at their work and the whiteboard and finding the same place.

They don't mean to do any of these things, but their brain isn't sending them the correct signals.

The vestibular system is inextricably linked to our emotional regulation. Babies are soothed by rocking which helps to calm them and regulate their emotional response. It's not unusual to see parents taking them for a push in their buggy or even for a drive in the middle of the night to get them to sleep. If your child or young person loves to swing, or go on rollercoasters, or go for a drive – this is why.

CASE STUDY
Jack, age 19 in the US

Jack has dyspraxia as well as being autistic, but his parents didn't discover that he seeks vestibular movement until he was diagnosed as a teen after significant mental health breakdown. He enjoys car journeys and usually needs to be taken for a drive in the car most evenings to help with regulating his central nervous system to prepare for relaxation and sleep.

SENSORY SEEKING, SENSORY AVOIDANCE, AND SENSORY OVERLOAD

Much of what we hear about autism and sensory issues is negative, but actually the ability to feel things intensely can also be fantastic! As we'll see it's a fine balance, but by understanding you can help create the environment for your child or young person to thrive.

When a child has sensory processing issues, they crave the sensory input their body and brain isn't giving them. They can be divided into sensory seekers and sensory avoiders, because they may be receiving too little or too much sensory information, although be aware that one person can be both for different senses.

What you need to know about sensory avoidance (hypersensitivity):

- Clothing can feel itchy or irritating or too tight.
- Lights can be too bright or noisy.

- Background noise can be impossible to filter.
- Touch can be painful.
- Smells can be overpowering.

What you need to know about sensory seeking (hyposensitivity):

- May crave touch.
- Spicy, salty, bitter, and very sweet foods can be favourites.
- May have a high pain tolerance.
- May move around a lot and be fidgety.
- May be unable to sit still on a chair.
- May like deep pressure activities like tight hugs, compression sheets, weighted blankets.
- May crave vestibular movement – swinging, driving, moving in vehicles or rollercoasters.
- May need activities which stimulate the proprioceptive sense like jumping on a trampoline.
- Favourite smells can soothe.

I can tell you that some children fulfil ALL these criteria, from both sections! That's why learning about interoception and the other lesser known senses can make such a difference to families. If you think that your child or young person may have a lot of sensory difficulties, it will make a big difference to have a sensory assessment by a sensory integration-qualified occupational therapist. Their assessment will look at four quadrants of your child's sensory profile:

- Sensation seeking (fidgeting, rocking, chewing).
- Low registration (does their nervous system have calm periods or are they on high alert all the time? fight/flight/freeze/fawn response).
- Sensation avoiding (bright lights, noisy environments, certain smells and tastes, light touch).
- Sensory sensitivity (in environments with lots of sensory stimuli, e.g. a busy classroom, canteen, supermarket, etc.,

your child will need to put in much more effort than their peers to stay focused and filter out the environment around them).

TASTE

Just a quick whizz around the topic of food and meals in a sensory capacity.

Points to remember when thinking about the sense of taste and about eating:

- Sensory seekers may like intense food, e.g., salt, vinegar, hot sauce, crunchy, or soft.
- Sensory avoiders may like bland food, not too crunchy or soft, which has a reliable consistency. This explains why food like McDonalds chicken nuggets is so popular with autistic children – it's bland, it always tastes the same and has the same texture and crunch every time.
- Mealtimes are difficult not only because of taste but proximity to other people eating and the sounds of chewing or plates and cutlery scraping (bamboo crockery makes very little sound).
- The texture of food may matter.
- The lip of a cup (or piece of cutlery) may need to be the right thickness or texture or weight.

SMELL

We experience the world through our senses, and while a sense of smell might be what most people think they could live without if they had to give one up, it's an important part of our lives. Some autistic people are hypersensitive or hyposensitive to smell. If you smell very little, you may not have much of an appetite and be unenthusiastic about eating. You may also not notice your own body odour! If you're hypersensitive to smell, it means you can smell both bad and good odours intensely. This means if you're in a restaurant and smell some-one else's food and it smells awful, you may be unable to eat there. Conversely, you may LOVE the smell of a particular food, and that can always tempt you to eat. From a chores point of view, it can be difficult to get a teen who is hypersensitive to smell to clean the bathroom, pick up dog poo, or take out the trash!

CASE STUDY
Adam, age ten in Australia

Adam is hypersensitive to smell. He has favourite smells, which can soothe him when he's anxious or upset, like the smell of fresh laundry. There is a scented candle which smells like this and he has a miniature version he can smell when he needs to. He also has smells he finds disgusting – quite a lot of them! He can't do smelly chores, and he couldn't even go into the dining hall at school because of all the different food smells (the noise and people didn't help either). His school lets him choose his food early and he eats in a small room with a couple of friends. He can manage more when he's calm, but when he's anxious or overloaded a bad smell will send his senses spiralling.

SOUND

Some autistic people have highly sensitive hearing and can hear sounds from a long way away or which are just whispers. I've learnt from experience not to assume my children can't hear anything I'm saying, however quiet, all around the house! Difficulty with auditory process-ing however means that it can be tricky to filter noises. Whereas most people can filter out all of the background noise from what someone is saying, some autistic people are unable to do this.

CASE STUDY
Grace, age 14 in the UK

Grace is autistic and is in mainstream secondary school. Before she was diagnosed, she was in a science lesson doing an experiment involving sound at a pitch humans couldn't hear. But Grace could, and she told the teacher so. The teacher said she couldn't possibly. Grace (who normally spoke very little in class) insisted she could. She got a detention. As Grace, like many of her autistic peers, is a strong proponent of social justice, this didn't go down well, because it wasn't just. (She didn't go to the detention!)

Misophonia

People with misophonia find everyday noises unbearable – noises that most of us would be able to filter out like someone chewing, birdsong, snoring – and depending on the severity of their reaction it can trigger a fight/flight response. Not everyone with misophonia is autistic, and certainly not everyone autistic has misophonia, but there is a sizeable crossover, and as with many sensory reactions it will be less bearable when anxiety is already high.

When your child or young person tells you they can't bear the sound of their brother chewing at the dinner table, listen. While it could be sibling bickering, it's also possible that the sound is physically painful, so don't just dismiss it.

Misophonia has only even been named in the last 20 years, so diagnoses are few and far between. It can be diagnosed by an audiologist, but your GP may not have heard of it so you might need to take some information along with you for referral if you do want to pursue a diagnosis. There's no treatment as such though, only strategies and therapies on dealing with it.

Ear defenders or noise cancelling headphones are going to be a must, and there are some good new (and rather expensive) ear plugs on the market which were originally designed for working with loud music.

TOUCH

The last of the senses we're looking at in this section is touch. This is probably an aspect of autism that most people think they know best – that autistic people don't like being touched or hugged. And this may be the case for your young person. But actually some sensory seekers DO love big, tight hugs – but only from the right people. Others are not too bothered about being touched, while others really do dislike it intensely. It will depend on your child or young person, but while they're young, they will depend on you to fend off all the distant relatives who want to hug them. Respect how they feel – civilisation won't collapse if Great Auntie Ethel doesn't get a hug from your son today.

It's also something to mention to teachers – however well-meaning, touching a child who is sensory avoidant to this will make them uncomfortable at best and dysregulated at worst. If their behaviour tips over, look back over what happened – how was the child or young person over-stimulated. Was there too much noise or touch, or unwanted sensations (for example, I've seen distressing clips of the build-up to dysregulation when someone was being made to take part in what was presumably art therapy with papier-mâché. There were at least three people crowded around them, one of whom kept touching his shoulders, all speaking at once and trying to make him touch the papier-mâché when it was obvious from his body language, facial expression, and speaking the word 'No' that he did not want to). Autistic people deserve to have autonomy over their bodies, and that includes the right not to be touched unnecessarily without permission.

SYNAESTHESIA

Synaesthesia is a relatively rare neurological trait whereby some senses that are usually separate become connected – 4% of the population have it, and it can cause some very interesting sensory variation! Because some senses have 'blended', synaesthetes experience the world in still a different way. They might see numbers as colours, or music might have a range of smells, or they might experience a taste when they hear a particular word. It's unusual but can by all accounts also be very beautiful, and can often run in families.

For example, the president of the UK Synaesthesia Association experiences sounds as tastes. Since we are pretty much always hearing some kind of sound when we are awake, he is pretty much always tasting those sounds as well as hearing them.

> If I hear my dog bark, I experience the taste and texture of runny custard in my mouth. The word 'like' tastes of yoghurt, the name 'Martin' has the tastes and texture of a warm bakewell tart. Individual voices have taste and texture, as does all music.[1]

Obviously this is highly personalised, and synaesthetes who see words as colour, for example, are going to have a completely different experience.

1   Giles, C. (2017) 'What it's like to have synaesthesia: Meet the man who can taste sounds'. *Independent*, 16 October. Accessed on 2 May 2022 at www.independent.co.uk/news/long_reads/synaesthesia-sound-taste-health-science-brain-a7996766.html?r=43762

Chapter 4

Co-Occurring Conditions

There are a selection of neuro-differences which tend to co-occur in autistic people and are part of the neurodivergent family of conditions. This doesn't mean your autistic child or young person will have all or any of them, but they might, and since some of them are even more misunderstood and difficult to get diagnosed, it's good to know about them.

ADHD

Just as the medical model of diagnosis for autism relies on pointing out deficits of behaviour, so too a diagnosis of ADHD, according to the DSM-V, needs 'clear evidence that the symptoms interfere with, or reduce the quality of, social, school, or work functioning'.[1] In fact, in England and elsewhere, unless you get a diagnosis privately, the decision on whether to prescribe meds is likely to be based on how much difficulty you are having at school. And as we've already discovered, schools aren't paying much attention to pupils who are not exhibiting externalised distressed behaviour. But ADHD is much more than the classic example of a hyperactive boy.

There are three types of ADHD:

- inattentive

---

[1]   CDC (2021) *Symptoms and Diagnosis of ADHD*. Accessed on 30 May 2022 at www.cdc.gov/ncbddd/adhd/diagnosis.html

- combined
- hyperactive.

Guess which one is the one most people know about? But in fact, some people, often those raised as girls, have either combined or inattentive type, in which the behaviours tend to be internalised. It's not a coincidence that, like autism, ADHD is underdiagnosed in girls. It's my opinion that autism plus ADHD is even more difficult to spot, because some of the traits camouflage each other, but there hasn't been any research done that could back me up there, so it remains just a theory. What's not theory though is that up to 80% of autistic people (estimates vary widely) also have ADHD,[2] and this is why I believe ADHD should be screened for at the same time as autism.

ADHD has many crossovers with autism, and one of the biggest is that some ADHDers mask their traits, unsurprisingly since they've been told they are undesirable behaviours. This means they are going unrecognised, and not getting support or indeed the meds which might help them to focus.

External ADHD behaviours used to aid diagnosis include:

- visible lack of focus at school
- poor grades
- impulsive, risky behaviour
- being unable to keep still
- being unable to sustain an interest in projects.

Those who are not exhibiting this behaviour which affects others are not likely to get referred in school, but I strongly believe diagnosis shouldn't be made on how others are affected but by how ADHDers themselves FEEL. There are lots of ADHD traits which are internalised and not external behaviour which will stop someone going under the radar. (Sadly though, an ADHD diagnosis is made on the basis of

---

2   Rusting, R. (2018) 'Decoding the overlap between autism and ADHD'. *Spectrum*, 7 February. Accessed on 2 May 2022 at www.spectrumnews.org/features/deep-dive/decoding-overlap-autism-adhd

reporting in two different settings, which means school not seeing it can stop any chance of getting the diagnosis.)

Hyperactivity is not just about behaviour but also about brain activity – a hyperactive brain can be constantly ON at full power, constantly restless, needing new stimulation all the time, with difficulty switching off to relax.

Impulsivity is not just about drinking too much or throwing chairs across the room... an impulsive brain can agree to things without really thinking them through, find it difficult to say no to anything (and we're back to the need for stimulation here), or trust someone without knowing enough about them.

Inattention is more than not paying attention to your teacher – much of the problems of inattention are likely to do with poor working memory, since it needs attention to be sustained to retain the information. When someone is doing all those things without friends, family, teachers, or bosses knowing they have ADHD, they are vulnerable to being shamed and made to feel bad.

Autism and ADHD together can make difficult companions. A love of order doesn't sit well with a love of chaos. A need for familiarity doesn't sit well with a need for constant stimulation. A love of rules doesn't sit well with a tendency to non-conformity. The need to complete a task doesn't sit well with abandoning it to start a new one. A focus on detail doesn't sit well with a tendency to ignore detail and see the big picture. And let's not even get started on peopling! ADHD meds can also be difficult for those who are also autistic. Quietening down a hyper-busy brain can mean that there's more capacity to notice all 'the sensory stuff' which the busyness might have distracted from.

CASE STUDY

Jess, age 18 in the US

Jess is autistic and also has ADHD. Her ADHD was diagnosed later at 15, and her paediatrician wanted her to try ADHD medication. At first Jess didn't notice a difference, but gradually she became hyper-alert to noise and life became unbearable, both for Jess and by extension her family. She stopped taking the meds. She realised that they had made a difference to her focus, and her brain became 'fuzzy' again, but the price of hypersensitivity to noise was too great to pay.

But ADHD can also bring great hyperfocus, great outside-the-box thinking, and a large dose of entrepreneurial spirit. Some CEOs and founders of some of the world's largest companies are neurodivergent – Richard Branson, Elon Musk, Ikea founder Ingvar Kamprad, creator of Pokémon Satoshi Tajiri, Bill Gates, Steve Jobs, Steven Spielberg, to name a few. Focusing on the deficits of a short attention span and ignoring the plus sides is not fair or even sensible when the world obviously needs people who can think differently.

How Can You Help?

- Be aware of the internal presentations of ADHD as well as the external ones.
- Advocate for your young person at school because internal ADHD traits are hard for teachers to spot.

REJECTION SENSITIVE DYSPHORIA

Rejection sensitive dysphoria (RSD) appears to be something that occurs mainly with ADHD, and is extreme pain and emotional sensitivity in relation to rejection, mockery, criticism, or disappointment – either people being disappointed in you or you being disappointed in other people. Everyone of course experiences feeling bad about being rejected, but this is as if the emotion has been hugely magnified. It doesn't occur in all people with ADHD, and it's not in any diagnostic criteria, but there's enough anecdotal evidence to be sure it's a 'thing'. So if your child or young person has what seems to be a very extreme reaction to criticism or rejection, this may be why.

Those who experience RSD will seek to protect themselves from it, either by extreme fawning and trying to please everyone, or by not trying anymore – not answering questions in class, not trying for that art competition, not asking out a girl they like, not applying to university. Each rejection, and ultimately each rejected opportunity, becomes part of a cycle of trauma – the more they don't try, the less self-esteem they have.

How Can You Help?

- Understand that RSD exists, and if it happens to your child or young person they are not being overly dramatic.
- Help with understanding and regulating emotions – professional help may be necessary.

DYSPRAXIA

Dyspraxia (also known as developmental co-ordination disorder) is a relatively common developmental condition thought to affect 2–6% of the population. Again, it is underdiagnosed in girls. DPD is diagnosed due to impairment of motor skills such as catching or throwing balls, using utensils or riding a bike among other things, but as dyspraxia it also includes difficulties with executive function, such as planning, organisation, and working memory.

If you suspect your child or young person is dyspraxic, it's a good idea to get a full sensory assessment from a qualified sensory integration practitioner (not all occupational therapists have this qualification). If you know your child or young person has a lot of sensory issues it's also good to get this assessment, and it may essentially tell you your child is dyspraxic, as it did for our family. (Please note though that the OT doesn't diagnose, at least in the UK – you would take this report to a paediatrician.) We had no idea. The report will tell you which aspects your child or young person struggles with and likewise teach you a whole new vocabulary! I never even knew praxis existed – now I could write a whole section on it! (Praxis is our ability to plan sequentially, to organise how we are going to carry out a task – what motor actions we are going to take, the order we will do them in, and how we will execute them.)

We talked about the vestibular sensory system, and how problems can stop your child or young person developing a complete picture or 'map' of their body and where it is in space in relation to their environment. Not having this accurate map affects how we learn new motor skills and develop praxis, which in turn means some everyday self-care tasks may be difficult because of body co-ordination for fine and gross motor skills.

While some tasks might be difficult, there are a lot of positives to dyspraxia. Dyspraxic people tend to:

- be creative thinkers
- be hard workers
- have good problem-solving skills
- have a great sense of humour
- have a unique outlook
- be determined
- be empathetic.

How Can You Help?

Dyspraxia is not well-recognised or supported, so it's important that you educate yourself as much as possible on it to advocate for your child or young person, and let their unique, humorous, determined creativity shine through!

DYSLEXIA

Because everyone's heard of dyslexia, they think they understand it. But dyslexia is much more than not being able to read. In fact many dyslexic people CAN read, much like Fern who was diagnosed at 16 and had never been referred or recognised by any schools, by CAMHS or by any of the social workers, psychologists, educational psychologists, or speech and language therapists who her parents had come into contact with over the previous few years. It was her, looking up information and asking her lovely new specialist school for an assessment they paid for, which led to the discovery that, like

10% of the population,[3] she's dyslexic. But it should never need to be that way. Her parents had mentioned things like spelling to her schools since the early days of primary school. Sadly the system failed her – there's no excuse for this.

Like autism, dyslexia is a neurological difference (classed as a 'specific learning difficulty' in the UK), and is part of the neurodivergent family. In fact it often runs in families, and can be experienced quite differently by different dyslexic people. It affects information processing, mainly but not only around reading and writing. It can also, like most of its neurodivergent cousins, affect organisational skills, co-ordination, and working memory. Many dyslexic traits cross over with other neurodivergent conditions, and include:

- Written work markedly different to verbal abilities.
- Poor handwriting and messy work.
- Spelling the same word differently in the same piece of writing.
- Trouble with grammar.
- Getting upper and lower case letters mixed up.
- Organisation difficulties.
- Finding it hard to take notes in class.
- Leaving out or adds words when reading.
- Trouble keeping place when reading.
- Difficulty in finding focus in a piece of comprehension work.
- Difficulty with times tables and mental maths.
- Difficulty with reading maths language ($+ - \times$ /).
- Difficulty with maths formulae.
- Difficulty with written language maths questions.
- Slow processing speed.
- Finding foreign languages tricky.
- Difficulty processing a string of instructions.

---

3   UK Gov (2017) *Statistics about Dyslexia*. Accessed on 2 May 2022 at www.gov.uk/government/publications/understanding-disabilities-and-impairments-user-profiles/simone-dyslexic-user

- Disorganised and 'forgetful' around appointments, home-work, etc.
- Difficulty interpreting body language.

Many dyslexic people find strategies around these problems but support and understanding make a huge difference. Once again there are many positives too, and many successful dyslexic people.

The positives of dyslexia:

- Like ADHDers, dyslexic people are often big picture thinkers.
- May be very creative.
- May be very fluent and talented in oral communication.
- May be good at seeing patterns.
- Often entrepreneurial.

How Can You Help?

- Educate yourself about dyslexia. There can be a culture of discouraging dyslexia assessments and therefore it's often not something that is brought up in school unless difficulties are severe.
- Trust your instinct if you believe – because of for example spelling – that your child may be dyslexic. Fern's parents raised it at both mainstream primary and secondary schools and were dismissed, only for a diagnosis to be given at 16 after raising it again at specialist school. With hindsight, they should have trusted their instincts.

DYSGRAPHIA

Dysgraphia is a lesser known cousin of dyslexia and dyspraxia. As you might guess from the name, it's a learning difficulty associated with the ability to write. Signs to look for:

- A poor, uncomfortable pencil/pen grip.

- Uncomfortable body positioning when writing.
- Poor spelling, or words which haven't been finished.
- Poor spacing of words and margins.
- Verbal ability much better than written.
- Pain and discomfort after writing.

Dysgraphia is likely to be much harder to get a referral for an assessment than its better known relatives. Luckily, with modern technology, and reasonable adjustments for exams, etc., most people can manage pretty well without needing to write too much.

How Can You Help?

It's unlikely school are going to flag this so your child needs you to be aware and be their advocate.

DYSCALCULIA

If you guessed that dysgraphia was about writing, we're not giving prizes away for guessing what dyscalculia is about! It's a learning difficulty which affects all aspects of maths and numbers.

People with dyscalculia may:

- Have difficulty with ordering numbers.
- Have difficulty calculating money.
- Have problems with mental maths.
- Have difficulty remembering maths signs and symbols and formulae.
- Have difficulty remembering phone numbers, times, appointment dates.
- Be tired from the extended effort.

Again, you're going to struggle to be referred for an assessment, but can sometimes arrange to have one together with a dyslexia assessment. With the right support (and no more maths lessons in adult life!), dyscalculia doesn't have to make too much difference or cause a lack of self-esteem.

The positives of dyscalculia are:

- creativity
- strategic thinking
- good with words
- good intuition.

How Can You Help?

Again, it's very rare for a child to be referred for a dyscalculia assessment without parents asking first. Be aware that one neurodivergent condition probably means more are present and keep an eye on the traits mentioned above in your child.

OBSESSIVE COMPULSIVE DISORDER

Like the other neurodivergent differences we've been exploring here, OCD does share some traits with autism. It also shares something else – the internalising of symptoms in some, especially those brought up as girls. Like autism, internalising OCD transforms what the condition looks like from the outside, and makes it more likely to be missed or misinterpreted.

Almost 20% of autistic people also have a diagnosis of OCD, and those who have OCD are four times more likely than those without the diagnosis to be recognised as autistic at some point.[4] What hasn't been discovered is why the two are so connected – is it because the traits really are related, or because autistic people in a neurotypical society are more likely to suffer mental health issues?

OCD is a mental health disorder, and contrary to what most people think it's not only about washing your hands or turning light switches on and off repeatedly – as well as compulsive behaviour it's also characterised by obsessive thoughts. These thoughts will be negative voices

---

4   Meier, S. M., et al. (2015) 'Obsessive-compulsive disorder and autism spectrum disorders: Longitudinal and offspring risk'. PLoS One, 10(11): e0141703. doi:10.1371/journal.pone.0141703.

or images which can cause great anxiety. Compulsive behaviours can also be different to what we might expect. They can be internalised behaviour – distraction, avoidance, and self-criticism can also be a compulsion.

Both autism and OCD have traits of repetitive behaviours, but for an autistic person the repetitive behaviour (or stim) is pleasant and soothing, whereas an OCD repetitive behaviour is just the opposite. OCD thoughts will make a person feel ashamed, and will target what they value.

What Can Help?

- Autism-adapted CBT (cognitive behavioural therapy)
- EMDR (eye movement desensitisation and reprocessing) therapy
- SSRI (selective serotonin reuptake inhibitor) medications.

Websites to find more help:

- Mind – www.mind.org.uk
- Young Minds – www.youngminds.org.uk
- OCD UK – www.ocduk.org
- OCD Action – https://ocdaction.org.uk
- Orchard – www.orchardocd.org
- Anxiety UK – www.anxietyuk.org.uk
- International OCD Foundation – https://iocdf.org
- National Alliance on Mental Illness – www.nami.org/Home
- Beyond OCD – https://beyondocd.org
- SANE Australia – www.sane.org/spotlight-on-ocd

CASE STUDY
Zach, age 17 in the UK
Zach has marked OCD with intrusive thoughts. These really cause him daily problems as he can't move on until he has been able to

be supported with whatever has popped into his mind. Although it does help him to know why this happens and that it is due to his autism, he equally gets very frustrated that he has this because he IS autistic. Any mental health interventions such as CBT have only had limited success because they are not offered in the understanding of the origins of intrusive thoughts for young autistic people.

TOURETTE'S

Tourette's is a motor and tic condition which is part of the neurodivergent family. More than half of people with Tourette's will also have OCD or ADHD, and 20% will be autistic.[5] Like autism, more males are diagnosed with Tourette's than females, and like autism it is much misunderstood. It is characterised by tics which might be movement or sound based, but it doesn't make everyone swear! In fact, 90% of people with Tourette's don't involuntarily swear.[6]

These motor tics are possible with Tourette's:

- blinking or rolling the eyes
- sudden head, arm, or leg movements
- pulling a face
- jumping
- repeating movements made by someone else (echopraxia)
- rude gestures
- touching things and people.

These vocal tics are possible:

- coughing
- sniffing
- whistling

5   Dattaro, L. (2021) 'Common variants link autism, ADHD, Tourette syndrome'. *Spectrum*, 2 February. Accessed on 2 May 2022 at www.spectrumnews.org/news/common-variants-link-autism-adhd-tourette-syndrome
6   Genius Within (n.d.) *Tourette Syndrome*. Accessed on 2 May 2022 at www.geniuswithin.org/what-is-neurodiversity/Tourette-syndrome

- clearing the throat
- grunting
- repeating words or phrases someone else says (echolalia)
- swearing or saying phrases that aren't socially acceptable.

How Can You Help?

While there are drugs that can help control Tourette's tics, none have been developed specifically for that. There are also behavioural therapies which can have success, such as habit reversal therapy. Some people have fewer tics when they are focusing on something deeply.

You can help by being matter of fact about tics, and educating family and friends so they do the same. If tics are disturbing sleep, a weighted blanket can help (though these are not recommended for children at night).

SENSORY PROCESSING DISORDER

In the last section we looked at sensory processing issues common to autistic people, but can you have a diagnosis of sensory processing disorder (SPD) without being autistic? The short answer is yes, you can be diagnosed as such, and some people with SPD are not autistic. However, we see plenty of instances within the Autistic Girls Network group of children who have been diagnosed with SPD and have then gone on to be diagnosed autistic as they got older. If your child or young person is already recognised autistic, it's unlikely a doctor would further pursue a diagnosis of SPD as they will already be presumed to have sensory issues.

SPD is diagnosed by an occupational therapist trained in sensory integration, and it is about how the brain receives and processes sensory information. It can be diagnosed quite young as some of the symptoms will be obvious to the trained eye even as a baby (though there aren't enough trained eyes!), such as arching the back away from cuddles and difficulty in falling and staying asleep. It's important to get a diagnosis, as just as with autism there are emotional costs to continuing to be unidentified and unsupported, such as isolation at school and eventually anxiety and depression. SPD can be helped and supported by a programme of sensory-integrated occupational therapy and the devising of a 'sensory diet', which has nothing to do with eating! The sensory diet can be used at school, at home, at grandma's house and eventually, and more discreetly perhaps, at work. It needs input from your child or young person on the things they find most soothing and most irritating.

Examples of a sensory diet:

- Touch – a weighted blanket, a compression sheet, a stress ball, a fidget toy, crunching ice, playing with slime or putty, having a bath or shower, not wearing shoes, a tight hug, putting on a face mask, stroking or hugging a pet, popping bubble wrap, stroking a particular fabric.
- Movement – walking, running, yoga, dancing, swimming, jumping on a trampoline, skipping, rocking, swinging, drawing, going for a drive, cleaning, going on rollercoasters, playing with Lego®.
- Sight – snow or rain, a fish tank, a bubble tube, a space projector, looking at photos, a ceiling mobile, photography, watching waves.
- Taste – spicy food, salty food, crunchy food, sour food, chewing gum, chewing ice, an ice lolly, yawning.
- Sound – a garden fountain, favourite music, a white noise machine, a rain or thunder storm app, a clock ticking, wind chimes, musical instruments, meditation app.
- Smell – fresh laundry (smell of a particular Yankee Candle), perfume, coffee, baking bread or cookies, cut grass, mint.

How You Can Help

- Notice your child's sensory likes and dislikes and look for patterns in them.
- Understand and respect your child's sensory needs and aversions, especially if they are different to your own.

IRLENS SYNDROME

Irlens is a visual processing difference which affects the way the brain processes full spectral light. Although it can affect the way people see words on the page, it is not to be confused with dyslexia, which is a language processing difference. You can have both Irlens and dyslexia (or indeed be hyperlexic).

Irlens can't be treated by a regular optician – indeed a regular optician might not even have heard of Irlens – but there are Irlens Centres globally.[7]

At an Irlens Centre you will be assessed individually to find the precise colour tint you need in glasses to (partially) correct your vision perception. On the website above, you can test what it looks like in different colours which may be helpful when you are trying to figure out whether you need to be assessed.

You can have Irlens without being autistic, but over half of autistic people have Irlens.[8] Since it isn't well known, many of these people won't know and won't visit an Irlens Centre for filters which would help their visual perception of the printed page. Your normal is your normal, and just as you can't experience something in the way someone else experiences it, so they can't experience it as you are.

Ways to Recognise if Your Child Has Irlens

- Print seems distorted which means reading and writing is hard work and exhausting.
- Difficult to stay focused on a subject.
- Hypersensitivity to some wave lengths of full spectral light mean it can be difficult to perceive patterns and contrasts, and bright lights or headlights can cause sensory overload and headaches.
- Depth perception may be difficult.

---

7   To find the nearest centre to you, please visit: https://irlen.com/find-an-irlen-test-center

8   Yates, T. (2017) *Autism and Irlen Syndrome*. Accessed on 2 May 2022 at www.autism.org.uk/advice-and-guidance/professional-practice/irlen-syndrome

- Everything may seem distorted, so sometimes it can be difficult going upstairs or walking in a straight line if perception is skewed.

How Can You Help?

- Visit an Irlens Centre if possible. This will determine the right colours for lenses, overlays, and even pens.
- Change the home environment to the colour tint mandated by the specialist – anything from wall paint to light bulbs. White walls are particularly susceptible to distortion.
- Remove bright and florescent lights and cut down on glare.
- Be aware that sanitary items – bath, shower, washbasin, and toilet – and crockery can be problematic since they are likely to be white ceramic.

PATHOLOGICAL DEMAND AVOIDANCE

PDA, or pathological demand avoidance, is a rather controversial term, both in name and diagnosis, and even whether it's part of an autism profile at all. Some people believe that it's a type of autism, and others feel that it should be a completely separate diagnosis, however currently it is not included in the diagnostic manual the DSM-V, although it was included within the review of the NICE guidelines on autism diagnosis in under-19s in 2021.[9] Lots would prefer it to be renamed extreme demand avoidance for obvious reasons (who wants to be classed as pathological anything?!). Those with a PDA profile are characterised by extreme avoidance and dislike of demands, usually led by huge anxiety. PDA is not diagnosed in many areas of the UK and is even less well-known in countries like the US, but in the UK we are seeing diagnoses of autism with a 'demand avoidant profile'. Australian

---

9   NICE (2013) *Individual Research Recommendation Details.* Accessed on 2 May 2022 at www.nice.org.uk/about/what-we-do/research-and-development/research-recommendations/cg170/4

autistic academic Dr Wenn Lawson has coined a rather wonderful alternative acronym – 'persistent drive for autonomy', and it's so apt!

PDA has some significant differences to a 'regular' autism profile and while all autistic children need a different way of parenting, a child with PDA REALLY needs one. To understand why, we first need to think about all the demands that are put onto a child every day. If you ask a child to do something, that's a demand. So, telling them to get up out of bed is a demand, telling them to brush their teeth is a demand, asking them to eat their breakfast is a demand. Even if you don't verbally ask them to eat their breakfast, putting a bowl of cornflakes in front of them with the expectation they will eat it is a demand. So they've already had multiple demands made of them and it's only 8 am – they haven't even left the house yet! Now imagine how many demands, spoken or unspoken, will be made of them at school.

What is a demand for a PDAer?

- Laws and regulations.
- Social expectations.
- Written instructions.
- Menus in a restaurant.
- Anything asking them to make a choice.
- Promises.
- Timetables, visual or written.
- Star and reward charts.
- Rotas.
- Questions.
- Lists of responsibilities.
- Terms and conditions.
- Wants and needs.

PDA and school has proven to be a difficult and sometimes explosive mix. Strategies used to engage autistic children often don't work with children who have PDA, and schools rarely have any members of staff who understand PDA adequately, so most young students are left unsupported and unaccommodated, which is a situation that can't end well. According to the PDA Society (who have excellent parenting resources on their website), 70% of children and young people with PDA are either not in school or struggle to attend.[10]

PDA traits:

- Extreme avoidance of everyday demands.
- Can seem fairly sociable.
- Use distraction and social banter to avoid demands and procrastinate.
- Often creative and imaginative in play (which would mean no autism diagnosis if the assessor didn't know what they were doing).
- Can have rapid mood swings which can get physical.
- Can seem quite controlling of others (anxiety-led).
- Can often easily see through bribery and other manipulation of that type by adults.

PDA is a huge subject which I can't do more than touch upon here, but there are some great resources out there and some great adults with PDA speaking out to educate us – look up Kristy Forbes and Harry Thompson on Facebook. There are also some good books on PDA listed on the Autistic Girls Network resources page.[11]

EHLERS-DANLOS SYNDROMES AND HYPERMOBILITY

The Ehlers-Danlos syndromes (EDS) are 13 conditions related to connective tissue (in skin, ligaments, blood vessels, etc.). Most are rare but the one we are most concentrating on here is hypermobile EDS (HEDS), which is not so rare and co-occurs a lot with autism. It is usually diagnosed in women.

10   PDA Society (n.d.) *Information for Education Professionals.* Accessed on 2 May 2022 at www.pdasociety.org.uk/working-with-pda-menu/info-for-education-professionals
11   www.autisticgirlsnetwork.org/resources

Symptoms of HEDS:

- hypermobile joints (e.g. may be able to bend hands and fingers right back)
- easily fatigued
- bruise easily
- joints easily dislocated
- clicking joints and pain in joints
- dizziness when rising from sitting or prone position
- digestive problems.

Both autism and HEDS seem to have the same difference in a part of our nervous system – the autonomic nervous system (ANS). The ANS is divided into two – the sympathetic (fight or flight) and the parasympathetic (rest and digest) nervous systems. In both autistic people and those with HEDS, the 'fight or flight' system is hyperactive, and the 'rest or digest' system is under active. This means that autistic people and those with HEDS are constantly on alert, which can cause anxiety, and the under active 'digest' system can lead to stomach problems and possibly constipation.

Schools tend to not be clued up on EDS, which can have very real and far-reaching effects on everyday life. People with EDS are also more likely to contract autoimmune conditions such as rheumatoid arthritis. EDS is about much more than being double-jointed. The dizziness and the tiredness particularly can be an issue at school, with PE classes often being difficult to manage and attendance unlikely to be as high as required for health reasons. Missing class, anxiety, and 'brain fog' can mean gaps in knowledge, isolation from friends, and decreasing self-confidence, so it's important that schools do all they can to make reasonable adjustments for their students to stop this cycle. The Royal College of General Practitioners has a new Ehlers-Danlos Hypermobility Toolkit available for school staff, and free and open to anyone.[12]

---

12 www.rcgp.org.uk/clinical-and-research/resources/toolkits/ehlers-danlos-syndromes-toolkit.aspx

How Can You Help?

I know I keep saying the same thing, but the lack of awareness around EDS means your young person needs you to advocate for them. As it's 'invisible', particular pushback may be needed with school around physical exertion and general exhaustion which might mean attendance is lower.

POTS

POTS (postural orthostatic tachycardia), often found in someone with EDS, is a different response in the ANS which causes the heart rate to increase when standing up. The cardiac function has been shown to affect sensory responses, which may account for light and sound sensitivity being a feature of POTS.

Possible symptoms of POTS:

- dizziness
- fainting
- blood pooling in the legs when standing too long
- light sensitivity
- migraines
- noise sensitivity
- bloating
- diarrhoea/constipation
- extreme fatigue
- tachycardia (fast heart rate)
- weak muscles
- problem in storing iron in the body
- sensitivity to hot/cold.

There appears to be an overlap with many symptoms of long COVID, so there is speculation that some cases of long COVID may actually be post-viral POTS.

How Can You Help?

Believe your child and advocate for them.

EATING DISORDERS

It's not unusual for autistic people to have a restricted food intake and to eat a very limited variety, and there's nothing wrong with this. Autistic people who ate very few foods as children tend to expand the number of foods they eat as adults. Roughly 35% of those with eating disorders are thought to be autistic,[13] although the actual number is likely to be higher given how many autistic people remain unrecognised or are recognised as they are older. Autistic Girls Network believes that all people coming into contact with eating disorder services should be screened for autism and ADHD as a matter of course, which will help the individual who has been struggling with feeling different, and make sure any treatment given is adapted to their neurotype.

If your child and young person seems to be starting disordered eating:

- Let them eat whatever their preferred 'safe' foods are (especially with ARFID – see below). Even food with poor nutrition is better than no food.
- Try to set up a loose schedule of regular eating and drinking.
- Don't force them to try new foods, but do work on reducing anxiety around new foods.
- If your child is demand avoidant, take care to avoid demands to eat (it's all in the phrasing) and offer a small choice every time. The PDA Society website has some great tips on how to rephrase potential demands.
- Don't take well-meaning advice to hide new food or

---

13   Brede, J., *et al.* (2020) '"For me, the anorexia is just a symptom, and the cause is the autism": Investigating restrictive eating disorders in autistic women'. *Journal of Autism and Developmental Disorders*, 50: 4280–4296. https://doi.org/10.1007/s10803-020-04479-3

medicine in their 'safe' foods, otherwise those foods might not stay safe.

- Choose high calorie options where it's possible to do so.
- Be aware of sensory issues around food and mealtimes – sitting at the table may not be comfortable, hearing other people chew or cutlery scrape against the plate may be distressing, some food can have an unpleasant texture in the mouth, etc.
- Provide predictable food at predictable times. Uncertainty = anxiety.
- Because of predictability, pre-packaged foods may be preferable to homemade.
- Don't offer items that take a lot of work to eat, e.g. chewing steak.
- Offer bland foods which don't hit any sensory triggers unless you know your child or young person is a sensory seeker. If they are, you may be able to entice them to eat again with a salty or spicy snack.
- Don't mix foods, e.g. with apple pie and custard, serve separately.
- Keep the plate simple and uncluttered.
- Take note of the texture of food they like and dislike – find a pattern.
- Relax all rules around eating – allow eating anywhere, with or without cutlery, with a fidget toy, with the TV on, with headphones and music – whatever it will take to reduce anxiety around mealtimes.
- Have a visual weekly meal plan so uncertainty is removed.
- If particular brands are 'safe' foods, don't substitute for other brands. You might not be able to tell the difference, but they can. Some autistic people can tell if their favourite brand has made a tiny change to its recipe – the families, who didn't believe them, were proved wrong when they checked with the manufacturer.
- Because this is not always going to be possible, have a 'safe'

meal backup plan which you've made in collaboration with your child or young person, consisting of always available food.

- Autistic young people need to feel rules are justified. Explain why it's important we eat regularly and (mostly) healthily – without calling any foods 'good' or 'bad' (because literal thinkers will jump right on that!).
- If you can work out meal plans or ideas around their passionate interests, embrace that plan with gusto, and get your child and young person involved.
- If you're involved with a psychologist, it's really important they understand autism and that treatment is adapted for autism.

Anorexia and Autism

There is a proven link between anorexia and autism – studies have shown that people with anorexia (mostly those raised as girls) are more likely to be autistic than people who aren't anorexic, but we don't know why. We do know that in general, anorexia in autistic people isn't driven by a fear of being fat or by body image, but it seems to be more about the relief from anxiety that control over eating brings. Interestingly, alexithymia (a difficulty in identifying emotions) is common in both autistic people and people with anorexia. Sadly there's no national pathway to adapted treatment for anorexia and autism, although a team at Kings College London are developing the Peace Pathway for Autism and Eating Disorders.[14]

The same techniques for lowering anxiety and creating a stress-free, low-arousal environment as we have already seen also apply with eating disorders, with the proviso of course that professional help is sought before the young person has become dangerously underweight or gone dangerously long without food. There are many adult autistics who had anorexia as a young person – they transitioned into more healthy eating habits and your child and young person can too.

---

14   www.peacepathway.org

ARFID and Autism

ARFID (avoidant restrictive food intake disorder) is much less well-known than anorexia, and many health trusts don't commission a treatment pathway for it at all, let alone one adapted for autism. Again, a high percentage of people with ARFID are also autistic. ARFID typically is not governed by a need to lose weight or look thinner, and it can also manifest among very young children, and through sudden trauma. Like anorexia and bulimia, ARFID is a mental health diagnosis, but it strays into physical health even more than the other two, since serious cases can need a peg or feeding tube.

How Can You Help?

- Many of the techniques that are applicable for anorexia are also applicable for ARFID.
- Most important – don't make mealtimes a battlefield, and keep 'safe' foods safe.

There is a very good ARFID-related Facebook group called ARFID Support for Parents & Carers in the UK/Ireland.

If your GP has never heard of ARFID, give them this link to look at: http://tvscn.nhs.uk/wp-content/uploads/2019/09/ARFID-GP-Training.pdf

Autistic Girls Network also ran a webinar on Eating Disorders and Autism with Dr Elizabeth Shea, Clinical Psychologist, which is available on our YouTube channel.[15]

CASE STUDY
Robin, age 13 in the UK (by mum Paula)
Robin has done lots of research on how an autistic brain works and has learned some of the reasons behind why he sometimes struggles. He has sensory needs which can cause many problems

---

15   www.youtube.com/watch?v=1P6f3XBorm8&t=86s

in a household of seven people, but we try as much as possible to be accommodating. He also finds it difficult to express how he's feeling so will self-harm as a way to cope with feeling overwhelmed, frustrated, or extremely low. Robin also identifies as transgender and prefers to be addressed as he/him. He has an eating disorder where he limits food, but what he does eat he will vomit back in the bathroom. CAMHS refuse to help as he's not seen to be losing a large amount of weight, but the physiological part of this is very worrying.

LGBTQIA+

Autistic young people are more likely to identify as LGBTQIA+ (a term used to encompass lots of different sexualities and gender identities)[16] than their neurotypical peers, and this puts them into a double minority, with double the chance of 'minority stress'. Some of this stress can be alleviated by you accepting them and supporting them whatever their gender identity or sexuality. How much you support and advocate for them needs to be led by them, but the importance of a simple acceptance of their identity can't be overestimated.

Both autistic and LGBTQIA+ students are at increased risk of bullying in schools, so that's something to monitor. The bullies may not even know that your child or young person is either autistic or LGBTQIA+ – they may just know that there is something different about them. While school leadership may be supportive, it's difficult to foster a truly inclusive and accepting atmosphere in a big high school. It's not impossible though and that should always be the long-term goal.

Social relationships may already be difficult to navigate for your autistic child or young person, and starting a new romantic relationship is always tricky. They are unlikely to welcome parental help here! So be there for support and if requested advice, but otherwise try to stay out of it unless they seem out of their depth. Of course, it's also

---

16 For a complete explanation see: https://abbreviations.yourdictionary.com/what-does-lgbtqia-stand-for-full-acronym-explained.html

possible your young person isn't interested in dating yet, and that's fine too.

How to Help

- Questioning your identity can be lonely – be there for them in a non-judgemental way.
- Let them know there's no rush. They don't have to get it right straight away, and they don't have to be like everyone else, including other LGBTQIA+ young people they know. But please don't imply that you don't believe them or that they don't know what they are talking about. It's likely they will have researched and thought long and hard about this before bringing it up with you.
- Try to find an online or face-to-face group for them if they are up for it – meeting other young people who understand will be important.
- If you need to seek therapy, make sure the therapist understands the intersectionality of autism and LGBTQIA+.
- Listen to your young person with your full attention when they talk about finding their sexuality or gender identity. At this moment, it's the most important thing in the world for them.
- Respect their wishes if they want to use new pronouns or a new name. Explain that you might sometimes make a mistake because your brain will naturally use the old pronouns/name for a while, but that you'll try to get it right as quickly as possible. And ask friends and family to do the same if that's what your young person wishes.

GENDER DYSPHORIA

It would be hard to think of an area where society has taught us the 'right' way more than gender. Many of us have grown up thinking of gender as a binary concept – male and female. Whatever your religion, there's probably a creation story that states that. But we know now that gender identity is a spectrum, and also that autistic people are more likely to identify in a gender diverse way. In fact according to a 2020 study, people who don't identify as the sex they were assigned at birth are three to six times more likely to be autistic.[17]

What Is Gender Identity?

When a baby is born, we, as a society, assign a gender – male or female. Those who continue to identify as the same gender they were assigned at birth are 'cisgender' or cis. Those who don't, come under the umbrella of gender diverse, because there are different genders they could identify as such as transgender, gender-queer, or non-binary, or they prefer not to identify as a particular gender at all, or to move fluidly between genders at different times in their life. Someone may choose to change the pronouns that have always been used for them, and this should be respected. While it's natural to find it difficult to use different pronouns and even a different name to the one you gave your child at birth, this is massively important for them and they need to see that you are making an effort.

Representation matters, and it's important for lesbian, gay, bisexual, transgender, queer/questioning, intersex, asexual, and other (LGBTQIA+) young people to see role models and literature with characters they identify with, just as it's important to see neurodivergent role models and characters. (And I apologise if, by the time this book is published, the accepted acronym has changed – language moves fast in this field!) Representation should also include inclusive sex education, particularly important when statistics show that LGBTQIA+ young people generally have poorer mental health than their peers.

---

17   Dattaro, L. (2020) 'Largest study to date confirms overlap between autism and gender diversity'. *Spectrum*, 14 September. Accessed on 2 May 2022 at www.spectrumnews.org/news/largest-study-to-date-confirms-overlap-between-autism-and-gender-diversity

What Is Gender Dysphoria?

Some of the gender diverse group of people above will feel there is such a difference between the gender identity they were assigned at birth and their real gender identity that it causes much emotional pain and distress. This is gender dysphoria, and it's this group of people who may seek gender-related medical care (if they do, make sure their care is autism-adapted). The dysphoria (meaning unease) can be physical (related to gender-specific parts of the body) or social (related to how people perceive their gender).

How Can You Help?

It's very challenging for a child or young person to reveal to their parents that they don't feel they have been identified as the right gender. They will have struggled a lot internally before they got to the point where they decided to tell you. No matter your initial views, the best thing you can do for them at that time (and every other time) is to tell them that you support them, and you love them no matter what. If it's something that you have difficulty coming to terms with, make sure your child or young person knows that's no reflection on them. They need a rock – be that rock for them.

Chapter 5

Autism Presentation in Different Groups

GIRLS

We have lots of families in Autistic Girls Network who quickly and easily got autism diagnoses for their sons but had to wait years for their daughters to get a diagnosis, and sadly that's because autism is either missed or misdiagnosed in a lot of girls – it's why the Network exists. Officially there are four times as many boys diagnosed autistic as girls (or people brought up as girls). But in fact, that number is almost certainly not presenting an accurate picture. In a recent study of mainstream students in England, one area diagnosed 13 times as many boys as girls and another diagnosed only two times as many.[1] That's not some strange geographical anomaly, it's a difference in diagnostic teams being able to recognise autistic masking. And masking is something that autistic girls can be great at, as can some boys and those brought up as girls who have different gender identities. Sadly, the stigma which leads to masking is not at all good for mental health.

It's important to note that there aren't different gendered types of autism. What we see a lot in those brought up as girls is an internalised presentation which is not well recognised or referred and therefore not

1   Roman-Urrestarazu, A., *et al.* (2021) 'Association of race/ethnicity and social disadvantage with autism prevalence in 7 million school children in England'. *JAMA Pediatrics*, 175(6): e210054. doi:10.1001/jamapediatrics.2021.0054.

well diagnosed. You can read more about internalised presentations in Autistic Girls Network's white paper.[2]

How Can Autistic Girls and Those Who Mask Present Differently?

- Strategise and come up with scripts to get through social situations they've observed.
- Camouflage and copy behaviour from their peers.
- Have friendship groups, but tend not to be leaders, more on the fringe.
- Tend to not obviously stim.
- Likely to have intense sensory issues.
- May become situationally mute (more on this later).
- They tend to internalise anxiety into negative thoughts.
- May be strongly perfectionist.
- May be shy and probably don't speak up much in class.
- May not get into any trouble at school.
- May become very anxious and their school attendance may drop before you realise they are autistic.
- Often strong willed.
- Often have a good sense of humour – humour is important to them.
- Support the underdog and social justice is important to them.
- Often love animals intensely.
- Their passionate interests are often things lots of girls are interested in – but their interest is intense.
- Often like to dye their hair bright colours.
- May well be able to make eye contact, no matter what the diagnostic guidelines say...
- May like to 'collect' – but it's just as likely to be information as things.
- Tend to avoid conflict.

---

2   www.autisticgirlsnetwork.org/keeping-it-all-inside.pdf

Why Do Girls Get Missed or Diagnosed Later than Boys?

Given that we have had all the information above for a few years now, why are girls STILL being missed, misdiagnosed, or diagnosed later than boys? After all, it's not that autism is different, it's that the girls are different. Certainly their ability to mask their autistic traits to fit in with their peers is one reason. But is our attitude towards girls different in society? At school, do we expect girls to sit and get on with their work? The way girls who are masking present is in a quiet, unassuming way until they can't manage to mask anymore. Schools are looking for this and it's not disrupting class – the more disruption, the earlier a child is likely to be referred for an assessment.

What's Different About Social Interactions and Friendships for Autistic Girls?

As a generalisation, a group of friends who are girls tends to be more complicated socially than a group of friends who are boys. At secondary school, girls' friendships can be destroyed over a perceived dirty look – impossible to understand for an autistic girl who doesn't know what kind of face she's making most of the time. Knowing what to say, when all seems to rest on using the right wording, can also be a social tightrope. If possible, make sure your autistic child or young person knows other neurodivergent people they can be themselves with, and with whom they don't need to communicate in neurotypical! Even as an adult, it can be difficult for autistic people to decipher if neurotypical people actually mean what they say because there are so many hidden meanings in social conventions (when you say you love someone's hair is that really what you mean?). Autistic people find it very hard and confusing to play this game, and would generally prefer it if people would just say what they mean.

How Can You Help?

- Encourage a strong autistic identity so they are comfortable with it and don't consider themselves 'weird' or an outsider.

(Or if they do consider themselves weird, that they think that's a good thing! There's #WeirdPrideDay now, after all.)

- Try to make sure they know and interact with other autistic people, especially girls their own age.
- Pay attention to their passionate interests and show you value them.
- Keep an eye, as much as possible, on their friendship group to make sure they aren't being bullied or pressured.
- Help them navigate the social world, and show them that friendships need to be a compromise with effort from both sides (though that doesn't mean they should be hard work!).

CASE STUDY

Rosie, age 11 in the UK (by mum Emma)

We have always known Rosie has been different from her peers in some ways. We've always thought so, but it took us eight years and five referrals for her to be diagnosed. School was not supportive at all until I put in a formal complaint and once they understood they are now super supportive and really keen to learn (the complaint went to: governors, OFSTED, LA, MP, etc.).

There have been many sensory issues and many meltdowns (her and me!). We have tried since she was two to get some help, but all referrals led nowhere. We have done parenting courses, paid for private help, tried everything we could think of to help Rosie. We had our first referral when she was four, then again when she was six, eight, nine, and ten. We only received our diagnosis because it was online during lockdown and as we were at home Rosie didn't mask. It was also the only time we reached the ADOS stage (ADOS stands for 'autism diagnostic observation schedule' and is the standardised assessment for autism most commonly used in the UK) – as prior to that we were discharged instantly with gems like 'neurodivergent children don't pick and choose where to display symptoms, and due to her being fine at school she cannot be neurodivergent', etc.

All three professionals on our ADOS were in agreement that Rosie is autistic. It has been a long journey.

PERIODS

Getting your first period is a difficult time for any young girl (or person who has periods), but because of the sensory issues it presents it can be particularly trying for autistic people. There's additional complication because recent studies have shown that autistic people may enter puberty early, meaning your child would be even younger when they go through this anxious time.

As for any big change, it's important that you prepare your child for starting their periods. There's a great book you can give them which is specifically written for them – *The Autism Friendly Guide to Periods* by Robyn Steward. As Robyn says in her book – you need to think about this from their point of view and be very specific about things. Saying 'You'll become a woman' is not helpful – they need practical, literal, and direct information about what to expect and when, before it happens, otherwise seeing blood is going to be scary. Prepare them for feeling different emotionally too, not just physically.

Using sanitary products is always going to be trial and error and personal preference, but you are likely to have sensory issues to deal with too. Not just how it feels when wearing it but how it feels to see it and touch it when removing it. There may also be executive functioning issues in remembering to remove it. According to posts in the Autistic Girls Network group, this is something lots of autistic people struggle with.

You may want to consider period pants – look at reviews to see which are judged the most absorbent and comfortable. These solve the issue of changing pads and tampons and are often – but not always – more comfortable. They don't however solve the issue of putting them in a specific place on removal (some need soaking before washing in the washing machine), so you may need to come up with a plan for this.

Also consider that periods often make us feel, quite frankly, pretty awful. And some of us more than others. If your child is already anxious about school, period pains can easily push them to overload. Alexithymia and interoception can also make it challenging for your child to know when their period is about to start, so one of the readily available tracker apps can be a good idea, as well as you keeping an eye on their moods for any monthly changes.

Executive function and planning ahead can also be an issue, and there is actually a fair amount of planning which has to go into being ready for a period to start when you don't know where or when that's going to happen every month. This is another reason period pants are a good idea – no health worries as there are for tampons, and you can wear them for longer. I realise money may be an issue, as they can be expensive, but high street stores are starting to sell their own brands of period pants, which should help to bring prices down.

As well as the physical inconvenience and the sensory difficulty, periods can also make us feel out of control, while progesterone and estrogen levels vary, and this can be intensified for autistic and other neurodivergent people. Some find the whole experience traumatic enough that finding a way to stop them having periods is paramount. You may well find that GPs don't understand any of the extra emotional and sensory labour that a period causes when autistic, and you'll need to be your child's advocate here.

PUBERTY AND HORMONES

Puberty is a difficult time for all young people. How many of us would willingly go through puberty again?! All those hormones whizzing through our body making us feel weird and act even weirder. No thanks. For autistic young people though, it's harder, for a variety of reasons.

First, it coincides with a period of immense change – the transition from primary to secondary school. We all know that change = uncertainty, and uncertainty = anxiety for our autistic young people. But this is one of the biggest changes they will go through in their lives – moving from a small primary school to a much bigger high school, going from one teacher to many, going from one classroom to moving round the school every hour... and it goes on.

Second, the areas that puberty hits hardest – relationships and a new awareness of all things sexual – are areas that autistic people can find challenging. The hidden social nuances are in full flow when we start new relationships – do we give them our number, do we ring first, do we call back, how eager is it appropriate to be, etc. These choppy waters are difficult enough for us all to navigate, but to someone who has difficulty reading non-verbal social cues they are a storm at sea! How do you navigate this minefield without knowing the 'rules'? It's all very confusing, and can be a time when autistic girls particularly start to feel isolated because they begin to realise just how different they might be from their friends.

Third, this is also an age when other co-related conditions start to show themselves, and that's probably not a coincidence, it's a perfect storm of dysregulation and confusion. This age is when eating dis-orders and mental health conditions start to become apparent, and likewise when autistic maskers often can't continue to mask anymore. When we did a survey in the Autistic Girls Network Facebook group it became clear that the February half term of Year 7, when a young person is 11, is the time when autistic girls start to really struggle. It's a time when young people need extra support and understanding but instead are expected to cope with huge transitions and their first 'proper' exams.

Lastly, there has been very little research on autistic or neurodiver-gent teens or the transition to adulthood – most research dollars are spent on younger children, and sadly on how to make children 'less' autistic rather than focusing on how to increase their happiness. We know that autistic young people are later to develop emotionally, and that they can find it difficult when their friendship group switches from, for example, talking about Roblox to talking about sex and rela-tionships. More autistic researchers are moving into this area now, so it's looking hopeful that within a relatively short time we will under-stand it better. This is particularly important given that puberty makes physical changes to our brains revolving around neural connections for cognitive functions, a sense of identity, decision making, problem solving, etc. Because these are all issues for autistic adolescents, we really need to know what changes are happening in the brain.

MASKING

We've looked at autistic masking in girls, but it's not just girls who mask. In fact we all mask to a certain extent, whatever our neurotype (have you ever been told you have a 'phone voice'?), but for autistic people masking is a survival mechanism. From an early age, behaviour is monitored and given approval or disapproval. Flapping hands, or meltdowns, or talking at length about passionate interests are rarely approved. We might have been asked to make eye contact, or speak up, or raise our hand in class. We might have been told to socialise, or work in a group, or go and play outside with the other children when we were happy in the library at lunchtime. But we are consistently told that our autistic behaviours and ways of communication are wrong or not enough, so we look at what our peers are doing, and we copy them. We do it to not get shouted at, to not get bullied, to not get called weird. We do it to survive, and a lot of the time it's an unconscious act, not something we do deliberately. It's an avoidance of stigma.

What Can Masking Behaviours Include?

- Rehearsing or 'scripting' a conversation.
- Looking between the eyes or at the nose instead of making eye contact (most people will never be able to tell – try it!).
- Practising facial expressions in the mirror so that you can try to use the appropriate one.
- Remembering details about people so that you can make 'small talk'.
- Stopping yourself talking about your passionate interest because you know it will bore people.
- Hiding or disguising stims, or using a less obvious one.
- Hiding the fact that you are anxious or scared.
- Hiding the fact that you are in sensory hell.

What Are the Downsides of Autistic Masking?

Firstly, masking makes it harder to get a diagnosis and to realise your own identity. An autistic young person will mask to make it seem as though they fit in, but inside, they still don't feel as if they do, which makes them wonder, what's wrong with me? The answer, of course, is that nothing is wrong, but while their autistic identity is camouflaged that's not a conversation they are going to be having, and they aren't going to be finding and talking to other people who experience the world in the same way as them. Although it is a survival tactic and can make an autistic person feel safer, research has shown that masking is damaging to mental health (though rather it's the stigma which prompts the masking which is damaging).

In addition, it's exhausting physically and cognitively, which is why so many children who mask all day at school go home and explode (or indeed, adults who mask all day at work are exhausted by the time they get home or self-medicate with alcohol). Hiding your real self means not only do you feel a disconnect in yourself, but you are making it harder to build real connections with others if they never see the 'real you'.

Now, I can see it in my child as soon as they leave the house, but for years, they masked all the time. It has only been the last few years where the mask has been allowed to drop at home. If your young person is diagnosed autistic as a teen, this is what you want, and what they need – to feel comfortable enough at home to be their authentic selves, though it may take them quite some time to figure out what that is if they have been masking all their lives. It may mean they change quite a bit at home, but this is the real them. Love and accept them.

CASE STUDY
Gemma, age 16 in the UK

Gemma was discovered to be autistic at 13 after serious mental health issues. Up to that point, nobody had ever mentioned the possibility of autism to her, or to her family. It was genuinely a surprise – that's how good she was at masking, because she had always been autistic. After her diagnosis, she was depressed and highly anxious. With hindsight, she was likely in burnout. It took a few months for her to take an interest in anything. In those few months, her family would have done anything to help her feel better, but what helped the most was dropping the mask at home. She allowed herself to stim, and with professional support she discovered what helped her to self-regulate. She re-evaluated what was important to her. She dropped out of all social commitments and saw nobody but her immediate family and professionals for a while. Now, she does put on the mask outside the house, even with grandparents, but at home she can be comfortably herself, and her mental health is all the better for it.

BLACK AND BROWN PEOPLE

When the average person thinks of a typical autistic person, they may well think of a white male (think *Rain Man*, *Atypical*, *The Big Bang Theory*, *The Good Doctor*), but just as it's not only males who are autistic, so (of course) it's not only white people. This may seem completely obvious, but sadly, research has shown that it's more difficult to get diagnosed as a Black or Brown person. This doesn't mean there are fewer Brown or Black autistic people, but that there are barriers to their visibility due to our unequal society. There are also cultural barriers, where some cultures have a different understanding of autism and a reluctance to be diagnosed. When we talk about intersectionality, we mean the difficulties for people with two or more different minority identities. For example, a Black, neurodivergent woman has three different identities and, unfortunately, three different ways to be discriminated against. She's also likely to be diagnosed autistic much later than a white autistic boy. If she/they were also LGBTQIA+, she/they would have four different identities and four possible ways to be discriminated against. That person is also going to have a considerably different experience of life than the white autistic boy.

Why Is Autism Less Recognised in Black and Brown People and What Can Be Done to Change That?

- There have been studies showing that professionals can attribute communication issues to ethnic background, and therefore don't refer a child for an autism assessment.[3]

---

3   For example: Begeer, S., *et al.* (2009) 'Underdiagnosis and referral bias of autism in ethnic minorities'. *Journal of Autism and Developmental Disorders*, 39(1): 142–148. https://doi.org/10.1007/s10803-008-0611-5; Wiggins, L. D., *et al.* (2020) 'Disparities in documented diagnoses of autism spectrum disorder based on demographic, individual, and service factors'. *Autism Research*, 13(3): 464–473. doi:10.1002/aur.2255.

- It's true that there may be issues with English as a second language, and there may be social problems where families have difficulties getting access to health care, but if children are going to school, theoretically all should have an equal chance of being noticed and referred – that isn't happening.
- If there is a reason why some cultures don't want an autism diagnosis, we need to work with those communities to raise awareness about why it's important, both to secure support for the child and to help them understand their own identity.
- There may be less information about autism, diagnosis, and support available in other languages – this can be a big barrier to some communities. We need better translation services and access to interpreters.
- There can be cultural issues around interacting with health/ social care/education professionals, and likewise these professionals may have little understanding of that culture, and may use inaccessible language.
- Some communities have a stigma surrounding disability in general, and autism can be included in that. Therefore some families don't like to be open about an autism diagnosis – sadly this will make the autistic person feel even more isolated and 'other'.
- Better awareness and understanding is needed on all sides, and all professionals should be aware that skin colour doesn't make a difference to neurotype.

Chapter 6

Autism Myths

There are far too many 'facts' circulating about autistic people which are not facts at all, and this is damaging to the autistic community. This is me passing on the baton to you to dispel these myths whenever you get a chance!

MYTH: AUTISTIC PEOPLE HAVE NO EMPATHY

There is a theory, put forward by Professor Simon Baron-Cohen (cousin to film star Sacha), that autistic people lack theory of mind. This means they lack the ability to put themselves in someone else's shoes, to imagine someone else's experience. I hope that this theory has been sufficiently debunked by other researchers by now, but it still seems to rear its head, especially around empathy. In fact, while everyone (or every neurotype) is different, many autistic people have a great deal of empathy, and to say that they don't in fact invokes another theory – the double empathy theory. This one was put forward by Dr Damian Milton, who happens to be autistic himself, and as we've seen it basically says that both parties, autistic and neurotypical, need to be empathetic towards the other. It's not enough for neurotypical people to accuse autistic people of lacking empathy, when it has become blindingly obvious over the years that most neurotypical people have not the slightest intention of putting themselves into an autistic person's shoes. If they did, the world would understand neurodivergence a great deal better, and I probably wouldn't need to write this book.

The double empathy theory is important – remember it when teachers, or social workers, or grandparents are trying to make your child (or you, if you're autistic) do something that's harmful for autistic people, for example making eye contact or going to a noisy, bright gathering. Ask them to put themselves in your child's shoes, feeling how they would feel – would they still make the same choice?

What some autistic people may find difficult is cognitive empathy, which is the ability to predict what other people will think and intend to do – though I suspect they might manage to do this successfully with other autistic people. When expecting an autistic person to do this with a neurotypical person, we are expecting them to predict an entirely different way of thinking, and that's something we very rarely ask a neurotypical person to do of an autistic person. After many years of practice in masking, I bet an autistic person would have a higher success rate than the other way round. Keep twisting the narrative. Many of the points that the medical model of autism insist are deficits are just different. You can help change that.

MYTH: AUTISTIC PEOPLE ARE LONERS

There's a myth that all autistic people are anti-social loners who want to live on their own away from society. And it is true that some autistic people keep to themselves, don't enjoy parties, and perhaps spend long periods in their own company. But let's think back to their childhood, when perhaps their awkwardness meant they were always picked last for team sports, or they were called weird for talking frequently about their passionate interest, or they were bullied for being quirky and, well, different. Or let's imagine the sensory hell of a party, with loud music and flashing lights and so many people talking that you can't concentrate on what anyone is saying to you. And let's not forget that autistic people, after they have 'peopled', NEED to chill out and have quiet time by themselves to get their energy back. For all these reasons, there will be times they will refuse invitations, or seem as if they aren't fully taking part in a conversation.

Loners, though? Well some, maybe, just as some neurotypical

people will be loners. There are introvert and extrovert people, grumpy and cheerful people, good and bad people of ALL neurotypes. But many autistic people do want friends, and a social life, on their own terms. They want people to share their passionate interests with, to talk about them, to action them if they are that kind of interest. They want people to talk about social justice with. They want people to understand them and support their point of view. They want to communicate their life experiences with people who understand. They want to laugh, and listen to music, and be entertained. They want relationships. Very few of us don't want most of that.

Many autistic people have grown up having to fit into a 'normal' social environment, and not doing it well. But the old idea of 'normal' isn't my definition of normal. It might not be yours. It almost certainly isn't your child or young person's. And why is my, or your, or their normal any less than society's 'normal'? Time to twist that narrative.

MYTH: AUTISTIC PEOPLE HAVE NO SENSE OF HUMOUR

Let's tackle the myth that autistic people don't have a sense of humour – originating, in all probability, from a study Hans Asperger did in 1944 when a group of children didn't laugh at his cartoons. Who knows what the reason was. Perhaps they just weren't funny? Perhaps sitting in groups being studied by Hans Asperger was a pretty serious business?

Whatever the reason for the myth – and this might be because some can have a flat tone of voice, or for various cognitive processing reasons, or because the joke was about a social construct the person didn't understand, or let's face it, just because their sense of humour is different – the existence of quite a few autistic comedians means a myth is all it is. We have Hannah Gadsby, doing sell-out world tours, we have Bethany Black, Dan Ackroyd, Rosanne Barr, Jim Henson, Fern Brady, Sara Gibbs, the comedy troupe Asperger's Are Us. And you only need to look at Greta Thunberg's Twitter feed to see what a brilliantly dry sense of humour she has.

Autistic comedian Kate Fox says:

> When certain psychologists say things like: 'Autistic people are not funny or don't have a sense of humour' – apart from the fact that it displays that they haven't spent any time in the company of autistic people – who personally seem to me to be the funniest people around – they're also ignoring the fact that the very condition of being autistic in a non-autistic world is funny. It's full of humour. It's full of incongruity and that's brilliant.[1]

CASE STUDY

Toby, age 14 in the US

Humour is really important to Toby. When he was in crisis, it was only professionals with a good sense of humour and a slightly irreverent manner who could get through to him. Going to stand-up comedy nights with his parents helped him leave the house again. Watching comedy on Netflix helps him self-regulate. He finds humour in lots of situations, and other people, whatever their neurotype, find him humorous. He thinks the fact that some people consider autistic people not to have a sense of humour is hilarious!

MYTH: ONLY CHILDREN ARE AUTISTIC

I don't think I need to spend too long on this one.

Autism is something you are born with. It's a difference in the brain, which means you think and experience the world in a different way to neurotypical people. Therefore, it's not something you can grow out of. What can happen is that you learn strategies to help you manage better, or you create, or those around you help create, an environment which suits you better. In that case, and if you are masking, autistic traits might be less visible than when you were a child. But you are still autistic, your whole life. There are far more

---

1   Rose, D. (2018) 'Do autistic people "get" jokes?' *BBC News*, 15 December. Accessed on 2 May 2022 at www.bbc.co.uk/news/disability-46555014

autistic adults at any one time than there are children, although some are undiagnosed as yet.

MYTH: 'WE'RE ALL A BIT AUTISTIC'

No. No we're not.

Many of us may have a couple of the traits which contribute to being autistic, but that doesn't make us autistic, and to say it does is invalidating the experience of autistic people. Saying that someone is 'a bit autistic' is like saying that someone is 'a bit pregnant'. It's not possible. The spectrum is not linear, you don't move up and down it according to 'how autistic' you are. Autistic people generally have what's called a spiky profile. That means they may be really good at some things but have difficulty with others, and there's not really a pattern – everyone is different.

When that phrase is said to an autistic person, it's likely to make them feel that their experience is being trivialised. And I have had health professionals say this to me in front of my child. 'No', I say, 'No, we are NOT all a bit autistic'. I don't say more because my child doesn't like conflict, but I'd like to!

MYTH: 'YOU'LL NEVER GO TO COLLEGE'

First of all, let me say that going to college doesn't need to be held up as some pinnacle of achievement. Lots of successful people – especially neurodivergent ones – never went to college. Richard Branson, who is dyslexic, dropped out of school at 16. His headmaster told him he would either go to prison or be a millionaire, and I guess he was right, although it must have been frustrating at the time.

However, can an autistic person go to college? Of course. Can all autistic people go to college? No. Can all neurotypical people go to college? Still no. And not everyone wants to go to college. However, the blanket statement that you'll never go to college (with the unspoken 'if you get labelled autistic') is wrong. There are autistic people in all walks of life including doctors, anaesthetists, psychiatrists, accountants, dentists, engineers, statisticians, teachers, and academics. They all went to university. If you're in the UK, Disabled Students Allowance (DSA) is also very useful in providing mentors and equipment or software if needed.

MYTH: IF YOU CAN MAKE EYE CONTACT, YOU'RE NOT AUTISTIC

Sadly, we hear about professionals saying this quite a lot on the Autistic Girls Network Facebook group. Children and young people have had autism assessments and even autism diagnoses refused because of this. And yet, autistic people who mask can make eye contact, because they've learned that they need to in order to fit in to that environment. This doesn't mean it's not uncomfortable, or even painful, as are many aspects of masking – that's why it's so exhausting and bad for mental health. It would be much better if they could be in an environment where it was made clear that it's perfectly OK not to make eye contact, and that it doesn't mean you're not listening to what someone says. Just the opposite in fact.

If this happens to you, please challenge it. And if your child or young person wants to SEEM as if they are making eye contact without doing it, tell them to look between someone's eyes or at the top of their nose. Do it to them (with their agreement of course), and see if they can tell.

MYTH: IF YOU'RE SOCIABLE, YOU CAN'T BE AUTISTIC

We've also had families refused an autism assessment or diagnosis because their child or young person has friends. What? Are these professionals seriously suggesting no autistic people are capable of friendships? Because that's certainly what it sounds like, isn't it?

We've just talked about spiky profiles. It's very possible that your child or young person, who perhaps struggles to make friends, has taken a shine to a boy in one of the groups they both go to. You discover that child also has a passionate interest in Pokémon. They talk together non-stop for two hours – about Pokémon. That doesn't mean your child would have talked to any other child for two hours, or would have talked to that child for two hours about any other subject than Pokémon, but the passionate interest got them through any social awkwardness and discomfort. It's equally possible that your young person is part of a group of friends, and is very sociable with them. She goes along with whatever they say, but they certainly all consider themselves friends. It's also possible your child has only one or two very special friends and guards them fiercely. We're all different. By the nature of autism, it's likely your child or young person will have a difficulty with social communication, but it doesn't mean they won't have friends, it certainly doesn't mean they're not capable of having friends. Far from it. And let's not forget that research has shown that much of the 'disordered' part of social communication disappears when an autistic person interacts with another autistic person. Let's not forget finding friendships with your neurokin.

Now of course, what we might traditionally call 'socialising' is about more than friendships. It's about networking, and small talk, and chit chat, and all the things, to be honest, that autistic people find tiresome and a little dishonest about neurotypical society. It's very performative, and as a generalisation, autistic people aren't interested in those kinds of performances. So often, it's not that autistic people aren't sociable, it's that they have social communication differences, and they also aren't interested in small talk – they prefer a meaningful conversation. Get one in the corner discussing their passionate interest and you might be there all night, but a ten-minute conversation about the weather probably isn't going to grab them. Or you either, if you're honest.

MYTH: THERE'S A CURE FOR AUTISM

The short answer is no, there's no cure for autism.

The longer answer is no, there's no cure for autism, and many autistic people wouldn't want to be 'cured' anyway. That's not to say they wouldn't want therapy for, let's say, sensory overload or executive dysfunction. But to remove their autism would be to completely change their identity.

So no, vaccines don't either cause or cure autism, and neither do bleach enemas, or CBD gummies, or a keto diet, or some strange supplement, or coconut oil, or conversion therapy, or Elon Musk, or anything else.

MYTH: AUTISM = INTELLECTUAL DISABILITY

While popular belief conflates autism and intellectual disability, the two are co-occurring in around 20% of autistic people but are separate.[2]

2   Kinnear, D., *et al.* (2019) 'Relative influence of intellectual disabilities and autism on mental and general health in Scotland: A cross-sectional study of a whole country of 5.3 million children and adults'. *BMJ Open*, 9(8), e029040. doi:10.1136/bmjopen-2019-029040.

Chapter 7

Autism No-Nos

Here are just a few things which are a source of controversy with autistic people and their allies.

AUTISM PARENTS

Obviously, this is not referring to all parents of autistic children and young people! What it means is the specific sub-section of society who call themselves 'autism moms', and under the guise of being an advocate for their autistic child, complain about how terrible life is and what a burden they are. While we all know that life can be tough sometimes, constantly complaining about your child's behaviour in front of them isn't a good look. We all need to find our identity, and to find like-minded people to talk to who will understand us, but using the term 'autism mom' is not like calling yourself a 'soccer mum'. Being autistic is part of your identity, of your culture; soccer is kicking a ball around a field. But if you're not autistic, you can't claim that as your identity. If you want to be an ally, this is not the name for you.

TONE POLICING

To tone police is to focus on HOW something was said rather than WHAT was said. It tends to be used to silence others who disagree with what someone is saying, and it takes the focus off the original point.

Tone policing happens quite a lot to autistic people. Some quite

literally tone police tone (of voice), because they either don't understand or don't take into account that some autistic people can't control
the tone of their voice well. Others tone police language used, such as
identity first (autistic person) over person first (person with autism),
with no sense of irony that they are telling an autistic person how to
speak about themselves.

APPLIED BEHAVIOUR ANALYSIS

The behavioural roots of ABA go back around 100 years, but what is
now known as ABA was started by Ivar Lovaas in the 1980s, though he
had been writing about it since the 1960s. His therapy aimed to change
observed behaviours by using repeated reinforcement – it's what gay
conversion therapy was based on. The data collected shows the rate of
change in behaviour, which is why ABA practitioners constantly call it
a scientific therapy. There is no one kind of ABA, it varies widely and
has a chequered past including electro-shock treatment and hitting
children. Modern ABA has moved on from such aversive techniques
but the principles – that 'aberrant' behaviours need to be changed to
more socially acceptable ones – still remain. Lovaas, astonishing as it
may seem, wanted toddlers and young children to be in ABA therapy
for up to 40 hours per week. That's a full-time job. Lovaas also came
up with this delightful gem:

> You see, you start pretty much from scratch when you work with an
> autistic child. You have a person in the physical sense – they have hair,
> a nose and a mouth – but they are not people in the psychological
> sense. One way to look at the job of helping autistic kids is to see it
> as a matter of constructing a person. You have the raw materials, but
> you have to build the person.[1]

My family are all very much people, thanks Mr Lovaas. Considerably

---

1   O. Ivar Lovaas (1974) Interview with Paul Chance. *Psychology Today*. Accessed on
     2 May 2022 at http://neurodiversity.com/library_chance_1974.html

nicer people in fact than the person who wrote or agrees with that statement.

What Is the Evidence Base for ABA?

Here's where it starts to get slippery. The ABA industry (and it is a HUGELY profitable industry) likes to consider there is loads of academic research proving success but actually a literature review shows very little. A recent study[2] showed up how common conflicts of interest are in autism research about ABA, and there was a study published by the US Military[3] (who use ABA for their troops' families) which showed that it led to no improvement at all. In fact, there has been research that shows ABA is abusive.[4]

What's the Problem with ABA?

- It doesn't ask for autistic views and presumes that autistic people want the same things as neurotypical people.
- It tries to stop behaviour it deems 'wrong' even if it is comforting behaviour for the autistic people (e.g. ABA teaches to make eye contact).
- It doesn't give autistic people rights of autonomy over their own bodies and decisions.
- It teaches to get rid of stims even when they are not dangerous.
- It teaches autistic people to mask.
- ABA teaches instructors to control autistic people.
- Sensory issues are very rarely ever considered.
- The ABA industry doesn't try to employ autistic trainers.

---

2   Bottema-Beutel, K. and Crowley, S. (2021) 'Pervasive undisclosed conflicts of interest in applied behavior analysis autism literature'. *Frontiers in Psychology*, 5 May. https://doi.org/10.3389/fpsyg.2021.676303

3   US Military (2020) *Annual Report on Autism Care Demonstration Program.* Accessed on 2 May 2022 at www.health.mil/Reference-Center/Congressional-Testimonies/2020/06/25/Annual-Report-on-Autism-Care-Demonstration-Program

4   Sandoval-Norton, A. H., Shkedy, G., and Shkedy, D. (2021) 'Long-term ABA therapy is abusive: A response to Gorycki, Ruppel, and Zane'. *Advances in Neurodevelopmental Disorders*, 5, 126–134. https://doi.org/10.1007/s41252-021-00201-1

- It creates trauma for autistic people that is still there when they are adults.
- The ABA industry, worth millions, does not listen to autistic adults who have had ABA therapy and dismisses their views.
- Independent research papers have not found any evidence that ABA works better than just letting a child learn as they grow.
- Research has also shown that what the ABA industry calls 'independent research' is not as independent as it seems.

What's Positive Behaviour Support?

In some cases, this seems to be ABA slipping in under a different name. There's no research that says PBS works for autistic people who don't have an intellectual disability. Much of the basis is the same as ABA and there is the same evasion of specificity on websites which makes it difficult to find out what actually happens – if you are offered this, please examine it very carefully to make sure it's not essentially ABA, trying to change autistic behaviour.

What's the Alternative?

Most autistic people need an understanding and accommodating environment more than they need therapy. Where they do, search for a therapy that's respectful to your child or young person's neurotype. Occupational therapy to help sensory issues can be very good, or an autistic mentor or advocate working individually with your child or young person to help them learn to self-regulate and to navigate a world not designed for them.

FUNCTIONING LABELS

Various functioning labels have been thrust upon the autistic community, despite that community being quite clear they don't want them. First there's 'high functioning' and 'low functioning' and I'm unclear as to why anyone thought this was a good idea. Who wants to be described as 'low functioning'? I think the folly of that one speaks for itself, but 'high functioning' isn't a good idea either. This is because those who have less visible disabilities may seem to 'function highly', but as we've seen, masking takes its toll, and they may well need support or accommodations that they don't get because everyone thinks they don't need them. How they are on five days of the week may be very different to how they are on the other two, when they may be overwhelmed by having to cope.

There are also levels 1–3 which are sometimes used in diagnosis. It's understandable that parents would use them, given that, just like the term Asperger's used to be, it's written on the diagnostic report. But those terms are also harmful for autistic people. While they don't say so, they are almost exclusively based on someone's IQ and verbal abilities, rather than all the other things which make up an autistic person's experience of the world such as sensory issues, executive function, and emotional regulation. They are based on how 'normal' and neurotypical someone can appear, without taking into account the support somebody would need from doing all that masking.

Consider also that, like all of us, autistic people function differently according to how tired, or anxious, or hungry, or in pain they are. How many spoons they have. There is no constant 'level' so support needs might change at any time or any given situation.

So What Should You Say Instead?

It's fine to just say autism or autistic, if you need to do so. No need to specify any further except to outline your child's needs if you are advocating for support.

ABLEISM

If we really dig deep, many of us will find that we actually hold some views which turn out to be ableist – prejudiced against disabled people. The key is to accept that, identify them, and root them out. Disability is not a dirty word, and we should not be ashamed to say it. Your child or young person may or may not feel disabled at any one point in time, but I guarantee they will feel disabled sometimes, and there's nothing wrong with that. Other conditions can add to that feeling, and it's not helped by the way our society and our government infrastructure is run being inherently ableist.

Let's take benefits/assistance. I'm in the UK, where you can claim Disability Living Allowance (DLA) for your disabled child (if you qualify for certain criteria). When that child turns 16, the benefit/assistance changes. Leaving aside the notion that a disabled person becomes an adult, with all of the bureaucracy that entails, at 16, the very manner in which you have to apply is ableist. You have to fill in the long form manually, which has pages and pages of blank space for writing. You have to send in supporting documents, on each page of which you have to handwrite your full name and reference number. We had to send 450 supporting pages, for someone who was autistic, dyspraxic, and dyslexic – expecting them to write on 450 pages is discriminatory. There are many, many other such instances in our society.

Your child or young person is likely to be a strong advocate of social justice. You will need to be a strong advocate for them. Open your eyes to the small and large instances of ableism all around you and challenge them. Be a role model for your child.

THE PUZZLE PIECE

Lastly in our no-no chapter, just a quick word on the puzzle piece. It has become synonymous with autism due to the US charity Autism Speaks (also a no-no for their support of ABA and their shocking I Am Autism video), but this is a symbol that's really controversial in the autism community and much disliked. Autistic people are not puzzles to be solved, you don't have to find their missing pieces and fit them together. Words and symbols are important. If you want to use a symbol to show support, the infinity symbol is preferred.

I know there seem to be lots of dos and don'ts here. It's OK if you haven't always understood these things in the past and you've made some of these mistakes. Probably all of us have. What's important is that you are now making the effort to really understand your young person and help everyone around them understand too.

PART 2

LIVING A HAPPY AUTISTIC LIFE

Chapter 8

Strategies to Help Support an Autistic Young Person

SELF-REGULATION

One of the really useful things you can do to help your autistic young person become a happy, independent (if appropriate) adult, is to help them learn to self-regulate. That doesn't mean to never have a melt-down, or never get angry or upset – we all get angry and upset. But it means that they learn strategies and techniques which work specifically for them and help them to regulate their emotions, feel calmer and less over-anxious. It's worth repeating though that uncertainty = anxiety, and to be truly relaxed they must feel safe.

When we feel threatened, we automatically respond in certain ways – flight (sort out the problem), fight (run away from or avoid the problem), freeze (don't think about the problem), or fawn (do whatever the other party wants to avoid them being angry). We are not necessarily in control of those responses, they are an instant reaction rather than a reasoned response. But if you understand this response to threat, your brain can allow yourself a moment to think about what to do – you can regulate your emotions instead of making a snap emotional reaction. An extra difficulty for some autistic people is their difficulty in identifying their emotions, so that feeling overwhelming emotion can be scary and disconcerting. Equally scary is when someone they love and trust – you – seems dysregulated and angry or upset, since you are their model for trying to regulate their emotions. Help them by trying to stay in control of your own emotions as much as possible – and this may be harder if you're autistic yourself. (We're all human. Don't beat yourself up if it doesn't always work out.)

The first step in helping your young person to self-regulate is understanding when emotions might be running high. Pinpoint the areas where your child might be having difficulty – is it being in a high-arousal sensory environment with, for example, fluorescent or flashing lights and lots of noise? Is it when they are put under pressure in class? Is it when they need to attend a busy social event? Make sure you and your young person know what their trigger points are, and the activities which will make them use up 'extra' social energy. For social events especially (and I include in that anything which involves socialising with people outside the house, whether it be school, a visit to extended family, or a festival) think of it as a finite cup of energy. The more energy you 'drink', the less is in your cup. The emptier your cup becomes, the less regulated your emotions are going to be. Eventually you and your young person are going to be able to figure out the optimum amount of socialising (or noise in a restaurant, or bright lights in a supermarket) that they can happily deal with and still have a half-full cup of energy. When you and they understand this, look at their schedule and help them to make sure there is chill out time built in after those energy-depleting days so that the energy store can be replenished. This will be useful throughout life, and learning to self-advocate for it is especially important.

Next, consider what activities (or lack of activities) make your young person happy or relaxed. What can they do to bring them joy? This might be related to their passionate interests. How can you facilitate things to allow them to dig deeper and get immersed into their passionate interests? How can they build time into their schedule to do some of the stuff that really makes them happy? We all need that in our lives. And you do too, so think about this for yourself. Even if you are muttering to yourself that you'll never have time for this, believe me, you will.

Lastly, help your young person to figure out what helps them in the short term – what techniques can they use to help them self-regulate in the moment when things have become overwhelming and their emotions threaten to boil over? This will be different for everyone at different times so it really is going to be about trying lots of things – at a calm time. Don't introduce anything new when your young person is already dysregulated.

Examples might be:

- pacing
- using a fidget spinner
- playing with Blu Tack, putty or 'slime'
- listening to music with headphones on
- hugging a special toy (you can get weighted toys too)
- stroking the dog/cat
- playing a console game
- dancing
- meditation app.

Or something completely unique to your child! As long as it helps, and doesn't hurt anyone, it works.

CASE STUDY

Jade, Robin, and Lucy, age 16, 13, and 12 in the UK (by mum, Paula)

Jade was diagnosed when she was 15. A referral was made when she was younger but she was not assessed for ASD but for ADD which came back as her diagnosis. We waited approximately six months for her autism diagnosis. Robin was diagnosed at age ten. For Lucy the referral was made and she was diagnosed within approximately nine months.

Jade wasn't supported much until an EHCP was applied for. School did apply for extra funding which enabled much more support as needed. Robin was not supported in mainstream at all and is now attending specialist school which is supporting his needs.

As autism wasn't recognised when it should have been, Jade got into lots of trouble at school, often excluded, given detentions, etc. Her mental health declined which in turn caused her to self-harm and have suicidal thoughts due to not being supported. She doesn't see the dangers that others see or know how to read certain situations and is therefore very impulsive. Since being diagnosed, she is able to recognise some of her triggers and will try strategies to avoid self-harm.

IDENTIFYING EMOTIONS

When you can't identify your emotions, or perhaps figure out what's causing them and you feel them strongly, then not only is it over-whelming but it's scary too. It makes you feel vulnerable, and you're much less likely to let anyone you don't know really well soothe you at this time. In an ideal world, your young person would have been identified as autistic earlier, and might have worked with a speech and language therapist on identifying degrees of emotion, but if they have been late-diagnosed, this almost certainly hasn't happened. Your young person may have picked up quite a lot on their own, but it's possible that they can only identify a small range of emotions – for example, happy, sad, and angry – and put all emotions into those buckets. If your child says that you look angry when you're not at all, this is probably why.

Not being able to understand and identify emotions (in your-self and other people) has a name – alexithymia, and (as we saw in Chapter 2) up to 10% of non-autistic people are alexithymic, but at least 20% of autistic people have alexithymia.[1] Some even estimate as many as half to two thirds of autistic people may fit the profile. It can lead to what society may describe as inappropriate responses, such as laughing when you are meant to be serious, and cause difficult social situations that can be difficult to escape. Those who are alexithymic

---

1   Autistica (n.d.) *Alexithymia*. Accessed on 2 May 2022 at www.autistica.org.uk/what-is-autism/anxiety-and-autism-hub/alexithymia

may be unable to answer direct questions about their emotions or reactions to other people's emotions, but this inability can be misinterpreted as a refusal to answer or a lack of empathy in a distressing situation. When you combine this with the possibility of not knowing what your facial expression is saying to others, it's obvious there is room for misunderstandings to brew. Combine that still further with a possible auditory processing delay, and there is no surprise that this is something there is often a fundamental communication misunderstanding about.

We've already looked at interoception – when the body doesn't send the signals to your brain about what it's feeling – and alexithymia is linked to this. It seems that both interpreting body signals and processing emotion take part in the same two areas of the brain (the anterior insula (AI) and the anteria cingulate cortex (ACC))[2] and it's not too surprising that someone who struggles to identify hunger or thirst should also struggle to identify fear or anger, both of which manifest with quite physical symptoms.

Alexithymia can affect people in different ways. Some people have difficulty feeling emotion at all, either all the time or some of the time (e.g. when stressed), and others feel too many emotions and can't identify them, which is scary and confusing. The former may tend to shutdown, and the latter may tend to meltdown more, or use strategies which help them to stop feeling emotions. These strategies may not be good lifestyle strategies, such as alcohol, drugs, or smoking. Often in those who have been diagnosed in adulthood, these strategies were used before someone knew that they were autistic.

How Can You Help?

- Be patient. Don't expect an alexithymic person (or one with auditory processing difficulties) to be able to instantly tell you how they are feeling. Processing emotions may take a long time – even weeks. In fact, take the phrase 'How are

2   Brewer, R., Cook, R., and Bird, G. (2016) 'Alexithymia: A general deficit of interoception'. *Royal Society Open Science*, 3(10): 150664. doi:10.1098/rsos.150664

you?' and 'How are you feeling?' completely out of your vocabulary. Find other, more explicit and more helpful phrases to use instead.

- Try to explain alexithymia to extended family if you can. Your young person may not identify with the same range of emotions (for example, guilt) as them, and may not react in the same way, and it's preferable they understand this so that they don't react inappropriately.

- Model what you teach. Get into the habit of subtly labelling emotions. For example, 'You look upset, has something happened?'

- If old enough, your young person can find all kinds of descriptive language around emotions in literature – read with an eye to searching it out.

- Tell your young person (in a way they will accept) that they seem to be more anxious and stressed, so that they realise why things may be becoming more difficult and they can self-regulate.

- If appropriate, buy them a bullet journal and incentivise them to write in it every day. It will take a little while but not only can this help with identifying or at least cataloguing what you're feeling, it can also be a good tool to build self-confidence, e.g. write down three things you have done well today. Have a look at the Five Minute Journal[3] – you don't have to dedicate a lot of time to this, it's the repetition that's important.

- Drama classes can also help, as these frequently tackle emotive subjects and how someone might behave in an emotionally charged situation.

- If your young person is stressed they may be less able to feel and identify emotions – don't be surprised at this or treat it as worrying.

Take a look at ELSA resources online (ELSA stands for emotional

---

3   www.intelligentchange.com/products/the-five-minute-journal?view=b

literacy support assistant).[4] While most will be for primary age children, others can be adapted for those older.

SOCIAL STORIES

The term 'social story' was first used by paediatrician Carol Gray in 1991, and has become widely used. What is called a social story may not conform to the parameters Carol laid down though, and it's important that they do. A badly designed social story can cause more harm than good.

What Is a Social Story?

It's an educational tool designed to show what to expect and even how to react in a certain setting or situation. They are usually designed to be short visual explanations, but can sometimes develop into 'social articles' for older audiences.

How Do You Write a Social Story?

There are ten social story criteria as defined by Carol Gray on her website.[5]

It's important to look at these criteria as social stories are often used in ways they were never designed for.

Often there are pictures for each stage of the story, so that there are multiple ways for the audience to understand it. Social stories should be mainly positive, and use descriptive language rather than 'should' or 'must'.

How Can I Find Social Stories Written by Others?

There are lots of ready-made social stories dotted around the internet which you might be able to use or adapt if you think your young person will find them useful (hint: not everyone likes them or finds them useful so do check this before you invest a lot of time or money). Pinterest can be a good source. Most social stories are written for children,

---

4   www.elsa-support.co.uk
5   https://carolgraysocialstories.com

so if you are looking for social stories to suit teenagers you need to search specifically for that, otherwise you will find lots with pictures that look too babyish to have any impact on your young person other than to annoy them.

When Is It Appropriate to Use Social Stories?

Social stories can be helpful in various situations, but in general they help to reduce uncertainty about a new situation (and as we know, uncertainty = anxiety). It can help to explain a rule or routine, can help prepare someone on what to expect at an event or appointment or can help understanding with a concept that's difficult to grasp. They can also provide a script for a social situation. Not all autistic young people will find social stories valuable, so do bear that in mind before you create one.

For teens, a social story might be about:

- What to expect at a job interview.
- What to wear for a job interview.
- Consent and saying no in relationships.
- How to recognise subtle bullying.
- How to keep yourself safe online.
- How to react if you are stopped by the police.

But other common social stories are about:

- Going to the dentist/doctor/hospital/optician.
- Getting a blood test.
- Getting a tooth filling.
- Getting a vaccination.
- Transitioning from one school/class to another.
- Going on holiday.
- Going to a wedding.
- Getting a pet.
- Coping when a pet dies.

Social stories shouldn't be used on their own, but as a conversation starter. They shouldn't ever be used to stop autistic traits or to make someone act more like a neurotypical person. But they can be useful in conjunction with educating your young person about some social cues – give them the information they need in order to 'read the room'.

EMPATHY

We previously looked at empathy – or rather the lack of it – as one of the myths about autism that people like to believe. And as we saw, it's simply not true that autistic people don't feel empathy. However, like all humans, not all autistic people are the same and some will feel too much empathy while others feel little. What may very well be a difficulty though, is expressing empathy, because much of how we express empathy in society is scripted and performative. Giving them the knowledge to navigate these situations if they want to gives them power – as long as we don't tell them that this is THE way and the only way to behave. Don't teach them to mask, teach them to advocate.

There are three types of empathy – emotional, cognitive, and compassionate. To explain them, let's imagine that someone we know has received some distressing news.

- Emotional empathy would help us to feel their distress.
- Cognitive empathy would help us to understand why they felt distressed.
- Compassionate empathy would lead us to try to come up with an idea or plan to help them feel better.

How Can You Help?

Body mapping can be a good exercise,[6] and you can use something like the board game Operation to make it more entertaining. Once an emotion has been identified, the challenge is to decide where in the body that emotion manifests, for example being anxious might feel like

---

6   Autistic Girls Network have a webinar on body mapping available on YouTube: www.youtube.com/watch?v=ABpdMR6xGjQ&t=1376s

butterflies in the tummy. If you were playing this game with a group, you could make tags to attach to a poster of the human body but it might be overkill with just your one person! This helps understanding around physical feelings related to emotion, and can help relate to sensations other people might be feeling.

You can use magazines and old photos to try to identify emotions from facial expressions – again, make a game of it if this is age appropriate for your young person. When the emotion has been identified, model what would be an empathetic social response in this situation.

Drama groups can also be really good for this and can help with modelling real-life situations and the possible responses to them.

Chapter 9

Autism at Home

A DIFFERENT STYLE OF PARENTING

You might have noticed already that traditional parenting styles don't work all that well for most autistic children and young people. In fact, some can do harm. You've taken the important step to understand your child's autistic identity and that's going to help enormously. Stop worrying about what other people think and go with your instinct to support and nurture your child as they are. While you may be invited on to a parenting course – indeed you may be forced to take a course in order to access some services or support – be aware that many of these are not adapted for neurodivergent families. Listen to other autistic and neurodivergent adults to understand what works for them.[1]

There are lots of phrases you might hear:

- 'You're spoiling her.'
- 'You're making a rod for your own back.'
- 'He's just playing you.'
- 'You're just giving in and making it worse.'
- 'You need to get tougher.'

---

1 Autistic Girls Network ran a webinar with the wonderful Chris Bonnello of Autistic Not Weird, which you can watch on YouTube: www.youtube.com/watch?v=7ijBtkindaM

But people saying these things don't understand autism and while they might think otherwise, they don't understand your child or young person. And I say that even if it's teachers or social workers saying this to you, because sadly there are plenty of professionals who don't yet understand autism well. Just stay in your own lane and be confident that you are setting your child up for a confident, happy, fulfilling life in a way that really didn't happen for autistic people when you were young.

The most important thing to realise is that your child might well be demand avoidant. This does NOT mean that they are naughty, but it does mean that anxiety compels them to resist demands. How far this stretches is different in every child, but the very demand avoidant child who might get a diagnosis of PDA (pathological demand avoidance) may resist every demand, no matter how much they want to do the activity they are avoiding. There are no easy answers here and I'm not trying to make it seem as if there are. But flipping your way of parenting WILL make a big difference to the calmness levels of your household.

How Can You Help?

Remember that your young person may have auditory processing differences which means they aren't deliberately ignoring you to wind you up – they need time to process what you're saying. Be patient.

Get educational psychologist and sensory-integrated occupational therapist assessments if you can, because this will tell you what your young person's struggles and strengths are, and enable you to build support around that. These can be requested as part of an EHCP assessment, a school may commission an educational psychologist, or you can commission yourself privately for a fee.

Flip your thinking. Behaviour which challenges is your child communicating with you. What is your child communicating? What are the problems which are causing the behaviour? Rather than focusing on changing the behaviour, focus on solving the problems.

Are your expectations unrealistic? Please don't misunderstand me. I don't mean that you and your young person shouldn't have lofty ambitions and aspire to achievements they dream about. Far from it. But to give an example, if they have executive function issues and you are telling them to tidy their room which looks as if a bomb has exploded in it, that's an unrealistic expectation. Instead of a blanket instruction, you need to break that task down into much smaller elements so that it's not overwhelming. The final task is still perfectly reachable, but broken down into achievable chunks. That's accommodating your young person's brain in just the same way as a ramp might be accommodating a wheelchair. And of course, the same applies in school.

When your young person is calm, talk about situations which are difficult. Get their input on why they perhaps behave in a challenging way. Find out what triggers that. Be prepared to learn that your own behaviour is not ideal, in the knowledge that they are not being rude or disrespectful to talk to you that way, since autistic people generally don't view authority in the same way as society dictates. Use co-production to solve problems. It's much more likely to be effective that way, and has the bonus that your young person sees that their view matters.

MASKING (OR NOT)

If your young person has only recently been recognised as autistic, it's likely that they learnt to mask or camouflage their autism at a young age. This was almost certainly an unconscious process for them, as they recognised that more obviously autistic behaviour got unwelcome attention from others, whether that be family, teachers, or peers. There is a stigma attached to seeming different, and often an enforced isolation. With hindsight you may look back and realise that certain events or behaviours were obviously autistic, but they weren't enough by themselves to make you aware – or indeed to make your child aware, as they may also have had no idea, although they were probably well aware that they felt different to their friends.

Sadly, when young people are recognised as autistic in their teens, it's often because their mental health has taken a battering. The child you know has probably felt they needed to conform to a neurotypical standard of behaviour, because that's what their peers do and anything else might make them stand out or be singled out for ridicule or bullying. This may well have spilled out at home too, so once your young person has essentially been broken by their masking and possible burnout, it can be a shock to see them behaving in a way which doesn't seem 'themselves'. And of course, part of that behaviour can be caused by depression and burnout, and will wear off once that passes. But it's still likely that once your child has accepted their autistic identity they will behave rather differently to how they did before. And that's absolutely fine, in fact it's perfect, because although it might take you some time to adjust, this is the real them, the one who can self-regulate, the one who is stronger, the one who can become independent and happy.

How Can You Help?

- Learn as much as you can about autism, and encourage wider family to do the same.
- Be an ally. Advocate for them to change their environment if they are unable to do so.
- Make your home a low-arousal sensory environment, and a place of calm and relaxation.
- Consider your home a safe space for your child. This means not springing surprise visitors on them, and it might even mean not having any visitors at all.
- Make sure your child knows what's going to happen (possibly with a visual chart/whiteboard) and when – eliminate uncertainty as much as possible.
- Don't react to behaviour you consider out of the ordinary (unless it's unsafe for your child or others).
- Facilitate self-regulating behaviour (such as finding somewhere to pace regularly).

TOXIC POSITIVITY

Most of us would probably agree that being positive about life increases happiness and is healthier for all of us. I'm all in favour of positive vibes. I'm a glass-half-full kind of person.

But when 'being positive' forces you to hide your own emotions it ceases to be healthy and becomes hazardous. Nobody should feel forced to be positive, or feel pressured by social media to present only a happy face to the world. Social media posts are often performative, showing only the 'best' side of a person, not the nitty gritty of their everyday life. Likewise, a person masking their autism has probably grown up doing the same – presenting a false performance of a neurotypical person, even though it's not the real them and masking is probably damaging their mental health. Add to this the fact that autistic people are often told to 'cheer up' because their natural facial expression is neutral rather than smiling, and they may not even be aware of how their face is presenting, and you have the perfect storm of toxic positivity.

How Can You Help?

- Instead of telling someone to 'Think positive', listen, acknowledge their stress/distress and ask if there is anything you can do to help. If there is, make sure you do it. This is a neurodivergent conversation and promises are expected to be kept – no meaningless platitudes here please.
- If there is nothing you can do, just listening to how they are feeling and validating that is useful too.
- The 'superhero' analogy is not a helpful one for autistic people. Yes some autistic people are particularly brave, or clever, or resourceful, just the same as people of other neurotypes are – we're all human and we're all different. It doesn't help to be told 'Autism is your superpower', it just puts pressure on autistic people to excel at something.
- Acknowledge to yourself that if you are neurotypical you don't experience the world in the same way as your autistic young person, and you cannot tell them how they are feeling.
- If you're autistic yourself and have worked out how to deal with toxic positivity, tell your young person and everyone else!

HELPFUL AND UNHELPFUL COMMENTS

There will be times you will need to make a choice between keeping quiet or letting rip because of unhelpful comments you receive. When I asked in the Autistic Girls Network Facebook and Twitter channels for examples of helpful or unhelpful comments autistic people and their families had received from both professionals and family or friends, the response was enormous. If you want to correct them, this book should give you a good basis on how to do it. Here are common unhelpful ones directly quoted to me (and I have experienced many of these):

- 'Everyone is a little bit autistic.'
- 'But she's only a bit autistic isn't she? She'll probably grow out of it.'
- 'She doesn't look autistic.'
- 'She's FINE once she's in school (she's no trouble in class).'
- 'Don't get her assessed she'll be labelled for life.'
- 'She's just a drama queen.'
- 'They just need more discipline.'

Actual quotes from professionals:

- 'You are married and have friends so it's unlikely you are autistic' (from a doctor).
- 'He isn't autistic, He talked to me and looked me in the eye' (from a doctor).
- 'We don't see that behaviour at school, it's bad parenting' (from a deputy headteacher).
- 'You need to be more resilient' (from a SENCO).
- 'Autistic people are known to make things up for attention' (from a doctor).
- 'She can't be autistic, she can hold a conversation' (from the GP).

Helpful things to say when hearing about a diagnosis (and what neurodivergent people might say to each other):

- 'Congratulations!'
- 'Yes I thought you must be!'
- 'Great that you have confirmation now.'

- 'Thanks for letting me know, and I'd really like to know if there's something I can do to support you, please feel free to tell me.'

TIPS FOR A HAPPIER HOME

Everyone feels happier when they've got space, permission, and even encouragement to be themselves. Here are some adjustments you can make to your home and family to help your autistic child thrive.

Be Their Rock

You are their most trusted people in the world. If you can't understand and appreciate them, who can? You may find your child or young person is particularly attached to you to the point of separation anxiety. Be patient about it. The world we live in is more difficult for them to navigate than for their neurotypical peers. The better you can educate friends and family about autism and about the way your child or young person thinks, the more likely it will feel safer for them to venture more widely.

Try Not to Explode

We all get cross sometimes. But for your autistic child, seeing you get cross with them may be both confusing and scary. The more you understand them, the less you're going to get cross about things which are basically misunderstandings between neurotypical and neurodivergent ways of thinking, which will help immensely.

Your Facial Expressions Can Be a Mystery

Your child has grown up trying to figure out what people are thinking, because they can't interpret social cues (like facial expression and body language) in the same way neurotypical people can. It may mean that your facial expression when you're worried, frustrated, or flummoxed can all be interpreted as you being angry. The more you and the rest of the family are aware of this, the more you can help, both by modelling what your facial expression looks like in certain situations and by (patiently!) verbalising what the issue is and how you are feeling about it.

Give Them Space

This space might not be their bedroom, because as you may have already found, their bedroom might not feel like an oasis for them.

But they will certainly need emotional space regularly, and they will need an area where they can be left to chill out/decompress (or whatever you might like to call it). The older they get the more likely they will need to do this, especially after a time they felt they needed to mask a lot. It will benefit them (and you) if you discuss with them, at a time when they are calm and not overloaded, how this decompression time will help. Make it part of their emotional regulation routine after they come home from school. And if they do spend hours in their room (as long as you know they are happy and not slipping into depression), don't shame them for it when they do come down and join the family.

Don't Ply Them with Questions

We all want to know what's been happening at school, but hold off on the 20 Questions. Your child or young person needs to just chill, quite possibly on their own, and you are not going to get the answers you want. You're much more likely to get answers on a walk, or a drive, where you're not facing each other and you can also throw in some questions about a subject they love.

Release the Need for Eye Contact

Don't ask for eye contact, or participate in any school or therapy initiative which tries to teach eye contact. Talk about it with your child to gauge their feelings on the subject – for some it will be physically painful, for others just uncomfortable. Have an honest discussion about how some people they will meet won't understand, and mention techniques like looking between the eyes or at someone's nose (test it out, most people can't tell when this is happening), but it should always be the autistic person's choice.

Embrace the Stimming

Don't make a fuss about stimming. Unless it's hurting them or someone else, stimming is a comfort behaviour. If we can be comfortable with people tapping their feet to music, or the British stereotype of making a cup of tea whenever something uncomfortable happens, we can get comfortable with our child doing their favourite stim or sitting with a blanket over their head when they are overloaded.

Respect and Join In Their Intense Interests

Likewise, be understanding about passionate interests. Don't mock them, don't tell people they're weird, don't – unless the interest is an alarming one – try to wean them onto something else. Just the opposite – show interest, have conversations about them. Join them for a little while in their happy place. Recognise that these interests make them very happy and are comforting.

Create a Sensory Dream, Not a Sensory Nightmare

Make sure your home in an inviting place, sensory-wise. You may want to make a sensory room for them (more on this later), but even if you don't, make sure the rest of the house isn't a sensory nightmare. Accept that they may only want to wear a limited range of clothes. Make sure lighting is toned down. Find out what they don't like about noises or smells and make sure they happen as little as possible in your house. Likewise, find out what smells and sounds might be comforting, for example they might like the smell of fresh washing (for which Yankee Candle's Cotton Fresh scent is an acceptable substitute) or the sound of rain (there are apps for your phone which have thousands of different rain sounds).

Release the Remote Control

Resign yourself to the possibility you may be listening to the same TV programme a lot. Everyone is different, but your child may find it comforting to have quite a limited range of programmes, and they may not even actually watch them, but the sound is comforting. Your child already knows how the programme is going to make them feel. They don't need to expend emotional energy worrying about what's going to happen, in fact the programmes can be used as a form of emotional regulation. As always, what you KNOW and what is predictable is comforting. And the opposite also holds true – some programmes might be more disturbing than you might expect, so if your child tells you they don't want to watch something or seems anxious about it, pay attention.

Don't Ban Screens

While we've touched on screentime here, let me suggest that you don't use the removal of screentime as a threat to make your child do something. As discussed, familiar programmes can be emotional regulators, and the same applies to gaming too if they are taking familiar actions. (Though where you might find friction in gaming is where your child is playing with others who insist on doing something in a different way.) A mobile phone, especially, for teens, can act as more or less constant emotional regulation. To take it away, especially when it can seem like a lifeline of easier social communication, is to immediately dysregulate.

Embrace Routine

While we're on the subject of sameness, routines are important for your child. There's a reason why they want you to drive the same route to school every day. Sameness feels safe. Now obviously not everything can be a routine, and life is always going to bring up some surprises, but try to give your child their routines as much as you can.

Minimise Transitions

And still on the same subject of change – you'll have figured out by now that your child doesn't like sudden change or transitions. Big changes like moving house or school are difficult for everyone but especially for autistic people. Your child's life, and by extension yours, will be much less anxiety-inducing if you keep change to a minimum and prepare them for things that are going to happen. That preparation is going to look different depending on your household, but it's likely to need repetition. And it's your job to make sure school are on the same page.

Keep Social Occasions to a Minimum

Don't over-schedule. Once you've recognised that social situations, like school, are very tiring for your autistic child, you'll also recognise that you need to build in a lot of downtime to recover. It's unlikely that your child will want to do lots of extra-curricular activities, but if they do, have a discussion with them about the need to rest too. Of course if they are in the happy position that their extra-curricular activity also happens to coincide with their special interest, it may be restful to them.

Protect Your Child's Boundaries

Be aware that your child may not really like to be touched – by others if not by you. As you are likely their special person a hug with you might be fine but a hug by Auntie Ethel might not. Don't make your child give hugs or kisses if they don't want to. Be on their side, not on society's side. It might be difficult to make Auntie Ethel understand, but you are all your child has got.

Allow Processing Time

It may be irritating when your child doesn't reply to you or takes a long time to make a decision on something. But many neurodivergent people have difficulties with executive function and need a longer time to process things. They are not being rude in this case. Give them time to answer, but also don't give them long strings of commands in one go. If you'd like them to tidy their room, for example, you may need to break that down into smaller tasks (depending on the state of the room of course!), but only a couple at a time. If you don't, it may be so overwhelming that they don't know where to start. As always, every person is different so be led by your child.

Chill Out Time Is King

Give your child time to decompress when they come back from school, without bombarding them with lots of questions. In fact, lots of questions at any time probably isn't welcome if it's not about one of their favourite subjects. It can be easier to talk if they aren't on the spot – go for a walk or a drive so that you're not looking at each other, and you might find it easier. If you're autistic yourself, you may have been surprised to discover during COVID lockdown that you used your commute to decompress... to turn from employee into parent. Working from home where you don't have that transition time can be difficult to adjust to.

Don't Make Mealtimes a Battlefield

We all know about fussy eaters. But a sensory aversion to some foods is not being fussy. Be understanding and open-minded about this, and prepare to be led by your child as much as is possible. It's likely that times of extra anxiety will exacerbate food issues, so don't be surprised if mealtimes get more difficult when your child is anxious. But do make mealtimes as relaxed as possible for them, even if this means tearing up the social rulebook as far as mealtime etiquette is concerned. If your child has very sensitive hearing and can hear everybody chewing from across the room, it's understandable if they don't want to sit at a table next to them when they're eating, don't you think? Be flexible. There's a good reason why you sometimes see small children sat on iPads in restaurants – it's a distraction technique, and it can work for your child too when they are anxious.

Don't Underestimate Supersonic Hearing Abilities!

If your child has really sensitive hearing (and remember you might not know that yet, because for them, it's their normal), be mindful of the fact that they can hear you however quietly you whisper and wherever you are in the house. And make teachers aware of that too. Don't say things you wouldn't want them to hear.

Your Home Is a Sanctuary

What we all aim for is for our children to feel safe and relaxed in their home. And with that in mind, be aware that for some autistic people, having strangers and 'extra' people come into their home can be very stressful. I don't mean grandma and granddad, or the next door neighbour who pops in regularly, but people – even those they know – who don't usually come in the house, and of course tradespeople. Don't be surprised if your child feels the need to hide in their room while someone is there. And obviously, prepare them for it to happen.

Remember You Are a Sanctuary Too

Remember that unless things have gone drastically wrong, you are also your child's safe person (usually but not always mum). You are the one they trust to fix things. You are the one they want to tell things, even things they find very difficult to talk about. So make it easier by promising to not be offended, to be open-minded and not judgemental, and not to overreact. And make every effort to keep those promises.

Truly, I promise, once you begin to understand autistic thought processes (or embrace them if you are now suspecting you might also be autistic), and show your child that you understand so that they feel relaxed enough to drop the mask at home, things are going to start to get better. But if you child has only been diagnosed as a teen, expect quite a change as the mask gradually drops. Remember, the new them is the real them.

If you read through this list again, it will become clear that doing these things will make for a more relaxed and less anxious household for everyone, parents and children alike.

CHORES

Hopefully what you have read up to now has given you more of an insight into your autistic young person. You'll understand how impossible it can feel to fulfil a demand, and change the way you ask to be less demanding. Your demand-avoidant child can often see through that too, but it's not that they want to defy you – their brain is telling them not to do that thing, and you asking them things they 'ought to do' makes them anxious. Remember too that they may not have the same priorities as you. For them, it may not seem important to wear clean clothes, or have a sparkling kitchen or a tidy bedroom, and it's very hard to motivate yourself to do something if it feels like a waste of your time.

Remember too that an autistic brain is focused on what they are doing and changing tasks is HARD. Asking them to stop doing a task they are enjoying for one they consider worthless doesn't build character, it builds resentment. Yes, they may well need to do some or all of these things as adults but it won't stop them being able to take the trash out as adults just because they weren't forced to do it as a child.

How Can You Help?

- Don't ask them to do too many things in one day.
- Have a plan to break large tasks down into smaller ones.
- Arrange the day so that you are not asking your young person to change tasks too many times.
- Incorporate passionate interests into chores as much as possible.
- Especially for older children make this feel like acquiring life skills rather than chores.
- Think about what chores are really necessary – a simple life is more neurodivergent-friendly.
- Consider your young person's sensory differences when allocating chores. If they have a very strong sense of smell, emptying the trash might not be the best chore for them even though 'they need to learn to do it.'
- Choose tasks which utilise their strengths. If they are very detail oriented, organisation might overwhelm them, but cleaning or painting every last spot on a cupboard might suit them well.
- Doing chores may well require downtime to recover – accommodate this.
- Encourage your young person to develop a routine for a chore if this is helpful. It will mean less cognitive load once the routine is embedded.
- Give them the right tools for the job, including sensory tools, for example ear defenders or headphones for vacuuming, gloves for cleaning.
- If in the right mood, support can help someone who has difficulty organising because of focus on details. As with all parent–child interactions, this can depend on the situation!

- If your young person constantly avoids a task, consider that it might not be suitable for them and stop asking.
- Music may help a task become more palatable.

HAIRCUTS

Going to a hairdresser can be a special type of sensory torture for an autistic person. Having somebody so close to them and touching their hair, the feel of cut hair on their skin, the sensation and noise of clippers, possible bright lights or radio playing in the salon, the noise of the hairdryers, the chat of customers and the smell of the hair products – it's all a perfect sensory storm.

Not to mention, sitting still for so long on a possibly uncomfortable chair. It's not surprising that many autistic children don't enjoy this experience. If your young person still hates this, and you can't avoid a salon visit, here are some tips.

How Can You Help?

- Choose a hairdresser who understands the needs of your autistic young person.
- Book an appointment at as quiet a time as possible.
- Consider using a mobile hairdresser who comes to your home, unless this will feel like invasion of a safe space.
- Prepare your young person in advance that the appointment is coming up – use your family whiteboard or whatever other visual calendar method you have.
- Look at photos and/or videos on the internet and YouTube to visualise what to expect. If you can, have your hair cut yourself in the salon and either video it or take your child with you.
- Use a timer so that your young person has a visual record of how much longer they have to endure the appointment!
- Use noise cancelling earphones or ear plugs to block out the noise of the salon.

- Take some fidget toys or simply a phone and get distracted – instruct the hairdresser that chat (and eye contact) isn't needed.
- Go for a special treat when it's over!

CREATING A SENSORY SPACE

They may not be there yet, but ideally your young person will self-regulate, and in order to do this effectively they need a calming, safe space. Presuming that they have their own bedroom, you can create a sensory space there without spending too much money.

First keep it simple, and be led (of course) by your young person and what they want. Let them choose colours which feel positive and/or calming for them. Let them choose sensory fabrics which work for them, for example my household prefers soft, jersey-type bedding. If adding cushions/pillows, etc., make sure they have some sensory input too, for example they might be furry. Let them look at videos of some of the products mentioned so they have an idea of what they do. Keep decor quite muted, because the sensory environment is going to be created by something else. Then choose from some of these products (please note that I'm NOT suggesting you go out and buy them all!):

- colour-changing LED bubble fish tube lamp
- colour changing night projector with stars/sealife
- magnetic whiteboard sheet which sticks to the wall – you can then easily add and change designs
- lava lamp
- white noise machine (or noise app)
- multi-coloured rope lights
- sensory sack or compression sheet
- spinner or fidget toys
- weighted blanket
- if there's space, a hanging swing pod chair.

Above all it needs to be a space which is comforting and soothing, and where they can chill out after a hard day 'peopling'.

CHRISTMAS AND BIRTHDAYS

I love Christmas. But I will be honest with you, the Christmas experience I have now is very different to the Christmas experience I had 10 or 20 or even 40 years ago. And that's fine, because it's the Christmas experience we have figured out works best for us as a neurodivergent family. We are lucky that we have a lovely and understanding extended family too, who don't put pressure on us to conform to a stereotypical idea of what Christmas should look like.

When thinking about Christmas for your neurodivergent family, there's no SHOULD involved. And your ideal day/week might very well look quite different to that of another neurodivergent family. And that's OK.

Why Can Christmas Be Difficult for Autistic People?

There seems to be an expectation in (Western) society that Christmas should be a very special time, full of joy and giving, and definitely happy families spending time together. But it's only relatively recently that images of bulging sacks and stockings became the image of Christmas, and lots of countries have quite different traditions too. This social expectation can feel quite false and performative to neurodivergent people.

Christmas brings change, and as we know, uncertainty = anxiety. While there may be Christmas traditions that your children learn, it's all a huge change from December onwards – different activities in schools (including pressurising activities such as school concerts or nativity plays), Christmas music and completely different aisles of goods in shops, and people making demands about gift decisions.

Christmas presents themselves bring uncertainty. What is under that wrapping? Will you like it? Will you be expected to perform the social function of pretending you like it when you honestly don't care about it at all? Magnify this for a whole sack or stocking of presents. Not all children will feel like this, but if your child wants to decide exactly what they want for Christmas, don't insist on surprises. The surprises are for your benefit, not theirs. Don't make, or allow someone else to make, your child unwrap presents with a whole room of eyes on them – that's a very uncomfortable experience.

Christmas dinner is another big change, and there is often huge pressure to sit at the table for longer than usual (if it's usual in your house) with extra people and different food to normal. Parents might also feel pressured to make it a special dinner, and for it to be perfect. Add crackers and hats and other sensory nightmares, and Christmas dinner might not be the special occasion for your child that you want it to be – it stands out for all the wrong reasons.

Which brings me to the elephant in the room – extended family. This is going to be different for everyone. We all have our family traditions, but at Christmas they often involve sitting down at a table with people you might not eat with very often. Those people may not be as understanding as you about your family's neurodiverse needs. They may have expectations about behaviour and traditions which don't fit so well with you anymore and which may cause your child to have a miserable day. If this is the case, try to educate and explain beforehand, but don't be afraid to put your own little family first. That's all I'm going to say on the matter!

How Can You Help?

- Talk it over with your child. Try to find out whether they love or loathe Christmas, and why.
- If you can discover triggers, you can change things so they don't occur. These could be anything from opening presents or having dinner with distant relatives, sitting at the dinner table hearing people eat or long hours expected to socialise with extended family because it's a 'special' day. They may wish fervently that it was a 'normal' day! But they may not, so personalisation is key here.
- Try not to go overboard with surprises. As with everything else, prepare your child for what's going to be happening.
- Don't overstay a welcome and ask your guests not to do so

either. Better to have a fun few hours rather than a miserable
many hours.

- Build in chill time either side of the big day. It's going to be
exhausting.
- Don't make a fuss if your child wants to spend time on
their own in their room. This may be necessary to avoid
overwhelm.

Birthdays

Much of this is applicable to birthdays too. While you as a parent may
want a big fuss, the older your child gets the less likely they will want
one. So be led by your child, and be prepared that the anticipation may
not quite match up to the reality.

I have seen threads in Facebook groups where parents are livid that
their child is being ungrateful in not wanting balloons, and cake, and
a big celebration. This is where a reminder is needed – it's not about
you. You gave birth to them, yes. But your reward was your baby. Once
they are old enough to say what they want to do for their birthdays
(within reason and financial capacity!), then the choice is theirs and
you need to respect it.

VACATIONS

If your young person was late diagnosed, it's possible you've never had
any issues with vacations. We didn't think that we had. Except when
we looked back, and realised oh THAT's why they didn't want to go to
kids' clubs after a certain age. Other memories started slipping into place
after that. Unknowingly, we had chosen holidays which suited them
fairly well – unsurprising given our own neurodivergence and aversion
to loud party resorts, or beaches and swimming pools full of people.

What your young person enjoys, or doesn't, in a vacation is going to
be very personal. But as you've probably found out, if they don't enjoy
it you won't either. And a vacation is BIG change, and BIG uncertainty
unless you've already been to the same place ten times. There's a reason
why neurodivergent families keep on going back to the same place.

How Can You Help?

- Talk to your young person about what they think is important in a holiday – our non-negotiables are no sharing bedrooms or sleeping in the living areas, good Wi-Fi, a comfortable-looking couch, and not being in a resort of apartments. There must be enough days out to entertain, although museums and churches don't count as entertaining for one teen, and shops don't for the other. Beach vacations are no good. There's a reason we don't go on vacation much!
- Prepare your young person as much as possible. Get them to find YouTube videos of where you are going. Ask questions so that you can build an idea of what a day there might look like. Prepare for the journey too, whether that be by airplane, car, or train.
- If your food is not provided in an all-inclusive way, research restaurants in the area and consider booking them. Searching for a restaurant and not knowing if there will be a table available or what they will be able to eat is likely to cause anxiety. If you're in an all-inclusive arrangement, look at the menus so that your young person can familiarise themselves with what they might choose. Hopefully there are some staples on there which can be a default if making a decision becomes too much of a demand.
- Plan your days – the aim is to remove as much uncertainty as possible (unless your child likes surprises, in which case, go wild!).
- Build in chill time when you get back after a day out. Doing new things which involve 'peopling' is likely to be quite exhausting.
- Accept that while going on vacation may well be enjoyable for your young person, it may contain so much change or so much needing to mask that it's not relaxing. Lots of chill time when they get home may be necessary.

WHAT CAN YOU DO FOR YOU?

I know that we've talked a lot about what you need to change, and how much effort you need to put into supporting your young person. This is going to seem daunting at times, all the paperwork and meeting preparation.

Ultimately though, you're no use to them if you burn yourself out. I'm not going to sit here at my desk and type about mindfulness and cups of tea and relaxing baths, although they might all be a good idea at some point. Those are too often suggested to parents whose children – and therefore themselves too – are going through serious crisis. And telling someone in crisis to have a cup of tea is not helpful. (I can attest to that personally, since it's happened to me.)

What I will say is, find something that you do for you. Whether it's knitting creations to rival Olympian Tom Daley, or conquering climbing walls, or wild swimming, it's something that you don't need to justify to anyone else, which helps you to settle your busy brain and brings some peace and a sense of achievement. Depending on what's going on with your young person, you may need to enlist someone to help you get some space and free time, but don't be afraid to ask. In fact, be as bold as can be. Maybe you'll find you inspire your own future mountain climber.

Chapter 10

Autism in School

Unless otherwise stated, the information below is based on the UK education system, but many of the roles will be similar elsewhere. The same principles of inclusive education and how autistic children are best supported in an education setting will be applicable everywhere.

KEY STAFF FOR SEN SUPPORT

The most important person for supporting your young person if they are in mainstream school is likely to be the SENCO (special educational needs co-ordinator, or special education coordinator in the US). They are responsible for supporting all students who have special educational needs of any sort, including neurodivergent children. You should have a chat with them when you first suspect your young person may be autistic, or before they transition to the secondary school.

The SENCO is the person responsible for co-ordinating and disseminating knowledge about your young person to all the staff they come into contact with. It's up to the SENCO to summarise their needs (and they may put together what's called a Student Passport, which we'll look at), and to advise teaching staff on the adjustments they need to make in and out of class. While it's certainly preferable that there's a whole school awareness of neurodiversity, it's sadly more common that this awareness is mainly restricted to staff responsible for pupils with special needs.

The SENCO will also be the member of staff responsible for

putting together or applying for support plans for your young person whether they be official EHCPs (in England) or IEPs (in the US) or other plans depending on where you are in the world. They should look at the needs of your child and whether they should be seen by the Specialist Teaching Service, educational psychologists, speech and language therapists, or occupational therapists. Sadly, the use of these services can often be driven by budget (or lack of) rather than need.

Depending where you are, there may be other staff available. The school may have specially trained teaching assistants, or they may call in specialist teachers or therapists.

EDUCATIONAL PSYCHOLOGY

Specialist schools may have their own dedicated educational psychologists (EPs), but in the UK most mainstream schools will need to bring one in from their local authority. An EP will be able to assess and support the learning needs of all children, but are likely to be very much involved with children with SEND (special educational needs and disability). Some EPs will be very knowledgeable about autism and other neurodivergencies, and others will have more outdated knowledge. They may be part of a multi-agency team who assess for autism in your area.

An EP is responsible for supporting any children and young people up to the age of 25 (in the UK) who are experiencing difficulties in their learning or in their social and emotional wellbeing. They will use different forms of questionnaires and assessments to identify needs, consult with parents and teachers, and put forward solutions to help smooth out the difficulties. They can also be involved with training teachers to solve particular issues. As is often the case, budget can be a barrier in getting EPs involved.

SPECIALIST TEACHERS

Specialist teachers are usually experienced teachers who have an additional qualification and specialisation in one particular area of SEND, in our case, autism. In the UK specialist teachers are usually a traded service between the school and the local authority, which means the school pays for all specialist provision. Naturally, this can again cause issues with lack of budget meaning lack of provision.

Specialist autism teachers are generally highly trained and knowledgeable, often either being autistic themselves or with autistic family members. They can be asked to visit a pupil either to give an assessment or to provide follow-up work, but usually since their services are only temporary in the school it will be up to the school to implement the recommendations written in the report. In our case, this sadly meant that an excellent and very detailed report written by a highly experienced specialist teacher after an assessment of my son, who had a private autism diagnosis, was completely ignored by the school. I'm sure this doesn't usually happen (why waste the money?), but it's something to be aware of.

Schools can bring in a specialist autism teacher to advise on how to support a particular child, in which case the advice will be very much tailored to that individual's needs, or to deliver general advice and training on how to support autistic students more broadly.

SPEECH AND LANGUAGE AND OCCUPATIONAL THERAPY

In a mainstream school, there is not likely to be a speech and language therapist (SALT) or occupational therapist (OT) employed by the school, but there will be a team available from the local authority who can be called in when needed – again, budget will apply.

SALT is one of the early therapies which may be employed, but it's less likely to be automatically given when your child is diagnosed later. In this case the child's support plan would need to recommend assessment, and the SALT report would detail what therapy was recommended. This would then be added to the support plan and a budget allocated to however many hours of therapy had been stipulated.

SAL therapy is often used with autistic children and young people because social communication difficulties are part of the diagnostic criteria. A SALT can also help a child to self-regulate by recognising emotions, as we've discussed. But you do need to be aware of the type of therapy being offered, as there are some which are not neurodivergent-friendly and can encourage masking and trying to appear more neurotypical. For example, I've seen sample worksheets which equate not making eye contact, or not wanting to be touched by non-family, with being 'not good'. Not only will this make your young person's self-esteem plummet, but it's teaching them that they shouldn't have agency over their bodies. If you teach them that anyone should be able to, for example, put a hand on their shoulders because otherwise that person would be offended, then you are leaving them in a very vulnerable position. Any SAL therapy should allow a neurodivergent person to behave in a way that's comfortable for them.

An OT is more likely to work with younger autistic children in a mainstream rather than specialist setting, but nevertheless you may find OT input particularly helpful if your young person has particularly strong sensory needs, or has a co-occurring condition like dyspraxia. A mainstream school is unlikely to engage the services of an OT unless you have professional input that says it would be advisable.

For sensory seekers and avoiders, a full sensory-integrated OT assessment can be invaluable in figuring out what is triggering for your young person and what is soothing, which can be really helpful for figuring out a self-regulation plan. The OT can also help advise school and make recommendations of all kind of things which can be adapted within the school environment, such as seating, position in the classroom, adapted PE lessons, etc.

TRANSITION TO SECONDARY SCHOOL

Transitions can be very hard for autistic children and young people, because uncertainty = anxiety, and all transition involves huge amounts of change. If you think about it, even as an adult, the transition from primary to secondary school (or the equivalent in your location) is probably among the biggest changes you've gone through in your life, and at age 11 for most children it would be their biggest.

I did some research in 2021 on transition to secondary school for autistic pupils,[1] and the overriding finding was that what mattered for a successful transition was the bespoke, individualised plan arranged with the new school. This was the case whether or not the pupil already had an actual diagnosis (of the respondents, 47% said that their child had been refused an autism diagnosis). The more familiar the pupil could become with the school before going was really important, along with having friends to transition with and having a trusted adult or two at the new school who they felt understood them.

Questions on transition experience	Yes	No
Diagnosed before the age of 11?	47%	53%
Received an EHCP in primary school?	12%	88%
Was the child more anxious than peers?	100%	0%
Was a different transition offered?	35%	65%
Did the transition make it easier?	44%	56%
Were secondary school aware of transition difficulties the child experienced during the first half term at secondary school?	92%	8%
Were concerns taken seriously?	59%	41%
Received an EHCP at secondary?	24%	76%
Were parents asked to do a parenting course?	47%	53%
Was it implied that parenting was to blame?	35%	65%
Were parents/child told they 'need to be more resilient'?	47%	53%

Reasons given for non-referral for autism assessment included:

- attachment to parent
- makes eye contact
- sensitive child
- mother is over-protective
- my child was said to be the bully

- you need to be referred by your GP
- could hold a conversation.

We asked, 'What could have been done differently?'; common themes were:

- Listening to parents and understanding that parental concerns are about seeking support rather than making criticisms.
- Training and education for school pastoral care and local authorities on how to recognise autism.
- Better communication.
- Provision of additional support for pupils.

Tips to make a successful transition more likely:

- Transition is a process that needs to start well in advance of September, and continue throughout Year 7 (age 11–12).
- Transition support plans should be needs-based and individualised.
- The autistic pupil needs to become as familiar as possible with their new school and teachers.
- Moving up to school with friends can provide insulation and a better experience.
- Having teachers that seem to (even if they actually don't!) understand the way you experience the world is very helpful and soothing.
- Being listened to and involved in the transition planning is important.
- A low sensory arousal environment is needed for autistic pupils.
- Schools need to be ready to make reasonable adjustments as soon as they become aware of a pupil's needs – on a case-by-case basis.
- Given that Year 7 is often the school year where autistic

masking breaks down and pupils go into crisis, teachers need to be aware of signs to recognise autism and what crisis may look like.

Examples of possible elements in a transition plan:

- A colour-coded map of the school, a timetable, and pictures or videos of processes such as getting lunch can all help.
- Summer school or activity clubs at the school before starting.
- A buddy system involving older pupils – well supervised to make sure there is no bullying.
- Help in the first few weeks with finding the way to lessons and navigating the school.
- Send a scrapbook of photos.
- A keyworker for extra school visits.
- A visit to the dining hall to eat lunch with a support group prior to starting.
- A support group.
- Meeting the SENCO in advance and learning about chill out spaces.
- Breaktime support.
- Whole school awareness to facilitate peer support.
- Interest clubs to facilitate social mixing.

There will be many more elements school could add which would benefit individual pupils.

TRANSITION TO COLLEGE AND UNIVERSITY

All of the same principles will apply when transitioning to higher or further education. A lengthy planned transition process is essential to familiarise the young person with what's going to be happening in the new placement. For college, it should be possible to have multiple visits before starting, and to meet with mentors or inclusion staff who will be supporting your young person. They should also be happy to show you around the college as much as necessary. We will cover university in a later chapter, but again it's best to find out as much in advance as possible. Often there are Facebook groups set up for those going into specific university accommodation, so you can communicate with others who are going to be living there.

PAPERWORK: EHCPS AND IEPS

Having a support plan in place can be key to getting the correct support for your autistic young person. Some schools will put the right stuff in place without the plan, but there is no legal obligation to do so, and everything can change in an instant with a new headteacher/principal or SENCO.

In the UK, the plan which has legal teeth is called an EHCP – an Education, Health and Care Plan (Wales has an Individual Development Plan which is slightly different and brand new at the time of writing this). It is obtained through a statutory process which should take 20 weeks (but often takes longer), and either school or parents can apply. If applying yourself (and I do suggest you do exactly that, it gives you more control of the process and should you need to appeal the school cannot do that anyway), it's easily done using the wonderful IPSEA charity's template email.[2] They also have lots of information about

---

2   www.ipsea.org.uk/making-a-request-for-an-ehc-needs-assessment

the whole process on their website.[3] An EHCP is divided into sections, and the three most important identify the young person's needs, the support needed to reach agreed outcomes, and the school placement. The plan (theoretically) lasts up to the age of 25, though few plans actually stay in place that long because education doesn't generally stay in place that long. It's worth knowing though that EHCPs are useful for college (though not university as they are not valid for higher education) and also for supported internships. If what's in the plan is not happening, you can either appeal or go to judicial review, depending on timing. EHCPs are needs-based, not diagnosis-based, BUT you will need professional evidence of those needs which can sometimes be difficult without a diagnosis. Most children with EHCPs are in mainstream school, but usually to be able to get a place at a special or specialist school the young person will need an EHCP. It is the legal obligation of the local authority to make sure the support detailed in the plan is being carried out, and to review plans annually, and they fund the requirements of the plan after the school has covered an initial fixed amount.

In the US, the plan with legal teeth is an IEP, an Individualised Education Program (or some say Plan). Like an EHCP, an IEP is a legal document, but is also a plan of educational support needed by the pupil to thrive in school. IEPs are for students aged over three at public school, including charter schools. Eligible students have one of the 13 conditions covered by the Individuals with Disabilities Education Act (IDEA), which include autism, ADHD, and dyslexia, as well as physical disabilities and mental health conditions. IEPs don't cover college. Most students with IEPs are taught together with students who don't have one in mainstream schools. IEP plans must be reviewed annually and re-evaluated every three years, and states are given additional funding for students with IEPs.

A 504 plan is fairly similar to an IEP but broader in its definition of disability and without such legal teeth. It also doesn't come attached

---

3   www.ipsea.org.uk/ehc-needs-assessments

with funding, although states do have obligations to meet their legal duties with regards to disabled students.

Without such a support plan, you are reliant on schools to 'do the right thing' for your child, which some will do but others won't. So how can you help schools to 'do the right thing'? Read on.

EQUALITY LAW

In Great Britain, the Equalities Act 2010 replaced multiple pieces of disability law with a single Act of Parliament which protects people from discrimination and harassment both in the workplace and in society as a whole. There are nine protected characteristics under the Act:

- age
- disability
- gender reassignment
- marriage and civil partnership
- pregnancy and maternity
- race
- religion and belief
- sex
- sexual orientation.

With autism, the protected characteristic would be disability (though whether an autistic person considers themselves to be disabled or not is a different and very personal issue). Under the act, people in Great Britain are protected in the following places:

- in the workplace
- in places of public service, for example schools or hospitals
- in places of business, for example restaurants, shops
- on public transport
- in clubs and associations, for example a sports club

- when in contact with public bodies, for example local councils.

For schools, the Equality Act 2010 covers every aspect of school life, from teaching to clubs to school trips. A child with any kind of disability must have full access to all facilities and services at school, and must not be disadvantaged in comparison to their peers. Schools must make 'reasonable adjustments' to accommodate the child's needs.

In the US, there are three Federal laws which protect disabled people from discrimination: IDEA (Individuals with Disabilities Education Act), Section 504, and ADA (Americans with Disabilities Act).

IDEA: relates to special educational needs and asserts that schools have a responsibility to recognise special needs and assess them. It covers children and young people who both have a disability and a need for support in school. IDEA is the legal process which must be followed to put in that support, from birth until 21 or until high school graduation. IDEA tries to encourage inclusion with the requirement that disabled children learn alongside their peers in the 'least restrictive environment'. When a child has been found to have disabilities, they must be provided with appropriate support and therapy through an IEP. Parents must be involved in this process and give consent to any therapy.

Section 504 of the Rehabilitation Act applies to K-12 (Kindergarten – 12th Grade) students, so roughly from age 5 to 18, their whole school career. Eligible K-12 students will receive a 504 plan which notarises their needs and the accommodations they should receive.

ADA is a Federal civil rights law which declares it to be illegal to discriminate against disabled people. It applies almost everywhere in the US, from schools to shops to workplaces. It includes people with any kind of 'a physical or mental impairment which substantially limits one or more life activities'. An autistic (or otherwise neurodivergent) child or young person would be protected from discrimination at school by ADA regardless of whether or not they were working at expected levels with their peers. Unlike Section 504 and IDEA, ADA isn't responsible for ensuring free appropriate public education, but all three laws may overlap and you are covered by whichever protects you most. ADA says that schools and businesses must make 'reasonable accommodations', but it is broader than IDEA and just because your child or young person is covered against discrimination by ADA, it doesn't follow that they automatically qualify for educational needs support under IDEA.

REASONABLE ADJUSTMENTS

So what exactly is a reasonable adjustment or accommodation (I'm just going to call them adjustments from now on), and what is classed as 'reasonable' in the law?

An adjustment here means any change that is made via tool, service, or rules to ensure that your child or young person is treated with equity (rather than equality) and not disadvantaged.

Equity vs Equality

Equality would mean everyone being given the same amount of support or resources.

Equity would mean everyone sharing the support or resources based on need so that the end result would mean everyone being level. However, the law (in either the US or UK) has no precise definition of what is 'reasonable'. Nevertheless, reasonable adjustments are made every day according to a person's individual needs, and examples of them at school might be the following.

Learning:

- Break down into smaller tasks.
- Give multiple forms of instructions (e.g. visual and written).
- Give sample work to model best practice.
- Consult child on seating in class.
- Provide scribe, laptop, reader, or reader pen.
- Allow extra time in exams.
- Allow extra time to process instructions.
- Provide a quiet space for exams.

- Use of headphones to prevent distraction.
- Use of special interests to help encourage learning.
- Provide notes of what's covered in class.

Sensory:

- Provide a quiet space to recover from overwhelm.
- Allow use of fidget items.
- Provide seating or accessories to aid focus, e.g. wobble cushion.
- Allow weighted blanket or lap cushion.
- Allow safe foods.
- Allow uniform rule relaxation.
- Change lighting/electrical appliance which flickers or buzzes.
- Allow child to leave class or school earlier to avoid crowds.
- Stop using the school bell.
- Allow child to eat lunch somewhere other than in the dining hall.

Communication:

- Don't enforce eye contact.
- Allow fidgeting/stimming while listening.
- Check understanding of instructions.
- Teach about non-verbal cues in a neurodivergent-friendly way.
- Provide a visual timetable.
- Provide visual instructions and/or checklists.

These are only examples and there are many more possibilities which can be adapted to the individual.

STUDENT PASSPORT

A student passport is a document that is co-produced with the child or young person and their parents (depending on age), and the school. It is something that is kept centrally so that it can be available to all teachers and support staff, even if they are temporary supply staff or visiting therapists. It's really important that it reflects the young person's strengths and ambitions as well as their needs, worries, and difficulties, and gets their input into what they would like teachers to know in order to help.

There is a free student passport template on the Autistic Girls Network website.[4]

If you'd like to read more about student passports, take a look at this article by Gareth Morewood here (included with his permission): https://blog.optimus-education.com/how-develop-student-passports-%E2%80%93-movie

CHECKLIST OF SUPPORT WHICH MIGHT BE NEEDED IN SCHOOL

It can feel to parents as if they are constantly needing to fight to get their child support which they are clearly entitled to under SEN law and regulations. Schools are meant to anticipate needs rather than react to behaviours coming out of those needs, but lack of workforce training on neurodivergence, government insistence on all the specifics of OFSTED paperwork, and time and budget constraints all mean that this doesn't always happen.

Other than reasonable adjustments, what support might be needed in a school to support an autistic pupil and put them on a truly level playing field with their peers?

- Whole school awareness and understanding of autism and autistic communication.

---

4   www.autisticgirlsnetwork.org/Student_Passport_Template.pdf

- Whole teacher awareness and understanding of autistic masking.
- Use of language that can't be misinterpreted (bearing in mind that many autistic people interpret things literally).
- Support with organisation and executive function.
- Mentoring and peer support group with other autistic pupils.
- A calm space which is not used as a punishment.
- Work on emotional regulation and literacy in a neurodivergent-friendly way.
- A buddy system (monitored to prevent bullying) at least for major transitions.
- Careful and timely preparation for change, and a recognition of how many things bring change.
- Support to understand and develop their autistic identity.
- Special interest clubs which are different to the norm (not just sports or chess).
- A sensory audit to discover how to improve the school environment.

FIDGETING

All school staff working with neurodivergent children and young people (and that's all school staff, with 72% of autistic children in mainstream school,[5] and 15% of the population at least neurodivergent[6]) need to be aware that being still may not be the best learning environment for autistic and neurodivergent young people. For example, there have been studies which show that pupils with ADHD perform better when they move.[7] For autistic pupils the repetition of using a fidget toy can bring the regulation needed to concentrate. In both cases, the movement is the opposite of a distraction, it's vital if the child is going to be able to focus on the teacher. Forcing a young child to be still in Circle Time, for example, just ensures that being still is all they can concentrate on.

MASKING AT SCHOOL

We've talked about masking (or camouflaging or adaptive morphing – whatever you'd prefer to call it) already, and it has probably become clear that a) autistic masking happens a lot at school, and b) we really need to be able to spot autistic masking in order to recognise autism earlier.

If, as a parent, a member of school staff has ever said to you that your child is 'fine in school', but they have come out of school and immediately gone into meltdown or shutdown, then I can categorically tell you that they are NOT 'fine in school'. In fact, they are masking their autistic traits in school in order to fit in with their peers, to avoid the stigma they have figured out comes from being obviously autistic. Of course, people's ideas of what is obviously or classically autistic

5   UK Gov (2018) *Special Educational Needs in England: January 2018.* Accessed on 2 May 2022 at www.gov.uk/government/statistics/special-educational-needs-in-england-january-2018

6   Acas (n.d.) *Neurodiversity in the Workplace.* Accessed on 2 May 2022 at https://webarchive.nationalarchives.gov.uk/ukgwa/20210104113255/https://archive.acas.org.uk/index.aspx?articleid=6676

7   University of California - Davis Health System (2015) 'Movement in ADHD may help children think, perform better in school'. *ScienceDaily,* 11 June. Accessed on 2 May 2022 at www.sciencedaily.com/releases/2015/06/150611082116.htm

are hopelessly out of date, and those stereotypes don't help anyone. I know autistic adults in professional positions who are told that they can't possibly be autistic so the stereotypes still very much abound.

So How Can We Identify Autistic Masking?

It's difficult, as that person has adapted (often unconsciously) specifically so that you don't spot it. But it's not impossible, once you know what to look for. Internalised presentations of autism (those most likely to be masking) may look like the following (and as always remember that there is no single presentation of autism and people may do none or all of these).

When speaking to your child's class teacher, you might want to ask if they have noticed any of the following:

- Rarely put up their hand or speak out.
- Blurt out whatever they are thinking (these pupils may also have ADHD).
- Have situational mutism.
- Have a strong sense of social justice.
- Have a love of animals.
- Have poor organisational skills.
- Dislike PE.
- Copy social behaviour.
- Have intense interests in subjects that aren't unusual topics for their peers.
- Find it difficult to join in if friends don't want to play their game.
- Are vulnerable to bullying and manipulation.
- React anxiously to changes in routine.
- Avoid or seek strong sensations with smell, etc.
- Have limited food choices.
- Are a perfectionist.
- Either have a single friend or are on the edge of a group of friends.

Something else to remember is that many autistic pupils will also have ADHD, and this can make their presentation a little different. Here are things to look out for:

Austistic Masking at School

What you see
- Hard worker
- Gifted
- Eager to please
- Well behaved
- Compliant

What you don't see
- Anxiety
- Exhaustion
- Social confusion
- Excessive worrying
- Panic attacks
- A need for perfection
- Stomach aches

autistic
girls network

SPEAKING CLEARLY AND LITERAL THINKING

It's really important that teachers and support staff understand autistic thought processes and consider what they say – and it's only fair since autistic people are second-guessing what they say and do most of the time! Autistic pupils need adults to speak clearly and literally, and for instructions to make sense. This means make sense both grammatically and logically. Instructions also need to ask for something to be done – saying 'You didn't tidy the pens away', is a statement not an instruction, and it's not asking the child to tidy up the pens. The child should therefore not be in trouble for not inferring that meaning from the sentence. Likewise, asking 'Would you like to tidy the pens away?' is also not a request to complete the task, so don't be surprised if the child simply says 'No'. School days are filled with such phrasing, and it's a constant puzzle.

TRANSITIONS

We've talked about the big transition from primary to secondary school, and there will be other big transitions at different stages, but the school day, particularly at secondary school, is filled with a succession of little transitions.

> All transition = change.
> Change = uncertainty.
> Uncertainty = anxiety.
> Therefore all transition = anxiety.

What are those mini transitions in a school day and how can they be made more manageable for an autistic young person?

Mini transitions:

- From sleeping to waking.
- From undressed to dressed.
- From home to school gate.
- From school gate to homeroom.
- From homeroom to assembly.
- From class to class (via school corridors of hell).
- From class to breaktime.
- From seated class to dynamic one (PE, food tech, etc.).
- From class to lunchtime.
- From lunchtime back to class.
- From class to circle time or homeroom time.
- From class to school gate.
- From school to home possibly via public transport or school bus.
- From regular class to unscheduled change.
- From school to school trip.

How can they be made more manageable?

- Prepare for any unscheduled change in advance.

- Allow child to arrive at and leave school at a different time or through a different door to avoid crowds.
- Allow child to leave a lesson early to avoid crowded corridors.
- Designate a calm room or a space the child can spend breaktime if needed.
- Remember the child may need extra processing time for all these changes.

LOW-AROUSAL SETTINGS

When we talk about a low-arousal sensory environment, what we mean is a space without sensory clutter. Somewhere that can be a calming space, without sensory triggers or input like loud noises or bright lights. Low-arousal areas are for teaching, and are not to be confused with chill out rooms or sensory rooms or other spaces where a child can go to escape sensory overload. A low-arousal environment or provision acknowledges that the child or young person who goes there needs this sensory calming environment all the time.

I would say it's impossible for a mainstream secondary school to be a low-arousal provision (though I would love to be proved wrong). Just the number of pupils alone will bring huge sensory input, unless they are going to walk around in their own little soundproofed bubbles all day. So any such provision is going to be either separate entirely or separate from the main building. It has become more common to attach autism 'hubs' to mainstream schools, but even if they have a separate entrance, this does not make them automatically a low-arousal provision, and if the young person needs to keep going into the main building during their school day, they are not in a low-arousal environment. They simply have a low-arousal area available to them.[8]

---

8 Autistic Girls Network ran a webinar with Professor Andy McDonnell from Studio 3 on low arousal and eliminating restraint and seclusion in schools which is available on YouTube here: www.youtube.com/watch?v=JfmmHuDosLk

How Is a Low-Arousal Environment Designed?

- Low-arousal paint colours are muted, with a balance of colour and grey.
- Studies have shown a preference for blue/green colours but individuals will have different preferences of course.
- Single-colour walls with no patterned wallpaper are preferred, and a minimum of pattern in flooring and soft furnishings also offers the least sensory input.
- Attention should be paid to where sunlight comes into the room, both in avoiding direct sunlight and avoiding shadow.
- In terms of smell, use low odour paint and avoid situating the area anywhere there are strong smells around, e.g. near the kitchen or dining room.
- Create a balance between a cramped space and one that will create echoes of sound.
- If different spaces in the area are used for different things, you may want to use different tones of colour.
- Avoid all flickering and fluorescent light, and any buzzing lights or switches (ask autistic people if they buzz rather than relying on your own judgement if you are not autistic).
- Indirect and hidden lighting is generally preferred.
- Avoid very busy wall and ceiling displays (this doesn't necessarily mean bare walls though).
- Avoid a school bell.
- Low-arousal behaviour from school staff – calm, quiet voices should be modelled.

RULES

This is a strangely tricky section to write. The idea prevails that autistic people like rules and always follow them, but this is not always true. Autistic people like rules to MAKE SENSE, and while your autistic person may still follow a rule which makes no sense to them, it's probably only because they are worried what will happen if they break the rule. There are lots of rules which are blindly followed which make no sense or which only made sense in another era. For example, the rule about children being seen and not heard has been largely discredited now, but we still cling to the idea that adults have automatic authority over children just because they are adults. In fact, there are plenty of adults who probably shouldn't have authority even over other adults, let alone children.

Then there are all kinds of rules which fall under the banner of 'manners' and which actually make no sense. Who decided that you shouldn't put your elbows on the table? Why? What harm does it do? Why should you eat with your fork in your left hand? Think about all the assumptions you have about accepted polite behaviour and see if it actually makes sense to be that way. If it doesn't, abandon it. The world will make more sense.

This doesn't mean that your autistic young person doesn't need to follow any rules. Of course they do, and some are more important than others and treated as such by figures of authority. But there will be much less conflict if rules are explained – for example, no running in the corridors because it could cause a painful accident if two people collide. Not just rules for rules' sake. This is particularly pertinent when talking about detentions. If your autistic young person is given detention, it needs to make sense and feel justified. If it doesn't expect argument and for it to be dwelled upon for quite a while as a topic of injustice. And of course, there ARE many instances of injustice regarding autistic and other neurodivergent pupils in our schools, when reasonable adjustment should have been made and the young person should not be punished for an act which arose directly because of their autism. Sadly, the young person arguing about detention, however eloquently and logically, is just likely to get them in more trouble so you may need to intervene here unless they specifically don't want you to.

TROUBLESHOOTING
Reward Charts and Behaviourism

Some governments have moved increasingly towards behaviourism in recent years. Behaviourism in schools basically means a process where students are constantly being given feedback about what they are doing and if it's right or wrong, good or bad. The obvious problem with that is when there is misunderstanding or subjectivity about what is good and bad. The SLANT strategy is particularly suitable for illustrating this. SLANT stands for:

Sit up straight.
Listen.
Ask and answer questions.
Nod your head.
Track the speaker.

SLANT sets an expectation of the positive behaviour that is expected from the student. You might initially look at that list and think that's just good manners, but look again in terms of SEND. I would argue that not only is it unrealistic and unfair to expect those behaviours from, for example, a pupil with ADHD, but enforcing it may very well breach the Equality Act 2010 in the UK. Let's look more closely.

Sit Up Straight

It may be very uncomfortable for an autistic or dyspraxic pupil to sit up straight on a regular school chair, and impossible for a full hour. This also proves true for sitting still which is similarly impossible for a young person with ADHD who NEEDS to move. Different kinds of chairs or cushions may be much more appropriate but are not really possible in a mainstream setting which involves moving classrooms every hour.

Listen

How do we know somebody is listening? We don't have access to their brain waves! A neurotypical person assumes somebody is listening to them if they are making eye contact, but actually as we have seen, making eye contact can be painful for an autistic person and stop them focusing on what's being said because all their attention has been focused on trying to look someone in the eye.

Ask and Answer Questions

Autistic students tend to be uncomfortable when picked on in class and are unlikely to actively ask questions in a mainstream class unless the topic is one they are very interested in. Some anxious autistic pupils are situationally mute in class.

Nod Your Head

A neurodivergent young person may not feel the need to nod their head – they already know they have listened to the speaker.

Track the Speaker

This is eye contact, and as we have shown, to expect it is ableist.

Doing one of these is hard. Doing all of them is impossible, if you want them to concentrate on what the teacher is demonstrating.

Reward Charts

Using reward charts generally doesn't work well with neurodivergent children (generally, because we're all different). Rewards charts slot firmly into behaviourism, a central tenet of which is that people can be trained to do things, regardless of any personality traits, neurology, or preferences.

Your young person has already been living much of their life being thought of as neurotypical. They have become used to having their sensory experiences invalidated, with people saying 'Oh that can't possibly hurt', or 'But it's not cold', or 'Look me in the eyes when I'm talking to you'. This will have led them to mask, as we've talked about, and very likely to fawn as a trauma response, overriding their own needs in an effort to please and to comply with what is being asked of them. When you understand this, you can see why I consider reward charts in general to be quite poisonous to autistic people. When used by someone who has no idea what's been going on or how your young person experiences the world, they are a form of coercion, of behaviour conditioning. That's not to say that you couldn't co-design, with the input of your young person, a reward chart that was more conducive to neurodivergent brains, but you would still be battling demand avoidance, because a reward chart is a big demand. Better to use alternative ways.

If School Doesn't Accept the Diagnosis

Unfortunately I do see regular examples of schools refusing to accept a pupil's autism diagnosis or declaring that they can't be autistic because they make eye contact, they have friends, they talk too much – take your pick from this range of responses to an Autistic Girls Network survey in 2021.

There is no legal basis for schools to do this. Obviously, it's unlikely any member of school staff would be professionally qualified to diagnose autism, and they should accept any diagnosis which is NICE-compliant (basically, which has used more than one professional to assess, for example a clinical psychologist and a speech and language therapist. Both don't need to be present at the assessment but one would need to review).

Schools' statutory responsibility is to use their 'best endeavours' to support pupils who MAY have additional needs. No diagnosis is actually needed before support is put in place (although in practice, this doesn't happen much). In the UK the SEND Code of Practice says that schools should use 'Assess, Plan, Do, Review' to assess a pupil's special educational needs, plan support for them, put the support into action and review how well the support is working. If a school ignores a medical diagnosis and doesn't identify needs or put support in place, you should firstly use the school complaint process (which will be available on their website). If this doesn't help you can take the matter to the Secretary of State for a determination under Sections 496 and 497 of the Education Act 1996. In the US, the multiple disability laws mean theoretically this shouldn't happen.

Remote Education

The pandemic has meant that we have all become intimately acquainted with remote education, although not under the best circumstances. I bring it up here because for many years families of children with extended absence from school have been asking for remote education to be available for their children, and have been told it was impossible. We now know for certain that's not true.

This is not to say that every autistic child would like or benefit from remote education. Some will find the lack of organisation oversight to be problematic, or the feeling of someone seeming to sit very close to them on a laptop screen to be uncomfortable. But it ought to be available as an option. Even better if it's part of some kind of flex learning system which is very geared towards anxious children and has a personal tutor/buddy/mentor who can visit weekly.

Trauma and Mental Health

Trauma is a subject that is being considered more in education now, and there are professionals who work in a trauma-informed way and lots of training courses helping others to do so. What's not so common is the idea that a relatively 'normal' school life can cause trauma for an autistic young person. But it can. I'm sure I don't need to tell you how by now – sensory stuff, ignorance about executive functioning and processing issues, behaviourist policies and an ignorance about neurodiversity among peers which can lead to bullying. Add to that the guilt and bewilderment and lack of self-worth over knowing that you're different but not knowing why for all those who are not recognised as autistic until they are older, and you can see why school might not be a happy place for all.

'About one in ten children aged between five and sixteen are diagnosed with a [mental health] problem every year and about 75% of mental illnesses are thought to start before the age of 25.'[9] Makes you think, doesn't it?

---

9   Nip in the Bud (2021) *Child Mental Health Conditions*. Accessed on 30 May 2022 at https://nipinthebud.org/child-mental-health-conditions

Mental health issues in our young people have become much more visible in the media recently, and schools have rightly been identified as the front line of mental health issues in young people. I'm not sure how realistic it is to expect schools to provide much in the way of anything but very surface-level mental health support, however, and I know that many senior leadership and pastoral teams are tearing their hair out at the difficulty of getting state mental health support for their most critically affected young people. At the moment we have a sticking plaster on a gaping wound, and it's not making a difference. What would help is a change in attitude and systems, so that a) mental health is given, as it should be, the same importance as physical health, and b) we remove the focus on attendance and exam results which drives the school system (at least in the UK and US) and concentrate on overall wellbeing and a truly rounded education which includes preparing for adulthood. School should not be a conveyer belt leading to a job and/or university. It shouldn't be about turning out productive individuals but about turning out happy, confident individuals, no matter their neurotype.

Until that can happen, families are often left coping with mental health crises on their own, and that can be a very lonely and distressing time. In the short term, having adults that will really listen, both at home and at school and in other services they may be referred to, will be a big help to young people. Too often, young people have tried to articulate that something is wrong and have not been listened to. If things escalate to crisis quickly, there are charities that can help as a stopgap to getting local help, and these are listed on the AGN website.[10]

CASE STUDY
Owen, age 18 in the UK
As an autistic person, my experience of CAMHS was not a positive one. I began attending CAMHS at the age of 12 and have recently turned 18, so I am a veteran of the system. When I was diagnosed

10 www.autisticgirlsnetwork.org

with ASD (by CAMHS) I didn't receive any support about what they meant, how to move forwards, and what support was available. As a young teen, who knew nothing about autism other than the non-verbal boys playing with trains that's portrayed in the media, receiving this diagnosis was confusing and scary. It didn't make sense. I could talk, I could do the work at school, I didn't like trains. Would I get worse? Would I ever be 'normal'? CAMHS provided no help in answering any of these questions.

In fact they provided almost no help at all, other than prescribing me anti-anxieties and anti-depressants. Once I received my autism diagnosis, they basically dismissed my mental health issues.

'Autistic people have anxiety', 'Autistic people have OCD', 'There's nothing we can do.'

This was what I heard. My OCD and anxiety were debilitating. I had PTSD and depression. I was struggling to eat and rarely left the house. As you can imagine, this didn't help my view of being autistic. From what CAMHS were saying, I would always be this way. For a 13-year-old boy that was terrifying.

As everyone knows, the education system in this country is not built for autistic people, and unfortunately neither is CAMHS. I was eventually given CBT, DBT (dialectical behaviour therapy), and attended group sessions. None of this was in any way modified for autistic people, despite the claims that it was. The DBT mentioned the importance of eye contact and that it's vital for connection. How 'meltdowns' shouldn't be rewarded by parents/carers because us young people are trying to manipulate you.

CAMHS has not helped me. Something I realised as I've gotten older is that you cannot place the responsibility of your mental health on anyone else. You cannot expect your mental health to improve if you don't put in the work and if you don't want to change. You yourself have to make a conscious effort to engage and make changes. Of course, support is vital, but you cannot expect a therapist or councillor to 'make you better'; you have to do that yourself, with their help.

When it comes to autism, I wish there was a service that provided support for neurodivergent people. Specialised therapy, support groups/social groups and co-morbidity assessments. This service does not exist. We get passed around the system. CAMHS say our mental illness is autism's fault, OTs say our sensory needs are mental illness, the GP says our sleep issues are a mental health need, the doctors say our pain is sensory. No one seems to listen. While there isn't any support readily available on the NHS, it can be found. There are some great YouTubers who talk about being autistic, support groups online, and books. The help can be found, it's just not necessarily easy to find.

I'm still trying to make my peace with the idea that I'll always be autistic. I still find it hard that I'll never be 'normal', but I'm starting to see the positives too, the skills I have because of my autism and the knowledge I have because of my experiences.

School Refusal

This section is called School Refusal so that you know what I'm talking about, but actually I HATE the term school refusal, which implies that it's the young person's choice not to go to school. In fact, the young person is too anxious to go to school. It's not a choice.

As a family, we have our own experience with what some call anxiety-based school avoidance (ABSA) and I call 'extended absence from school', and I know that many of the families within the Autistic Girls Network group share our experience. There are some really heartbreaking stories in fact, where schools ask parents to drag their children into school quite literally kicking and screaming, and in some cases to hand over their screaming, crying child to a member of staff to take away. I'd like to be totally clear here. PLEASE do not do this. Please do not ask a parent to do this. If your school asks you to do this, you can say that for the mental health of your child you refuse to entertain such a scenario. I know the school are going to say that your child is 'fine in school' once you are gone, but they just can't know that with an autistic child or young person. It's more likely that they are masking because school doesn't feel safe for them, and they won't release that trauma until they get home.

But for many, it won't be quite that dramatic. There may be numerous tummy aches. They may feel sick. They may promise to go in tomorrow if you let them stay home today. But a school-avoidant young person is not 'playing' you. School genuinely makes them highly anxious and traumatised, in fact it makes them ill. Mental health is just as important as physical health for all of us, including schools. What's important is to find out – if possible – the reasons why school has become something which causes such huge anxiety. Research seems to show that there is a pattern of ABSA around transition, especially transition to secondary school, and that would fit with the pattern within Autistic Girls Network of the spring term of Year 7 (the first year of secondary school) being very difficult.

If this has been caught quite early, then reasonable adjustments made by school may be enough to make school a safer place for your young person. But it's really important that any promises made are kept. And it's important too that school doesn't try to take it too fast. We hear lots in AGN about promises being broken, and young people being told they need to come in full time because they've managed a couple of weeks part time – that's very unlikely to work, and all that's happening is a reinforcement of the idea that school is not safe.

CASE STUDY
Greg, age 13 in the UK (by mum Kathryn)

Greg was diagnosed when he was ten and it was very difficult and only happened after multiple A&E visits for suicidal ideation. When we moved areas and therefore started afresh (with much greater knowledge on our part) it became easier. Primary school was awful, didn't see the problems, and didn't put anything in place to help even after diagnosis. Secondary have been great – he has a 1:1 and fantastic understanding of his anxiety. But it's still very difficult and he's not able to go to school at the moment, despite wanting to.

When my son was seven his great grandmother died. This affected him greatly and he started talking about wanting to die. This was the first time we were seen by CAMHS, but were dismissed after one meeting with no help, being told 'Children this age don't commit suicide'. There were no concerns from school as he was always perfectly behaved, with good eye contact and good grades, so autism wasn't considered. He saw the school therapist (awful) and a bereavement therapist from a charity (better) but it didn't really help. He had friends at school but was always a little different in his interests and wasn't challenged much by the school work which he found frustrating. We needed to move house and areas when he was in Year 5. He started to have big mental health problems again after we visited possible new schools and we ended up at A&E a couple of times due to suicidal ideation. So back with CAMHS, under the crisis team, with regular meetings where we had to discuss feelings (which he found very painful). I brought up autism with the therapist but he wasn't even considering it (despite the fact that his younger brother was already diagnosed). When we moved we managed to transfer to CAMHS in the new area. One conversation with them put us on the waiting list for an assessment (I think having not met him actually helped here). However, we did end up at A&E again which eventually triggered psychiatric (and medical) support.

The autism assessment was surprisingly easy, as the person doing the assessment seemed to know on instinct. She said her partner was autistic so she didn't get held up on details like eye contact. We had pages of notes to give her and stories to tell, and we got the diagnosis that day. However, due to him performing so well at school, his diagnosis didn't trigger any support at all. We knew he was unhappy and had a meeting with the teacher and SENCO, but nothing was put in place and no warning was given that his teacher was leaving mid-year. He couldn't cope with this, it was the final straw after so many big changes. His anxiety peaked and he was unable to go to school.

We had an awful year trying to get support for him while battling against judgement about our parenting (which must always be to blame, right?). I had started educating myself thanks to the many wonderful social media groups I belong to. I applied for an EHCP and got 32.5 hours support (despite being told a number of times that I wouldn't get one because he was achieving academically). I got home tutors put in place (again because of my own extensive research as the school seemed unaware of their legal duties). I battled the attendance officer who was either ignorant of the law or chose to ignore it. Meanwhile I also did all this for my other son.

Then 2020 struck and we went into lockdown. It actually helped him because everyone else was off school too. The (internal) pressure lifted and with an awful lot of support he managed to go back to school after a whole year off to do the final weeks of Year 6. All because he desperately wanted to go to his new school, a grammar school, with subjects he was desperate to learn and a quite traditional structure that he liked. The only school he ever considered.

Luckily it has a great SEN department and he had a full-time 1:1 due to the EHCP. But it's been a bumpy ride. He hasn't fully unmasked, we're still learning how being autistic affects him personally. His hyper-empathy means that if anyone in the class is told off he feels it personally and painfully. His social anxiety has made it impossible to make friends. He has only just discovered that it's more difficult for him to read people and this combined with the unwritten rules all teachers have is making his life extremely difficult. He loves many aspects of being autistic and thinks it would be very dull not to have intense interests to 'geek out' over. But I wish the people supporting him understood anxiety from an autistic perspective as they've done a lot of damage.

Social Skills

At Autistic Girls Network we're not massive fans of regular 'social skills' training, because it tends to be training young people to behave like a neurotypical person, i.e. masking. As you'll understand by now, that's not a good thing.

Instead, we'd like professionals to come to the situation with the acknowledgement that there are multiple ways to have a conversation, and no way is the 'right way'. That social skills don't involve being forced to look people in the eye, and that neurotypical people should be educated that some people don't look others in the eye much and it's not being rude, as well as autistic people being told that people may expect eye contact. It's always a two-way street. Often autistic young people can be socially isolated because they seem a little bit different, but if their peers had an understanding of autism they would be likely to be a lot more accommodating and there would be less miscommunication. It's not only autistic people who lack social skills!

In school, staff should be sensitive to when a young person wants to be on their own – it doesn't necessarily mean that they're miserable or have no friends, it can just mean that they'd prefer their own company for a while and have had enough 'peopling'. Likewise working in groups can be exhausting. Recognise that neurodivergent pupils will be tired out from socialising, and just treat that as a fact of life.

Sensible scheduling of breaks and not pursuing the idea that more socialising in breaktime is necessary will help. Not everyone wants to socialise in the same way – we are all different. Autistic people make fantastic friends though in general – loyal and with a strong sense of social justice. Supporting with friendships should include the whole class not just autistic pupils – teach where misunderstandings arise so that they can be understood and overcome, and teach to accept difference as part of being human. Get rid of 'unspoken' social rules too. These are alienating for an autistic young person who is expected to know what they are but won't have picked them up automatically.

Autistic young people brought up as girls tend to get diagnosed later than male peers, and this can be partly attributed to social skills they have learnt growing up. As a society, we tend to steer girls towards being 'likeable', and discourage girls from being too assertive or from questioning authority. There's a huge need, particularly in tweens and teens, to 'fit in'. But we can't expect autistic girls to advocate for themselves if they are also being told to be compliant and fit in. Nor does it help when non-conformity is labelled as dramatic or bossy – instead, flip the narrative and see the strengths being displayed. Give them the support to understand social situations better and develop those leadership skills.

When looking at 'friendship' patterns of teens and tweens, particularly girls, ask yourself which neurotype is actually lacking in social skills. The one which speaks the truth? Or the one which bitches behind someone's back? Both of those ideas are generalisations of course, but we need to see that stereotypical social groups in schools can be rather toxic. How can we help steer them to a better way? I suspect teachers will be able to answer that a lot better than me, but educating about difference and bringing children up to accept it would certainly help.

One of the best ways schools can 'encourage' pupils to find friends is through clubs and societies – and I don't mean endless sports clubs. Things like board games, computing or coding, literature, feminism, Pokémon, anime. It's much easier for neurodivergent pupils to form a relationship while doing something they love, not just 'socialising'.

Drama groups – if led in a neurodivergent-friendly way – can also be very good to help young people make friends and socialise in a non-pressured environment. An organisation which does this very well is Act for Autism, based in the Midlands, UK.

Working with young people in our drama group we noticed that through being together in a safe environment and 'playing' together with laughter and support, social awareness and confidence grows.

Once the group feels safe talking about who they are and how they feel, learning from each other and sharing experiences comes naturally. This a great environment to explore who you are in relations to others with no judgement. The group help each other build a greater understanding of self and others and also share outside of the group via films and social media, helping other autistic individuals and parents feel connected and understood.

Never underestimate the need and the value of connection with self and others but also recognise how challenging this can be if autism is not understood. (Tessa Morton, Act for Autism)

Act for Autism have a book which helps you follow the system they use: *Connecting and Communicating with Your Autistic Child: A Toolkit of Activities to Encourage Emotional Regulation and Social Development*.

Tricky Lessons

Some lessons are going to be more challenging for some neurodivergent pupils, either because of sensory issues or unpredictability. Lessons like PE often cause a challenge for a variety of reasons. First, it involves a speedy change of clothes, which both involves sudden change and a big demand, and also means you are vulnerable in front of your peers (when changing). Second, what happens in the lesson changes from week to week, not only which activity but within the activity. Third, autistic pupils can often be dyspraxic and therefore not enthusiastic to be involved in team sports. Having a ball thrown at your body when you're possibly not likely to be able to catch it is not fun. Nor is always being chosen last for a team. Not doing PE is a reasonable adjustment for pupils who become very anxious about it.

Other lessons may be a challenge depending on individual needs. Subjects like design and technology can involve a high degree of fine motor skills, strange smells, and pupils walking randomly around the classroom. Food tech has the same issue with smell and unpredictability. Pupils should be listened to if they express worries about lessons like this.

Homework

If your young person has only just been diagnosed this might be the first time you realise that many neurodivergent young people have a problem with homework. The main problem is that it shouldn't exist. School work is for school. Home is a safe place for being yourself, and it shouldn't be corrupted by school. This can be difficult to reconcile with heavy exam years I know, but better to know what you're dealing with!

Homework relies on executive function processes – recording it while listening to the teacher, knowing how it fits in with what has been learnt, recording when it needs to be done by, planning it, and completing it along with your usual schedule. Any of those may be a challenge. During the week, your young person is likely to be exhausted from a day's peopling and learning at school. Planning and executing homework too is a tall order. It's also a further demand.

Your young person may also be a perfectionist, so anything less than perfect is less than acceptable to them. Creating a perfect piece of homework is another huge demand. Not receiving homework is another reasonable adjustment it's possible for school to make.

Home Education

While I don't and will never agree with anyone being effectively forced out of the education system, many families do decide that their child or young person will be happier in a home educated environment. The home ed community is full of neurodivergent families, and particularly children and young people who are recognised (or not!) as PDA or extremely demand-avoidant. This makes sense when you consider that being in school is a non-stop demand, and it would take a very different kind of school (so different that it would be classed as alternative provision) to be able to step outside of the education system enough to remove those demands.

So if you've decided that your child or young person will be happier being home educated, in whatever form that takes, that's great. If you feel you are being forced out of school then it's possible for you to stand and fight for your child's right to education, and you need to read the EHCP/IEP section and possibly delve into EOTAS which is 'education other than at school'. There are some great Facebook groups around and if you decide to home educate I strongly advise you to join the various Home Ed Facebook groups, both national and local. Local ones can be particularly useful for meet-ups and organising home ed visits and trips. Remember that home education doesn't have to follow a curriculum, but that if your young person wants to take the traditional route of GCSEs and A levels in the UK, you will need to enter them for the exam privately at an exam centre and pay for it yourself (this can get very expensive for a clutch of GCSEs so do research this so that it doesn't come as a nasty last-minute surprise!). Otherwise, you can spend as much or as little on home education as you like. There are many resources available online and a history lesson can be a visit to a free museum, for example.

There are many different ways to home educate. Some will arrange it by the 'school at home' method, teaching themselves or increasingly as their child gets older using a tutor or online school – because how many of us can teach maths A level after all? Other people are entirely child-led, with activities revolving around the child's interests and no set times or days of the week for education. Then there are many more who do a variation of both. There's no right or wrong, only the best way which brings the best outcomes for your child (and those outcomes may not be related to qualifications).

Recommended home education resources for the UK:

- HE-UK – www.home-education.org.uk

- Education Otherwise – www.education-otherwise.net
- Ed Yourself – http://edyourself.org
- Home Ed in the UK – http://home-ed.info
- https://he-exams.fandom.com/wiki/
  Finding_an_exam_centre
- https://he-exams.fandom.com/wiki/Exam_Boards

CASE STUDY

Millie, age ten in the UK (and her mum Ellie)

This year (aged nine) Millie received her diagnosis, although I have been asking since she was around five and suspected since she was three. We had to go down the private route after CAMHS rejected her application for support following the school report (which schools need to write to contribute to an autism assessment).

Millie had a tricky start to school, she was one of the oldest in her year and academically able but was often fighting with the other children and seriously injured other children more than once. As she got older, our parents' evenings consisted of being told that she was an overly chatty perfectionist who never completed work. She told stories of wandering around the playground at breaktime struggling to find other children to play with, or hiding in lunchtime clubs with older children so that she would have some company. When she came home from school she would lose all control, often injuring herself or us. We raised autism several times with the school but they said they didn't have any concerns. When the country went into lockdown, we tried a few of the tasks sent by her teachers but it was clear that the anxiety around them was too high for her to complete anything. Instead we did a lot of topic-based learning, exploring the world through books and online tours, cooking meals from different countries, and learning new languages.

During this time her love of learning shone through and she became a happier, calmer child. There was no more self-harm and the family home was a much more comfortable place for everyone. She never returned to school, it was a difficult decision in lots of ways, and one we had to make for her guided by her behaviour. We now home educate both her and her younger brother (also autistic), it's not always the easiest balancing act but I knew that the path we were on was only going to lead to something destructive. Millie continues to lead most of her learning and has recently received her autism diagnosis. She recognises the strengths that being autistic gives her and we use those to facilitate her education. I won't say it is always easy, but I feel like we are laying the groundwork for her to live a happy life, in whatever form that might take.

Chapter 11

Autism in Society

FINDING YOUR TRIBE

Whether officially or self-diagnosed, your identity as an autistic person is important. We all need to identify as something, and feel as if we belong with a group of people. It might be being female, being Black or Brown, being a feminist, loving Pokémon, enjoying cosplay, being a fanatical Man United or Liverpool or New York Giants fan – whatever it is, it's important to you.

If your child has been diagnosed late (whether that's in secondary school or even later), they'll already have known that they felt different to their peers. An outsider. They might be regarded as weird. They might feel weird. So it's going to be a comfort to know that there are OTHER PEOPLE who experience the world the same way they do. Finding them and communicating with them, whether virtually or face-to-face, is going to give your young person more of a sense of belonging to a group or movement.

A study in 2021 found that 'more dissatisfaction with autistic personal identity predicted lower self-esteem, and more autism pride predicted higher self-esteem'.[1] We have an identity that is personal to us and might revolve around our own interests and values and talents, and an identity that is social and is framed by how we are positioned socially and our similarities with social groups. We might intersect

---

1   Corden, K., Brewer, R., and Eilidh, C. (2021) 'Personal identity after an autism diagnosis: Relationships with self-esteem, mental wellbeing, and diagnostic timing'. *Frontiers in Psychology*, 12: 699335. doi:10.3389/fpsyg.2021.699335.

some of those groups, and I've already mentioned intersectionality which looks at the possible conflict between different identities, e.g. Black, female, autistic, dyspraxic, gay, etc. The younger you discover your autistic identity, the more likely you are to be at peace with it and the higher your self-esteem is likely to be. After all, if you are diagnosed late, but still knew yourself to be different, you may have endured other 'labels' such as slow, weird, lazy, stupid (upsetting, but labels that autistic women in our group said they had heard about themselves). Even though those labels are wrong, being called them is bound to have a long-term effect on your self-esteem.

As parents, your role is to understand as much about autism as you possibly can, and be positive about autism and neurodiversity to help your young person have higher self-esteem and a positive outlook. Being in school, where peers who don't understand neurodiversity may have said upsetting things about autistic people or used the word as a slur, will not have helped self-esteem, and a positive autistic identity is going to be linked to psychological health. How we understand and consider ourselves is going to be very important in shaping our life experiences. So if at all possible, it's vital to shape a positive identity before 'graduating' to adulthood. Building up a sense of self is partially going to be decided by personal choices, but someone who is not aware of their autism or who has no positive feedback about it is not going to choose to identify as part of that group. And to complicate matters, an autistic teen may be anxious about exploring different choices in identifying their self. Your role is an acutely balanced one here – their identity must be their (and ONLY their) choice, but they need authentic information to make their choice. Does society and school life give authentic information about autism and neurodiversity? I'd have to give that an emphatic no. So it's up to you.

How Can You Help?

Support your child to experience a range of different topics and interests. Depending on your child, you may not need to do much here, but the aim is to introduce them to lots of different topics and ideas that they might enjoy. And it goes without saying that this is also a balancing act – there's a fine line between offering topics for enjoyment and forcing someone to do something. If your child is adamant that they don't want to become a Scout, or start yoga, or read about radical feminism, then their choice should be respected. Nor should you be stopping them from pursuing whatever is their passionate interest at the time. Talk to them about it being important to learn about different things so that they can find other things they can become passionate about – we're definitely not trying to lose the passion! They should be in control of the choices in this process.

Ultimately your child is more likely to find lasting friendships among other people they have lots in common with. And they are more likely to develop relationships in a safe, calm environment where they are busy doing stuff, and like to talk about that. There's no pressure to 'socialise'. So a good way to find people who you are more likely to 'click' with is to join groups coinciding with interests you are passionate about, or to join groups of people who experience the world in a similar way to you. If a young person joins a group of neurodivergent young people, they are more likely to find people they click with there than in a group of neurotypical people. Everyone's different of course, which is why you need to give yourself the best chance. Now, I'm not suggesting it will be easy for your young person to join a group. It might in fact be very difficult, because socialising and doing something completely new = uncertainty, which we know = anxiety. But if it's the right group, it will have been worth it.

As humans we crave acceptance. Research has shown we actually live longer if we have relationships, compared to those who do not,[2] and there are differences in stress and cognitive responses, sleep and even cardiovascular function. Many of us feel the need to find others who understand us, who listen to us, who make us feel good, who can pick up where we left off even if you don't see or contact each other for months. But not everybody deserves a spot in our tribe. Only those who accept you for you get in. It's an exclusive club!

---

2   Holt-Lunstad, J., et al. (2015) 'Loneliness and social isolation as risk factors for mortality: A meta-analytic review'. *Perspectives of Psychological Science*, 10(2): 227–237. doi:10.1177/1745691614568352.

What If It's Difficult for Your Young Person to Accept Their Autistic Identity?

When you're recognised as autistic later, it's not unusual to be resistant to a diagnosis. After all, you've probably been masking for most of your life, and you're aware that at least some of your friends might have difficulty accepting that you're autistic. You want things to continue the same, even though things might be pretty awful. You don't want to stand out. You want to appear the same as your peers. You're a social chameleon but it's only just beginning to dawn on you how exhausting that is. It may take something to resonate before you are open to the idea of valuing and accepting your autism, and that might be different for each person. It might be the growing notion that you felt very alone before, and you're coming to terms with the idea that you're part of a recognised group who can validate lots of what you've been feeling. Imagine being at a festival (or conference) and it being only other autistic young people there! Social media has meant this is much more possible (admittedly virtually) now. But it will come, especially if you are surrounded by autism positivity, and a family who builds your self-esteem daily.

Once this happens, it doesn't mean you need to announce that you're autistic, or start advocating or being an activist. You don't need to be loud and proud unless you want to be, but I hope at some point you get to the point of being quiet and proud! Just feeling able to be yourself without (much) masking is a huge consideration when thinking about self-identity. Understanding why your past self needed to disguise your autism so much is a good step towards liking and accepting yourself. But it's fine if it takes a while!

A tribe doesn't need to be lots of people. Just two or three who get you works just as well. And once you've accepted your place in the autistic or neurodivergent tribe, you might find yourself belonging to others – those who share the same interests (music, specific TV programmes), or religion, or politics, or social commitment. You just 'click' on those topics. You don't feel you have to hide your special interest. You understand each other. There's little miscommunication.

There's no judgement. There's no censorship. You just get it. Your world has expanded.

NEUROTYPICAL FRIENDSHIPS

It's likely that many of the friendships your child has had growing up have been with neurotypical children, and that's great. But as they get older, it takes more understanding and acceptance of difference to build cross-neurotype relationships. Please understand that I'm emphatically not saying they're not possible. That would be ridiculous. But I am saying that they work better and entail less miscommunication on both sides when the neurotypical half of the equation understands neurodivergence or at least values difference. And I stand by that.

It means that it's really important to help educate your wide circle of acquaintances and family as much as you can, so that your young person can have the best pick of relationships among people that understand and accept them for who they are, who accept that sometimes they want to be alone and who they feel safe 'unmasking' with. Get them to buy or borrow this book and read it with your young person in mind. The world needs more people who embrace difference.

Chapter 12

Future

HIGHER EDUCATION

More and more autistic students are going to university – or perhaps more and more university students are now being recognised as being autistic. Either way, there's a considerable university autistic population. This shouldn't be a surprise, as there are plenty of autistic engineers, GPs, anaesthetists, psychiatrists, teachers, accountants, actuaries, coders, scientists, and researchers. However, while university doesn't have all of the difficulties of secondary school, it's still not always a comfortable environment for autistic people.

Applying to University

Naturally, because of discrimination law, universities can't and are keen not to be seen to be discriminating against neurodivergent students. So it won't affect your application to disclose that you are autistic should you wish, and if you want to receive support you will need to do so. How universities make reasonable adjustments for their autistic students and how much support is available will vary, and sadly it can even vary at the same university for different students, according to the level of knowledge of individual staff. But in general, things are much better than they used to be.

Applying in the UK

Pupils in the UK apply via UCAS (University and College Admissions Service). If you're at school they will help with the application; if you're home educated this help won't be available and it will be slightly more complicated to find suitable references. You can choose up to five courses on your UCAS application. Once you have some offers, and probably before they are confirmed, you can apply for a student loan from Student Finance, and it's at this point that you can also apply for DSA (Disabled Students' Allowance). The student loan comes in two parts: the fees loan and the maintenance loan. The fees loan will cover your university fees and (probably) be paid directly to the university. The maintenance loan has a basic amount which is not means-tested, or you can apply for a full loan where you'll need to input financial details. Be aware that the basic maintenance loan doesn't even cover the full amount for accommodation for most students, so if this is all they'll be entitled to, it will need to be supplemented by quite a lot, either by you or by part-time employment. After A level results are released, universities will firm up their offers and if you didn't get your first choice you can just change the institution with Student Finance.

If your child has a diagnosis of autism it's very likely they will be entitled to DSA. It's not a monetary award, but it provides equipment and mentoring and is FAR easier to navigate than any other SEND-related benefit. Basically, you say what you need support with and they will tell you what they can offer you – it might be a laptop (you have to pay the first £200 at the time of writing), voice to text software, a dictaphone, student support mentoring, wellbeing mentoring. You can be entitled to up to three hours of mentoring per week, but you might not necessarily want all that if you have a heavy work schedule. If you have strong sensory needs and, for example, would be unable to share a bathroom, DSA will sometimes pay the difference to get studio or ensuite accommodation. As well as DSA, do also contact the learning support team at your chosen university to see what they can offer. There is a very good Facebook group called What I Wish I Knew About University – WIWIKAU, and there are often threads in there about which universities offer good support for neurodivergent students.

Applying in the US

In the US, there's no central body like UCAS and you apply for each university or college separately. So when researching the institutions you're interested in, part of that research will be to see what accommodations are made for autistic students, and what reputation that support has amongst alumni. Whereas potential students in the UK are applying for a course, those in the US are applying for a university place, not a course, as majors will be decided later down the line. For finance, it will depend very much on your chosen school and any bursaries, scholarships, or loans you may be entitled to. And lastly, there's no national program of support for autistic students, so a conversation with student support centres at your chosen universities around technical and emotional support is essential.

What to do after school or college is another huge decision and transition.

EMPLOYMENT AND JOB INTERVIEWS

Autistic and other neurodivergent people are at a disadvantage in the recruitment process due to lack of knowledge about neurodiversity and disability law, and lack of interest in addressing that lack of knowledge. But things are changing slowly. Diversity – and that includes neurodiversity – in the workplace has become much more than a tickbox exercise. US recruitment agency Tallo recently carried out a survey of Gen Z-ers (born after 1996) and found that an incredible 99% of them said that diversity, equity, and inclusion were important, 87% of them saying they were very important.[1] The same survey reported 80% of respondents saying they would be more likely to apply to a company which had readily accessible information for neurodivergent employees available. And 20% said they had been put off applying to companies who didn't have such information available.

Some big companies such as Microsoft, SAP, J P Morgan, Hewlett Packard, Ford, and EY have neurodiversity programmes. *Harvard Business Review* even ran an article recently talking about autism as a 'competitive advantage'. I'm not in favour of trying to turn autism into something 'productive', and singling out those with those skills as somehow better than autistic people who don't have them. All of us have value. We're all different, and we need to find the path in life which makes us happiest and most fulfilled. If employment is in your young person's future, then what will make them happiest and most fulfilled is something that aligns with both their talents and their interests. If that equals what Microsoft or EY are looking for, happy days.

---

1   Tallo (2021) 'What companies need to know about Gen Z's diversity, equity, and inclusion expectations'. Tallo, 12 July. Accessed on 2 May 2022 at https://tallo.com/blog/gen-z-workplace-diversity-equity-inclusion

Really what this tells us, if we need specific programs to attract autistic employees, is that there's something wrong with the recruitment process. If we can't attract diversity then perhaps our recruitment process is not inclusive, and that affects the running of the whole company. Senior leadership at SAP said that the program forced them to get to know their whole workforce and made them better managers. So we can all encourage our local government and employers to both recruit in a more neurodivergent-friendly way and to support their neurodivergent employees. No point in spending to recruit them if you can't retain them.

What Might Autistic Young People Find Difficult About the Recruitment Process?

Interviews – we are told to shake hands and make eye contact but even if autistic people can do that it can take all their focus. Sticking to the topic of a question can be difficult. Surprises are never welcome (remember uncertainty = anxiety) so not knowing what questions are going to be asked in an interview makes the whole experience very stressful, which is not conducive to making a good first impression. In general autistic people like to be honest, and the whole recruitment process is prone to exaggeration and blatant lies, not a comfortable place to be.

Assessment centres – I probably don't even need to tell you that these are an autistic nightmare come to life! A whole day or even weekend of peopling, and trying to predict social cues and what people actually mean when they ask you something. Universally hated I know, but justifiably so for neurodivergent people.

What in General Can Autistic People Find Difficult at Work?

- Communication skills.
- Being a team player.
- Emotional intelligence.
- Persuasiveness.
- Customer service skills.

- Networking.
- Not speaking their mind.
- Conforming to standard systems and processes.

What in General Are Great Strong Points of Autistic People at Work?

- Innovation and creativity – ability to 'think outside the box'.
- Loyalty.
- Analytical skills and pattern-spotting.
- Ability to focus.
- Honesty.
- Reliability.
- A great sense of humour.
- Unique viewpoints.
- Increased perceptual skills.

These might not all apply to your young person, so the key is to look at strengths and challenges and not try to fit a square peg into a round hole. And if you're an employer thinking about employing autistic young people, please do so. Providing a calm sensory environment will benefit all your employees, not only neurodivergent ones. Remember that just as you'll need to train (like all new staff) your autistic staff, you'll also need to train your existing staff to be accepting and understanding of differences. And allocate work on the basis of strengths rather than sticking rigidly to role titles or societal ideas of how genders should behave. For example, if you have an autistic employee in an insurance company who hates 'people stuff' but is great at processing and picking apart complicated cases, let them do that. As always, understanding that your way is not the only right way is key.

REASONABLE ADJUSTMENTS AT WORK

What companies like SAP running neurodiversity programmes at work have found is that their neurodivergent employees need to be able to deviate from 'the norm' that is expected. This is not an intuitive thing for a big company to allow, being generally governed by scalability and economies of scale, but it's what works for both the employees and, in the end, the company. Reasonable adjustments should be both to draw out the strengths of autistic employees as well as to protect from any environment or action that might be harmful – accommodating for the classic 'spiky profile' in fact. For managers to be able to individualise the work environment to suit an autistic employee, they have to know that employee quite well. This can also lead to them knowing their other employees better too and that's a win-win situation. It's worth knowing that in the UK you can use Access to Work to secure some funding for things like mentors, coaching, and technical support and equipment, and sometimes even transport to work (much like DSA for university students). For the US see this list of available resources: www.dol.gov/general/topic/disability.

When autistic adults mask a lot, it can be difficult for employers to realise or remember that they need to apply reasonable adjustments. If you are being open about your diagnosis and you want reasonable adjustments, it's good practice to get that agreement in writing – this can then be shown to anyone at any point who decides to question the validity of the agreement. It also serves to remind the employer of their legal obligation – however well the autistic adult appears to be coping.

What Reasonable Adjustments Are Possible in Job Interviews?

- Knowing the questions that will be asked in advance.
- Reading time and planning time.

What Reasonable Adjustments Are Possible at Work?
How long is a piece of string? Anything is possible, but more will be possible at some companies than others. These are the kind of things which may help to make the environment more welcoming for autistic employees:

- Clear instructions without the need for inference.
- Adjusting lighting so that it's not fluorescent, not too bright or too direct.
- Providing seating which is comfortable and helps with focus (may apply more to dyspraxic people and those with ADHD).
- Allowing employees to work at times which avoid commuter rush hour.
- Allowing remote working.
- Providing noise-cancelling headphones.
- Providing a quiet area to self-regulate.
- Allowing adjustments if there is a uniform.
- Limiting meetings and allowing them virtually.
- Minimising sudden changes.
- Flexible hours.
- Meeting agendas finalised and sent in advance with slides if possible.
- Having a work therapy dog.
- Important verbal conversations followed up with a written version.
- Normalising fidget items.
- Allowing sunglasses inside if necessary.
- Use of private meeting rooms.
- More time and feedback with manager/supervisor.
- Speech to text software.
- Peer mentoring system.
- Management team to use clear instructions which reduce the need for inference.
- Choice of desk location (within reason!).
- Use of standing desks and/or wobble boards to help concentration.
- No team-building exercises! Or neurodivergent-friendly ones.

You may notice that 'extra time' is not in there despite that being among the most common reasonable adjustments in school – often the only adjustment. This is because in school there are fixed practices and systems which are disadvantageous to neurodivergent young people, whereas in a workplace there is the freedom to set up systems of appraisal which are more suited to the individual. If there was a disadvantageous system of appraisal in a workplace, that would be grounds for reasonable adjustments of the system or a discrimination case.

But the most important and valuable adjustment in a workplace would be everyone understanding and accepting autism and putting these strategies in place without rolling eyes. It should be noted too that there may be different societal expectations of women which may mean different reasonable adjustments are needed. For example, some men are allowed to be 'the strong, silent type' without judgement, whereas women who act in the same way (avoiding eye contact and small talk, being brief and to the point in emails) may be perceived as somehow lacking in social skills. A respondent in a 2021 study said 'I have had managers before that have told me that I am obviously untrustworthy as I don't look them in the eye'.[2] While I will fight this everywhere I see it for our daughters' sakes, I can't deny it still happens.

CASE STUDY
Jillian, age 32 in the UK
Jillian worked in retail management for a well-known high street chain store. She often felt that she was treated differently to her male counterparts, even when they did the same things that she did. She clashed with some of the staff, but so did they. The difference was, they were male, and she wasn't neurotypical. She was actually sent by upper management on a training programme to improve her interpersonal skills. Their interpersonal skills were apparently fine! Jillian felt that the company weren't good at making reasonable adjustments, but that this was directly related to her being both autistic AND female.

---

2   North, G. (2021) 'Reconceptualising "reasonable adjustments" for the successful employment of autistic women'. *Disability & Society*. https://doi.org/10.1080/09 687599.2021.1971065

HEALTHCARE

While some health professionals like psychologists and psychiatrists will be very knowledgeable about autism, other more general practitioners may have received very little training on it at all, and this can have negative consequences for your young person without an advocate in their corner. It can be useful to prepare a so-called autism passport (but call it whatever your young person wants it to be called!) with all relevant strengths and needs, especially if there is going to be a hospital stay. But even visiting your GP or your local A&E/ER department can be a minefield when doctors and nurses don't properly understand their autistic patients.

What follows will be a list of things I'd like all GPs to know. It will help you advocate for your young person if you feel they are being disadvantaged in some way. (And if your young person is over 16 in the UK and wants to go into GP appointments on their own this can become more challenging, as we found out.)

What I'd like health professionals to know:

- Making appointments by telephone is difficult for autistic people. Online appointment booking is much easier.
- Coming for a doctor's appointment is stressful. The autistic person may be in a heightened state of anxiety because of this.
- Waiting in a waiting room with others who may be noisy, or stare, or smell, is stressful. Bright lights can be painful.
- Many autistic people don't like to be touched so please do it only when necessary and explain what you are doing and why.
- Don't make a diagnosis based partly on facial expression. This may be different from how you expect a neurotypical person to present.
- Don't make a diagnosis or prescribe meds based on what you feel pain levels are – listen to the patient or their advocate. Autistic people may not feel pain in the same way as neurotypical people, and it may be heightened or lessened.

- An anxious autistic patient may become situationally mute, or may take longer than usual to process sentences. Please be patient, and if necessary offer other ways of communicating.
- An autistic patient may be uncomfortable making eye contact – please don't make any assumptions about this.
- Some autistic people have different reactions to medication – please listen to the patient and act accordingly, even if what they say seems unusual. It may only be unusual for neurotypical patients.
- Autistic patients may have problems with interoception and have difficulty identifying the source of pain, for example.
- Use clear and precise language, and remember that autistic people can have difficulty with inference – what you say may be interpreted literally so make sure it makes sense that way.
- Some autistic people have executive functioning difficulties and it may be preferable for you to write down the main points of importance in the appointment.
- During inpatient care, autistic people are often in an environment which is very stressful for them – bright lights, too many people, too much noise, no control over their environment. Mitigate as much of this as it's possible for you to do.
- In the UK, a learning disability nurse may be useful to point out strategies to help which you may not have thought of.
- Autism can present quite differently in different people so unless you are an expert yourself, please don't suggest that a patient may or may not be autistic when they come asking you to refer them for an autism assessment. Especially not when that person is a 16-year-old who has reluctantly brought along a letter from his mum asking that he be referred! Telling him that you don't think he's autistic may have set back careful work done on preparing him for a diagnosis.
- An internal presentation of autism is quite different from the more stereotypical one, and tends to be how most girls and women present. You need to research autistic masking to understand.

There is an autism passport template on the Autistic Girls Network website.[3]

EMERGENCY SERVICES

Now we know that uncertainty = anxiety, but by its very nature contact with the emergency services is going to be unplanned and therefore uncertain. There's nothing we can do about that in the moment, but we can plan and prepare our young people for contact with paramedics, police officers, fire fighters, etc. This is even more important in the US where it's more likely that police officers will have access to firearms making an uncomfortable situation into a potentially dangerous one. What you do and how you prepare is going to very much depend on your young person and how you think they are going to react in an emergency.

Emergencies may bring with them scary and even life-threatening situations, noise and sirens, and sensory overload. In that moment, your young person may be hard-pressed to behave calmly in the face of uniformed and unfamiliar emergency personnel. If this is going to be an issue, it may be a good idea to make them familiar with what might happen in certain scenarios. For incidents involving the police particularly, it's important to know that some traits common to autistic people such as not making eye contact, delay in following or refusal to follow commands, or reacting in what's deemed an unusual way to sound or lights (sensory overload) may cause police officers who don't know someone is autistic to consider them non-compliant or under the influence of drugs.

In the UK

If you may have difficulty making a phone call to the emergency 999 number you can use a confidential app called Relay which is integrated with 999 emergency services. It needs to be installed on your phone so you might want to do it now before you need it.

---

3   www.autisticgirlsnetwork.org/Hospital_Passport_Template.pdf

Many police forces in the UK have alert card schemes where the autistic person or their parent/carer can carry a card showing they are autistic. More details on the schemes can be found here: www.npaa.org.uk/alert-card-schemes

Of course, these schemes rely on the person being happy to carry the card (which may carry stigma) and being able to produce it in a stressful situation.

In the US

Some states support an autism ID card scheme – find out if yours does, and discuss with your young person whether it would be a good plan or not for them to have this card, and whether they would be able to produce it if needed.

SELF-EMPLOYMENT

As your child gets older conversations will need to be had about future independence. Presuming that they can work, they need to start thinking about possible career paths. For the adult autistic people in our group, getting employment right has been a big part of their lives. One refrain we hear often is that working for themselves is much more suitable than being employed in an office. This might be an option you want to explore with your young person as a future aspiration. Setting up your own business is a big leap and can feel risky compared to employment. But there are a lot of advantages to self-employment for autistic people:

- You're the boss. Nobody is going to tell you to do things another way (though you may need to comply with a client's methods).
- You set your own deadlines (though they may be dependent on when a client needs something).
- Theoretically, you work the hours you want to work. Boundaries are important here – you may need to be strong in ring-fencing certain hours, days, or weeks for you or your family.

- You provide your own sensory environment – in these days of Zoom calls, and depending on the nature of your business, you should be able to work remotely.
- You set your goals and are responsible for measuring your success.

The downsides of self-employment (for any neurotype):

- You are dependent on attracting clients/sales yourself.
- You need enough self-belief and self-confidence to feel able to set up a business yourself – imposter syndrome can be strong.
- You need to do everything – production, marketing, design, sales, insurance, payroll, accounting, etc., until you make enough to be able to outsource these.
- In times of crisis (e.g. during the COVID pandemic), you may lose business and be ineligible for government help.
- You need a certain level of organisation and therefore executive function to keep a business flowing – but you may be able to outsource the organisational side.
- Depending on your setup you may be vulnerable to financial/legal hits to your family income and property.
- It needs a strong will sometimes to maintain a good work/life balance, for example blocking out holiday time.

How to Start Your Own Business

As a mentor for the Mayor of London Business Growth Programme, I advise start-ups on their marketing strategy, but these are businesses that have been trading long enough to be able to invest a little. However, I also founded a membership for freelancers and small business owners with some colleagues, and I understand exactly the kind of imposter syndrome which stops someone from starting out on their own. Women particularly may have taken a career break to look after children or be a carer to children (not being sexist here – statistically this tends to be women) and it can be difficult to drum up the self-confidence to start again. But you or your young person can do it, if you follow sensible and realistic steps. For your young person, they may want to get some employment experience behind them first.

First, write down your ideas and research your market to validate those ideas. What is your target audience? Is it big enough? What would they pay? Can you price your product or service with enough profit margin to make a living? What's the competition? Are they successful? What do you need to make in your first few years to support your family or yourself?

Second, what resources do you have available? If the business is by your young person, are they eligible for any grants or mentoring schemes? What can you use to bootstrap your business – make it successful for a minimal investment?

Third, plan the brand of your business. Research domain names and social media handles BEFORE you decide on a business name. You need to come up with (by yourself or with the help of a designer) a brand identity – not just a logo but brand colours and fonts, what your brand stands for and values, and what tone of voice you want to use on your website and in marketing materials and social media posts.

What is the legal structure of your business going to be? You'll need to research what structure is best as well as thinking about any permits or licenses which might be needed, or any training you might need to prove you've undertaken.

Next, if you're going to ask the bank for a loan or apply for a grant you'll need a fully costed business plan, but even if not you need to at least plan out your costs and projections for the next six months at the minimum, remembering things like insurance and software subscriptions.

How and where are you going to market your business and find new clients/customers? You need a basic viable strategy for this.

If you're not familiar with tax and accounting this is the first thing I'd suggest to outsource. But with new online bank accounts and integrated accounting software like Xero and Dext it's easy to at least stay on top of the bookkeeping.

If you're serious about starting a business I'd recommend reading *The Autism-Friendly Guide to Self-Employment* by Robyn Steward.

PART 3

DIAGNOSIS AND BEYOND

Chapter 13

Diagnosis

Perhaps you have been reading this book but your child has not yet been formally diagnosed as autistic. If that's the case, in this chapter we will take a look at how and when you should pursue a diagnosis and what you might expect to happen.

DIAGNOSIS

Understandably, we get a lot of questions in the Autistic Girls Network Facebook group about diagnosis. My child has these traits x, y, and z, should we get a diagnosis? We've been waiting for three years, should we pay for a private diagnosis? My daughter was diagnosed and now I think I might be autistic, should I ask my GP for a referral to get a diagnosis?

While I've used the 'D' word for this section heading, I actually prefer to use the word recognition. Diagnosis sounds rather too medical for me, and autism is not an illness. But the fact remains, a diagnosis has to be done by a medical practitioner (or multiple practitioners to be NICE compliant), and although it shouldn't be the case, to get support in place you often need to have a diagnosis.

In some areas in the UK diagnostic services for children have a waiting list of up to four years at the time I'm writing this. I'm hopeful that by the time this is published that wait time will have reduced as the government realises we are at crisis point and pours some money into local councils, but I won't be holding my breath. Unfortunately, this means that some young people are going unrecognised or are not receiving the support they should despite their needs being recognised, just because they don't have the piece of paper declaring them autistic.

DIAGNOSTIC CRITERIA

There are very specific criteria recorded for an autism diagnosis, and it's not a simple procedure. There's no genetic marker, and no blood test that can tell medical personnel that someone is autistic. Professionals will use the diagnostic manuals ICD-10 (ICD-11 from January 2022) and DSM-V, and NICE guidelines state that this should be a multi-disciplinary approach. If you want the diagnosis to be used in a school, with CAMHS, or as part of the EHCP process, make sure you heed that last part, or they may refuse to recognise the diagnosis.

So What Are the ICD-10 and 11 and DSM-V?

The International Classification of Diseases, 10th and 11th editions, present autism under the heading 'Disorders of Psychological Development'[1] and the sub-heading 'Pervasive Developmental Disorders'.[2]

As you can tell from that language, the autistic community does have issues with these diagnostic manuals. Autism is not a disease – why should it be included in the ICD at all? Many would argue autism is not a disorder, and the same could be said for ADHD (attention deficit hyperactivity disorder) and the 'P' in PDA (pathological demand avoidance). Language is important, and a definition which concentrates on 'reciprocal social interaction, communication, and restricted, stereotyped, repetitive behaviour'[3] is never going to be welcomed with open arms.

The DSM-V (*The Diagnostic and Statistical Manual of Mental Disorders*, 5th edition) is not too widely used in the UK, but it was recently updated, making quite wide-ranging changes to how we name autism, and this has had an effect on the amendments in the 11th version

---

1   https://icd.who.int/browse10/2015/en#/F80-F89
2   https://icd.who.int/browse10/2015/en#/F84
3   https://icd.who.int/browse10/2016/en#/F84.5

of the ICD. In summary, the DSM-V gets rid of the classification of Asperger's as a separate diagnosis and gives only a diagnosis of autism spectrum disorder. It also brings in sensory difficulties which is an important addition and may help more girls to be diagnosed. Those who are already diagnosed with Asperger's do not lose their diagnosis or have it reclassified.

SHOULD YOU GET A DIAGNOSIS FOR YOUR CHILD?

As a parent, it's going to feel quite urgent to you to get this situation resolved. You may have friends, family, teachers, or doctors telling you not to 'label' your child. But a diagnosis is SO MUCH more than a label.

Let's examine the scenario for a moment. Let's say your child's school SENCO tells you that autism is a label that will stick with your child for the rest of their life, and may stop them getting a job (yes, this has happened). I have a few problems with this statement. First, I'd really like SENCOs to stop having such a negative view of autism – plenty of autistic people have jobs (despite depressing statistics – but many autistic adults are not recorded as diagnosed, so not part of any statistics). Next, while an EHCP or IEP is needs-based rather than diagnosis-based, having a diagnosis certainly helps a child access support when needed. It also gives them protection under the Children and Families Act 2014 Part 3 and The Equality Act 2010 Section 6 in the UK, and equivalent legislation in other countries.

Under the Equality Act, autism is classed as a disability which is one of the nine protected characteristics. The Equality Act 2010 (Section 6) says that someone has a disability if he or she has a physical or mental impairment that has a long-term and substantial adverse effect on his or her ability to carry out normal day-to-day activities. In the US, autism is also a disability under the Americans With Disabilities Act. This means that at school, and later at college or university and in work, your child will be entitled to what's known as 'reasonable adjustments' – these are the things which can be changed to make life easier. In school, examples of reasonable adjustments might be a relaxing of the uniform policy to accommodate a sensory need, access to a quiet place to decompress, having a written note of all homework required. Of course, there is a wide variety of adjustments that might be needed, some needing an EHCP/IEP or a specialist school to work, and some being those that any mainstream school in the country ought to be able to put in place.

Let's not also forget that a diagnosis can be important for parents too, so that you know for sure that you're treading the right path for your child (and so many parents of autistic children go on to realise they might be autistic themselves). Knowing their neurology is going to enable you to plan life better, and adapt your child's environment to make things easier for everyone. There will be those who don't get behind you, or don't agree with the diagnosis. Frankly speaking, no matter how close you are to those people, saying these things is not helping you, or your child. There are lots of resources on the Autistic Girls Network website, which you could direct them to if you think they are willing to read and learn. It will help them understand why it's so important for your child to know – far more important than any 'label'.

Which brings me nicely to the most important reason for getting a diagnosis – so that your child can understand that they are not different to everyone else, that there is a sizeable proportion of the world's population that has the same neurotype as them, that thinks and sees the world in the same way. Studies have shown that neurodivergent people are more likely to get on with each other than with neurotypical people, so it's only fair that your child gets to know some other people like them, who instinctively understand them. Your child needs to know that despite how the world might make them feel sometimes, there is absolutely nothing 'wrong' in the way that they behave, or think, or feel. It's just that they are not in the majority. And you need to know and understand that too, so that you can make sure your child is brought up with the love and understanding that shows them that difference is not deficit.

CASE STUDY

Grace, age 12 in the UK (by her mum)

Since being quite young my daughter has stated that 'no one understands me or what I'm thinking', (usually mid-meltdown!). Now I know this wasn't a precocious version of teenage angst, but a genuine cry for understanding that she sees and experiences the world differently from most people she knows, family included. Since we've been having discussions around the likelihood of her being autistic, she's done her own research and is beginning to understand some of these differences. She still has trouble understanding other people's experiences or points of view, but I hope that may come as she gets older. For myself, I wish that I'd had this knowledge when Grace was much younger – it would have helped me to understand her better at a younger age, to be more tolerant and less judgemental of her and also of my parenting.

SHOULD YOU GET A DIAGNOSIS – FOR ADULTS?

Increasingly, we are seeing mums in Autistic Girls Network who only realised they themselves were autistic when they started to investigate autism for their own child or children. This brings up a question I've pondered for a while now – the official stats are that 1 in 100 people in the UK are autistic, and 1 in 44 in the US. The latter only includes 8 year olds, and both figures are incorrect. So many still are missed. What are the true statistics for autistic people, and for neurodivergent people? Common sense tells us it's likely to be a higher number than previously thought. (Autistic professional Ann Memmott puts a good case for it being 1 in 30.)[4]

Either way, the chances are high that if you have an autistic child, one of their parents will be autistic. A 2016 study put the likelihood at 64–91%.[5]

---

4   http://annsautism.blogspot.com/2016/11/autism-1-in-30-missing-most-females.html

5   Tick, B., *et al.* (2016) 'Heritability of autism spectrum disorders: A meta-analysis of twin studies'. *The Journal of Child Psychology and Psychiatry*, 57(5): 585–595. https://doi.org/10.1111/jcpp.12499

That piece of paper stating an autism diagnosis can be important to fight for an EHCP, claim DLA, PIP or other benefits, or get support in further education, but let's get one thing straight right at the beginning of this section – self-diagnosis is completely valid and might well be enough. Getting an adult diagnosis can take a long time and involve dealing with services which ironically you may find difficult to access because you're autistic. A private diagnosis can cost anywhere between £800 and £2500 ($1200 and $3200 in the US), so it is out of reach for many. Like us you may already have had to spend money on private diagnoses for your children because of the long waiting lists on the NHS for assessment.

You might feel you don't really deserve a diagnosis, because nobody has spotted that you're autistic so far – but everyone who is autistic deserves to know that they are.

You might worry that the authorities will feel that you're not as capable at looking after your children, but this is not the case.

You might worry that it will be on your medical records and that you will suffer discrimination at work because of it. While some autistic people do sadly suffer discrimination, you are not obliged to tell your employer. If you do tell them, they need to make reasonable adjustments.

If you want to 'test' whether or not you're autistic there are good resources online. Treat the online tests with some scepticism – they are a useful starting point to the conversation but they can't boast accuracy. There could be lots of reasons why you think you might be autistic, but whatever they are, it can be a nerve-wracking time.

Your first port of call to start the diagnostic process will probably be your GP. Experiences will vary according to the GP – some are much more enlightened than others! If you ARE autistic, this might be difficult for you but it's the only free way to start the process. It's likely you've masked for many years and you'll carry on masking to the doctor. You might smile, meet their eyes, make small talk, all the things you've learnt to do to feel like you fit in, which will mean there's a possibility the doctor won't think you qualify for an autism assessment referral. You might also have a job you like, and be married, and have children – and while we know those are absolutely possible while being autistic (of course!), some GPs are stuck in a more pathological view of autism. In England, Wales, and Northern Ireland, GPs should be following NICE guideline 142. In Scotland, GPs should be following SIGN guideline 145.

Autistic masking is still not well known among GPs (but we're working on that at Autistic Girls Network). Presuming the doctor does refer, your postcode will affect how long you'll need to wait – I've heard wait times varying from six months to five years.

Once you've cleared that hurdle, I'm afraid not much may happen for a while. The GP will have passed on a brief summary for a psychiatric assessment, and this is where a professional who is not clued up on autistic masking can let you down again by refusing the referral. At this point you may want to consider going private if that's a possibility. If not it may be back to the GP with research to back up your case.

There are a variety of tests which the doctor will go through with you, most of which put a ridiculous amount of emphasis on very early childhood and all of which basically assume you are a man. The doctor may also want to talk to your parents about your early childhood.

It seems a lot of effort to go through, but some adults have had their lives transformed by getting an autism diagnosis.

Maybe you always felt weird or the 'odd one out' as a child. Maybe you found friendships difficult. Maybe you made decisions or exhibited behaviour that others found difficult to understand – and therefore so did you at the time. All of that now makes sense.

Maybe you've always felt you needed to behave in a way you now know is neurotypical, and do things you didn't really want to do or which exhausted you. Now you can understand why you were exhausted and put strategies in place so that you can avoid sensory overload.

For some women, an autism diagnosis can correct a previous incorrect diagnosis. Unfortunately it has been all too common for women to be misdiagnosed with bipolar or schizophrenia when in fact they are autistic.

If you disclose your diagnosis to your employer they can make reasonable adjustments to support you to work in a more comfortable way with them.

In addition your diagnosis can be the catalyst to start receiving support and finding your autistic tribe.

ACCEPTANCE AND UNDERSTANDING

Some of you reading this are going to be shocked at your child getting an autism diagnosis, and may feel sad and disappointed, or even angry about it. Others of you may be relieved – perhaps you have known for years or have been trying to get a diagnosis for a long time, and the confirmation is what you needed. Either way, for your child's sake, you need to move past any emotional barriers and go forward. So, don't suppress your feelings, feel them all, there's nothing wrong with them. But accept that they don't help you moving forward.

If you are in a relationship, you may find that your partner processes the diagnosis differently to you. Men, for example, tend in general to have more difficulty accepting it, and their female partners may feel they aren't getting emotional support at a time they need it. But no matter how differently you come at it, you both need to talk about it and end up on the same page. What's important after all is your child.

Now it's time to throw yourself into researching autism – in the right places. There is often a negative narrative but that doesn't need to be your story. Listen to autistic adults so that you can avoid some of the difficulties they have had growing up. Times are very different now and attitudes and understanding are changing. Part of the reason for the depressing statistics around the mental health and employability of autistic people is that society hasn't understood or accommodated autism. You can be part of changing that. Be part of bringing up a generation of happy and supported autistic people who are confident of their place in this world.

TELLING YOUR CHILD

How you talk with your child about autism is going to shape how they think about autism. It can inform their whole identity and idea of self-worth. Of course, how your child finds out their diagnosis is going to depend on their age and the circumstances under which the diagnosis took place. A child who was diagnosed at age three is going to have a very different experience to a young person who has been undergoing huge mental health issues and has been assessed as part of that, which is going to affect the whole family's feeling about the diagnosis.

It's hard at first to be positive when your child is harming themselves, but time will allow you to understand that these mental health issues were caused by NOT being diagnosed, by your child having to mask their whole life until they couldn't anymore. In fact, once your young person has come to terms with the diagnosis (which they may have been reluctant to do in those circumstances, because what teen wants to be different and draw more attention to themselves?), learning more about autism and developing a sense of autistic pride is only going to help them. We all want to feel more comfortable in our skin.

You may want to delay telling your child or young person. But I believe that children know when they are struggling. If you don't give them the words, the explanation, for what's going on, they are going to come up with their own, and they are likely to be negative. Unless your child is very young, this may already have started happening, and schools have a tendency to choose negative language too when they don't know that SEN is involved. Give your child the self-awareness to be their own advocate, and to choose if they want to find friends within their own tribe. If there are people in your extended family who are autistic, do tell them that they are also in 'the tribe' – the more matter of fact you can be, the better. I don't ever advocate not telling your child. To do so is to make the assumption that autism is a 'bad thing', and it's not. Simple as that.

When is the best time to tell them? Well there's no best time. But if something comes up organically, for example they bring up something that's bothering them, whether it's struggling in school or friendship difficulties, that would be a good time to bring it into the conversation. Be casual and matter of fact. It's just a difference in the way your brain is wired, and you might find, for example, that social chat or sitting still is difficult but you're great at being loyal or trying hard, being kind, caring about animals, and having a strong sense of social justice. Highlight the strengths which are more general rather than something particular like being good at science, so that you can foster a growth mindset. In case your child is so used to hearing what they CAN'T do, make sure you have some examples of the strengths you're talking about. We're interested in turning round that internal narrative to something positive.

As their parent, it's now your job to shape their environment to suit them as much as possible. Try to leave behind the social rules and regulations which say you 'shouldn't' do certain things. Consider deeply if things really need to be done that way – or done at all. Shake off some social conventions. What you want is to produce a happy, well-adjusted adult, who can live (if possible) an independent life, right? Do they need to be working in a building with thousands of other employees, noisily walking the corridors every hour and crammed into small offices with 30 desks in? Probably not. So school is NOT practice for that, no matter how much a teacher tries to tell you so. Open your mind to the idea that society is not always right, and your autistic child, who will probably overtake you sometime soon on the social justice front, will thrive.

Your young person might like to read this blog by one of Autistic Girls Network's trustees, who was herself recognised as autistic only after mental health trauma, at the age of 17: www.autisticgirlsnetwork. org/autism/for-newly-diagnosed-young-autistic-people

FRUSTRATION WITH PROFESSIONALS

Reading this book you're probably going to be able to detect a certain level of frustration with some professionals. You may be feeling this too, or you may be a professional yourself, in which case I apologise!

Unfortunately, my journey as a parent of two autistic teens has not been a particularly happy one with regards to professional input. We've had to pay for private diagnoses and were lucky to be able to research those and choose from excellent recommendations, but have had interactions with social care, CAMHS, and school which have been spiky, problematic, or just ineffective. Other than a handful of people I'm very grateful for, I haven't come across many professionals at all who really understand autism and this is problematic. I know from interactions in the Autistic Girls Network Facebook group and other groups that my experience is the norm. In fact, there are many others who have had much worse experiences than me. Parents have had to upskill themselves with the knowledge needed to advocate for their children so that well-meaning professionals didn't damage them still further by not understanding their neurotype.

It's not acceptable, and this is why Autistic Girls Network campaigns for better awareness of autism in girls among health and education professionals. Let's not have diagnosis taking years, let's not have any more schools refusing to refer children because they are 'fine in school'. Please LISTEN to parents. Please take the time to understand autistic masking, and WHY children and young people behave differently at home than at school. Please make yourself (and all your staff) aware that these children and young people will mask until they just can't anymore, but by that time the damage is done. It doesn't have to be that way. Autistic people shouldn't need to be diagnosed by deficits and only recognised when they are showing distressed behaviours, but if you do have a child exhibiting distressed behaviours, find out why before they are put in detention, or shouted at or excluded.

Fast forward ten years – we have changed the structure of schools to be more comfortable not only for neurodivergent students, but for all students. We have removed florescent lights, stopped the school bell, and built more schools for autistic pupils who can't stand mainstream. We have calmer, more regulated students. We have less mental health issues. Wouldn't that be a nicer place to be?

WHAT HAPPENS NEXT?

Your young person has got their diagnosis. They have been officially recognised as being autistic. What happens next? The most common answer to this is probably not much! There's no real pathway of support when your young person is diagnosed as an older child or teen. It's likely that you'll be signposted to various charities which may invite you for parenting classes, and if you're lucky there may be a group your child can join to meet other autistic young people. (And as long as this is a good, neurodivergent-led group, this is probably the best possible therapy!)

Chapter 14

Post-Diagnosis

AUTISM ADJUSTMENTS

Some young people (and their families) will have been expecting their diagnosis, have had time to adjust to the idea and can get on with their life in the knowledge that their expectations have been proven right. For others, particularly those who find out suddenly in traumatic circumstances, it can be a less welcome realisation. It's natural for young people to want to fit in with their peers, and for some receiving a diagnosis they perceive as immediately making them different is not welcome. Listen to them, and validate how they are feeling. Try to find ways, in conjunction with school, that they can receive support without standing out too much. Things will change, but it will take time, and it will be a less distressing process in a school that is already autism-aware and has made efforts across the whole school to educate all pupils about neurodiversity. Having friends who understand and accept will make a big difference here.

As your young person adjusts to their autistic identity, you may find that they start to behave quite differently at home. They are dropping the mask. Some people (including you) may think that they are becoming 'more autistic', but it's not that. It's just that they are beginning to realise that they don't need to hide it anymore, at least at home in their safe place with their safe people. This is the first step to a better way of living for them, and it is to be quietly accepted and applauded, not anything to be alarmed about. You might, in fact, end up with what sometimes feels like a completely different young person than you started with. I did. But the newbie is your real young person, learning that they don't always need to pretend, consciously or not, to be someone else. It can be a good idea to have a word with the other close people in their life, to warn them not to make a fuss about this. It's a good thing, though for a while it may seem like a retrograde step.

What's different? Well, your young person is coming to terms with the idea that it's not wrong to have such strong sensory reactions, and so these might seem to increase for a while. They may start to realise that pacing up and down helps them, so they may start doing it frequently. They may understand that it's acceptable for them to have a limited food repertoire, so food choices may become more restricted. They may understand why they have difficulty with social communication, and stop trying to mask it so much. They may also understand that it's not wrong for them to want to be alone, and stop wanting to go out so much. If they've had trauma from being unrecognised as autistic, I promise you they are tired out. They need a lot of rest and downtime now. It's also likely that they are thinking back over their life – or as much of it as they remember – and realising why they felt or thought a certain way that seemed different to their peers. That time they couldn't do something all their friends could. That time they overshared and everyone looked at them strangely. That time nobody seemed bothered by the buzzing noises from the electrics. Suddenly all these mysteries are solved. It's going to take some time for everything to reach a new normal. But it will.

OTHER THERAPIES

I don't want anyone to assume that their child or young person automatically needs any kind of therapy just because they get a diagnosis of autism. That doesn't follow. The difficulty is, the later your child has been recognised as autistic, the more likely that trauma has occurred, and that 'extra' support will be needed, not necessarily BECAUSE they are autistic, but because they have been unrecognised and unaccommodated as autistic. And each young person is going to be different here, and need a different level or type of support. It will always help if the person giving the support has a good understanding of autism, and as we've already covered, avoid anyone who talks about ABA or PBS, or who tries to get your young person to mask autistic traits.

Understanding individual sensory needs can definitely help, so therapy with a sensory-integrated occupational therapist can help, and working with a knowledgeable speech and language therapist can be good for working on understanding, recognising, and expressing emotions. But the most valuable might be for your young person to be able to talk with an autistic adult (which might be either of those professionals, in an ideal world) and understand their identity, and how to interact comfortably and safely in a neurotypical world. What I'd like to see is a national programme which appoints an autistic mentor for a period after diagnosis, and for all areas to have good groups for autistic and other neurodivergent young people. Autistic Girls Network have opened their first face-to-face group to nurture a positive autistic identity, and they plan to open many more as they secure funding. You can get involved to help us.

Chapter 15

Support

DISABILITY BENEFITS

We had already been under CAMHS and Social Care for more than a year before anyone mentioned to us that we could apply for DLA (Disability Living Allowance) in the UK. Of course, we should have figured that out for ourselves, but when you are living on the edge of crisis 24/7 it's the last thing that occurs to you. It would have been helpful had someone mentioned it to us earlier because you can't backdate claims, so we lost out on some money we would have been entitled to which would have (partially) offset our horrendous petrol (gas) bills from needing to go out for an hour's drive every night for vestibular movement. I know that not all of you will be in the UK, so wherever you are, please find out your rights as to disability benefits.

In the UK, if you have a child with a health need or disability under 16, you may be entitled to DLA. It isn't means-tested, nor is it taxable, and it doesn't affect any other benefits you receive, if any. At the time of writing, this is changing to Child Disability Payments in Scotland. A diagnosis is not necessary, but the child must have needed support for over three months and be likely to still need it for at least another six months. In order to qualify they must need substantially more care than other children their age. I'll be honest with you, filling in the form, particularly if your family is in crisis at the time, is fairly heartbreaking. But the money can be used for things which will make life more comfortable or enjoyable for your young person.

DLA has both a care component and a mobility component and is scored in points for both. It will also make a difference if you have to give significant amounts of care at night. Any of the big charities for parent carers will go into detail about what qualifies for low, medium, and high rate of care and mobility, and how they are scored. There are also a couple of very good Facebook groups where people can help you to fill in the form.

Once your young person is 16 they no longer qualify for DLA and you will need to apply for Personal Independence Payments (PIP). These are scored on the amount of support a person needs to live independently, so the emphasis is different than for DLA where it was all about how much extra care parents needed to give. You may think – and you may be right – that it's ridiculous this happens at 16, when we generally wouldn't expect a young person to be independent, and indeed some of the questions such as ones about driving or paying bills are not even relevant to them yet. The form for PIP is long and fairly agonising, and again there are charities and groups such as Fightback who can help you to complete it.

In the US, child disability benefits are called Supplemental Security Income, and they are payable to those under 18 who qualify under some fairly strict medical and financial criteria. The benefits are means-tested on the family's income, so are only available to low-income families, and the child must be 'severely limited in activities by their condition', as well as having the condition for at least 12 months (apologies for the medicalised language – this is Social Security language, not mine!). This means that unlike in the UK, it's not an automatic benefit at a certain level of support need.

I know that around the world there may be other child disability benefits you may be entitled to, so I would urge you to see if you qualify. For our family, I was unable to work for quite a long time, and if I had been employed full time I would certainly have lost my job. Luckily, I had a very understanding boss for a part-time flexible role, and I ran my own businesses. I had some very understanding co-directors who held the fort for me, and some lovely friends and family who helped us financially, but our finances took quite a hit, and along with private assessments, etc., we actually had to remortgage the house to stay afloat. Not everybody has that option, so it's even more important to understand your benefit rights.

CHILD MENTAL HEALTH SERVICES

I hope that you won't need to experience Mental Health Services for your young person, and that in ten years' time this will be a rarity. You may have picked up in this book so far that we didn't have a great experience with Child and Adolescent Mental Health Services (CAMHS) in the UK. CAMHS is under-resourced and has been severely underfunded by government for years, and that affects staff morale too. I know that there are good people within CAMHS, trying to make change and disheartened by the system, the huge waiting lists, and the lack of resources. None of this is criticism of individuals, who are doing their best in a broken system.

In the UK, we have CAMHS as the child element of national mental health services. CAMHS are the go-to service up to the age of 17 or 18 (depending on area), when there is a handover to adult mental health services. Sometimes, this handover is less than ideal and basically means that the young person is put on a waiting list all over again. There is a long waiting list for CAMHS mental health services, which is not to be confused with CAMHS neurodevelopmental services who carry out autism and ADHD assessments, although there is also a very long waiting list for these services. How long you wait will depend on your area because each CAMHS service is commissioned by your local Clinical Commissioning Group or, as they are changing to as I write this book, Integrated Care System. The commissioning will be different in each area, for example some areas will prioritise young people under CAMHS for mental health within their neurodevelopmental waiting lists, and some won't.

CAMHS will triage each new mental health service request that comes in according to severity of need. It has tiers of service, of which the highest is tier 4, admission to an inpatient mental health unit. What qualifies for the lowest tier has to change according to demand, so that some families whose child is presenting with 'just' anxiety may be on the waiting list for many months because CAMHS are too busy supporting children and young people who are attempting or thinking about suicide. It's an awful situation, and particularly with the increasing numbers presenting with mental health challenges, it needs financial governmental input. But the main issue we had with CAMHS was staff lack of knowledge around autism, and the pretty much constant refrain that anxiety and depression are 'just part of autism'. While autistic people, and particularly demand-avoidant ones, may be more anxious than the average person, they are not depressed to the point of needing medication to avoid suicide. And even anxiety is not part of the diagnostic criteria of autism.

Within Autistic Girls Network, we have found that it's a national problem that CAMHS are declining to provide treatment to some autistic people if they are depressed, or have an eating disorder, or have gender dysphoria. Whether this is related to commissioning issues or not, it's something which needs to be addressed. So if you are a parent seeking support for your young person, this section is not meant to depress you, but to invigorate you in your fight – if CAMHS says any of those things to you, tell them that it's against NICE guidelines and the diagnostic criteria does not include any of those points mentioned.

In the US, there is no national service like CAMHS co-ordinating Children's Mental Health services, so what happens in each state is going to be different according to state law and insurance coverage.

What I can say is, the more you and those around you learn about neurodivergence (since it's quite likely that your young person isn't 'only' autistic) and adapt your parenting and your young person's environment, the more likely you will be able to support them to improve their mental health.

TRAUMA

Within the health sector, there is a movement towards trauma-informed care. But what many people don't seem to be clear about is how autistic people experience and react to trauma, or what actually constitutes trauma for them. We tend to think of trauma as 'big' one-off events – being in a car accident, rape, being attacked, being bullied – but actually, continually being invalidated in a system that makes you an outsider can also be traumatic. I remain convinced that it's very possible for an autistic pupil to suffer PTSD from being in an unsupportive mainstream school, or one that hasn't recognised their neurodivergence. So when professionals start throwing around the words 'trauma-informed' I start to wonder how informed THEY actually are.

There is the additional complication that autistic people – and girls and women particularly – can be more vulnerable to manipulation and abuse. Sadly, autistic young people are more vulnerable to being bullied, with some research showing up to 94% of autistic young people have been bullied.[1] (This is why at Autistic Girls Network we advocate whole school training – peers who accept difference are much less likely to bully you over it.) They are also more likely to suffer some degree of sexual abuse. And they are also more likely to suffer 'mate crime', which is to be seriously taken advantage of by someone you thought was a friend,[2] because they rightly expect to be told the truth and not gaslit.

In the US, ABA is the chosen therapy by many insurance providers, and there are plenty of autistic adults who consider their experiences within ABA to be traumatic. In the UK, behaviourism seems to be the current flavour in favour at the Department for Education, and behaviourist attitudes which don't take into account neurodivergent traits are traumatic for neurodivergent pupils. Isolation units and the use of restraints can be hugely traumatic. Autistic people can also be disbelieved a lot regarding particularly sensory issues. 'Oh that light's not so bright, you're overreacting.' Not believing what an autistic person says about their own feelings and senses is teaching them not to

1   Maïano, C., Normand, C. L., Salvas, M.-C., Moullec, G., and Aimé, A. (2016) 'Prevalence of school bullying among youth with autism spectrum disorders: A systematic review and meta-analysis'. *Autism Research, 9*(6), 601–615. https://doi.org/10.1002/aur.1568
2   Gray-Hammond, D. and Adkin, T. (2021) 'Creating autistic suffering: In the beginning there was trauma'. *Emergent Divergence*, 29 September. Accessed on 2 May 2022 at https://emergentdivergence.com/2021/09/29/creating-autistic-suffering-in-the-beginning-there-was-trauma

trust their own bodies, and that causes more vulnerability. For sensory, emotional, and behavioural reasons, school is a traumatic place for our young people.

It is the combination of systemic failure and trauma which causes suffering for autistic young (and older) adults. In this sense, an untraumatised autistic adult is rare indeed. Even what is looked for in the diagnostic criteria of autism (upset stimming, repetitive behaviour) is for many autistic people the behaviour of a traumatised autistic person. Changing this cycle of trauma by educating and changing environments will transform the wellbeing of our current autistic young people when they are adults.

LIFE SKILLS

It won't be any surprise to read that individual need is going to be greatly relevant to this section. Some of your young people will already be able to cook a three-course meal. Others need prompting (can also turn into nagging of course) to take a shower. If they are going to eventually live independently what they will all need some direction on, in common with all their peers, is what used to be called running a household – paying bills, organising repairs, cooking and cleaning and ironing, and general admin stuff like insurance. I also think that budgeting and finance is a really important topic for ALL teenagers, especially given how easy it can be to be given a large spending limit on a credit card. If they go to university this can be a good middle ground, where they have to pay a couple of bills and feed and clean up after themselves but don't have full responsibility of a house or flat/apartment. Some young people won't be ready for this of course, and some may always need your input even if they are living independently. Others will need some kind of assisted living arrangement – what matters is that they are comfortable and happy with the amount of independence that they have.

Now you may have read that last paragraph and thought 'Oh my child can do all of that already', or you may have thought 'I can't imagine my child ever doing that!' That's how different our young people might be from each other, but have faith in them. They'll get there, but it's not too early to start showing them how to do stuff if they're willing to be shown. It's likely to be the organisational part which might be difficult, so strategies and/or apps to help with keeping track of what needs to be done (such as renewal dates of insurance, etc.) will be helpful.

- Tiimo is a good app for this (and includes family sharing if needed) but any kind of calendar/tracker will do as long as you can input recurring tasks.
- Resources such as Money Saving Expert's Teen Cash Class are good for teaching basic savvy finance (UK resource but applicable in any currency).[3]
- Goodbudget is a budget planner app which can be shared across phones and helps to create a budget but also a visual representation of your spending.
- The bizarrely named Decisive Wife is a meal planner app which will help you decide what to eat if you don't like making decisions.

Useful skills to teach (using whatever methods work for your young person):

- Laundry – what goes together, what to use in the machine, which clothes can't go in the machine.
- Food storage – sensible guidelines on how to store and cook fresh food and how much attention to pay to 'best before' dates.
- Job interview skills and whether to disclose that you're autistic – if so, reasonable adjustments you can ask for in an interview.
- Staying on top of bills, insurance, credit cards, and other household admin.

---

3   www.moneysavingexpert.com/family/teen-cash-class

- Reading a bank statement and keeping an eye on outgoings and incomings.
- Understanding and maintaining a credit score.
- Basic tax management (and compliance!).
- Getting medical treatment in an emergency.
- Basic plumbing – how to turn off the water supply in a house and unblock a sink or toilet.
- Basic electrical safety and when to call an electrician.
- What to do if you smell gas.
- How to meal plan (if their eating habits allow for this).
- How to ask for repeat prescriptions and fulfil them.
- Basic first aid.
- How to recognise fraud, spam, and phishing emails.
- How to register to vote.
- How to keep track of important dates (such as your birthday!).
- How to be clear about and respect consent.
- Basic car maintenance.

SOCIAL CARE

If your young person may struggle with some of those life skills, it's a good idea to investigate Social Care involvement. Anyone who has a need is entitled to a social care assessment in the UK. (In the US this will depend on insurance coverage or qualification for Medicare.) The assessment will determine what kind of support you need, and should consider the person's strengths and ambitions as well as needs. Obviously, the person doing the assessment ought to be well trained about all forms of neurodivergence but often this is not the case and some advocacy or education is needed. It's worth remembering that the assessor can only take into consideration the needs which are covered during the assessment so it's worth planning what needs to be said. Worth remembering also is that the assessor needs to consider not only your needs but also your hopes and wishes. Theoretically, your council, if asked, will provide you with the questions that are going to be asked in advance.

The assessor will look at the person's 'care outcomes' which are their ability to do things such as:

- Prepare and eat adequate food and drink without help.
- Wash themselves and their clothes.
- Use a toilet and manage all their toilet needs.
- Dress themselves appropriately for the weather.
- Move around their home safely.
- Keep their home safe and habitable.
- Have enough contact with other people.
- Take part in activities, like volunteering, training, or learning.
- Use services like public transport and shops.
- Caring for their child or a child they are responsible for.

The kinds of things Social Care can support with are:

- support groups
- an outreach worker or targeted support worker
- respite centres
- day centres
- therapists
- supported employment.

I wouldn't like to imply that it's easy to get these services – often it's not. But they do exist. If you think that your young person may need them as they get older and more independent, it's worth getting in touch. It may be a long battle.

HOW TO BE A GOOD ALLY TO AUTISTIC PEOPLE

I run Autistic Girls Network with the ethos that change needs all of us working together to make a difference – autistic people, non-autistic people, professional, and not. Systemic and attitudinal change can't be imposed on people, so we need to bring awareness and understanding, and gradually that's what has been happening. Look back ten years ago – people are much more aware now, even if there is still a long way to go.

How you can be a good ally to autistic people:

- Advocate for your young person where needed, but don't talk over them. Make sure you're advocating for their views, not yours.
- Listen to autistic adults.
- Use identity first language (autistic person, not person with autism) unless an autistic person has a preference for another form.
- Don't use functioning labels like high or low functioning or 'levels' of autism.
- Take every opportunity to spread awareness that there are different ways of experiencing the world.
- Be positive about autism, while also advocating for support. Spiky profiles mean it's very possible to be successful in life AND need support.
- Support neurodivergent-led charities and research. Likewise, don't donate to charities like Autism Speaks, or take part in research which is damaging to the autistic community such as research using ABA.
- Support social and interest groups for autistic and neuro-divergent people. Your young person would benefit from joining one.
- Read articles by non-speaking autistic people – there's a great collection listed on NeuroClastic.[4]

---

4   https://neuroclastic.com/category/culture-identity/nonspeaker

Appendices

BOOKS, APPS, YOUTUBERS, AND #ACTUALLYAUTISTIC BLOGGERS
Books with Autistic Characters

A Kind of Spark by Elle McNicoll

Blue Bottle Mystery by Kathy Hoopmann

Can You See Me? by Libby Scott and Rebecca Westcott

Counting By 7s by Holly Goldberg Sloan

Geek Girl series by Holly Smale

M is for Autism by the Students of Limpsfield Grange School

Mockingbird by Kathryn Erskine

Notes on My Family by Emily Critchley

Rules by Cynthia Lord

The Boy Who Made the World Disappear by Ben Miller

The Curious Incident of the Dog in the Nighttime by Mark Haddon

The Infinite by Patience Agbabi

The Secret Life of Rose by Rose Smitten

The Someday Birds by Sally J. Pla

The State of Grace by Rachael Lucas

The Underdogs series by Chris Bonnello

Books to Help Understand Autism

Diary of a Young Naturalist by Dara McAnulty
How to Be Autistic by Charlotte Amelia Poe
Neurotribes by Steve Silberman
Odd Girl Out by Laura James
The Autism-Friendly Guide to Periods by Robyn Steward
The Awesome Autistic Go-To Guide: A Practical Handbook for Teens & Tweens by Yenn Purkis and Tanya Masterman
The Girl with the Curly Hair by Alis Rowe
The Reason I Jump by Naoki Higashida
The Spectrum Girl's Survival Guide by Siena Castellon

There are many more books in many more categories listed on the Autistic Girls Network website here: www.autisticgirlsnetwork.org/resources

Apps

Booster Buddies
Calm Harm app
ClearFear
Daylio Calm app
FearTools app
Glenn Howard relaxation
Headspace app
Kooth Online app
MeeTwo
MindShift app
PanicShield
Rain Rain app
SAMapp
The Mood Gym
Wellmind app
Worrytime app

YouTubers

Agony Autie

AspieComic (Michael McCreary)

B Blushes

Chloe Me Just Me

How to ADHD

Indie Andy

Invisible I

Jaime A Heidel the Articulate Autistic

Just A Skinny Boy

Neurowonderful – Amythest Schaber

Princess Aspien

Purple Ella

School of Life

Autistic Bloggers

Actually Aspling
https://actuallyaspling.wordpress.com

Ann's Autism Blog
http://annsautism.blogspot.com

Aphantastic Writer
https://aphantasticwritercom.wordpress.com

Authentically Emily
www.authenticallyemily.uk

Autistic Not Weird
https://autisticnotweird.com

Autistic Science Person
https://autisticscienceperson.com

Autistic Self Advocacy Network
https://autisticadvocacy.org

Autistic with a Chance of Weather
www.facebook.com/AutisticWxVlog

Autistic Women & Nonbinary Network (AWN)
> https://awnnetwork.org

@autisticgpshh
> https://secretlyautisticgp.wordpress.com

Autistictic
> https://autistictic.com

Embrace Autism
> https://embrace-autism.com

Emergent Divergence
> https://emergentdivergence.com

Jaime Heidel – The Articulate Autistic
> www.thearticulateautistic.com

Mind the Flap
> https://mindtheflap.wordpress.com

Neurodivergent Rebel
> https://neurodivergentrebel.com

NeuroClastic
> https://neuroclastic.com

Neuroqueer
> https://neuroqueer.com/neuroqueer-an-introduction

Rosie Weldon
> https://rosieweldon.com

Sally Cat PDA by PDAers
> www.sallycatpda.co.uk

Sarah Boon
> https://autisticallysarah.com

Spectrum Women
> www.spectrumwomen.com

Steve Asbell
> www.steveasbell.com

The Aspie World
> www.theaspieworld.com

The Autistic Advocate
> https://theautisticadvocate.com

The Autistic Panda
  https://theautisticpanda.wordpress.com
The Autistic Psych Student
  https://theautisticpsychstudent.wordpress.com
The Participatory Autism Research Collective
  https://participatoryautismresearch.wordpress.com
Thinking Person's Guide to Autism (TPGA)
  www.thinkingautismguide.com

PRODUCT RECOMMENDATIONS

Deodorant – roll ons might feel slimy, and spray deodorants might potentially hurt, but either stick deodorants (Mitchum and Dove both get the thumbs up in the Autistic Girls Network group) or a crystal/Himalayan Salt Rock deodorant seems to be acceptable for a wide selection of autistic girls and women in the group. And it has the advantage of being much more environmentally friendly for your social warriors.

Noise-related products include:

- ear defenders
- Flare Audio – Calmer ear plugs
- white noise machine
- noise cancelling headphones (with Bluetooth).

Fidget toys include:

- fidget spinner
- pop it mats
- Rubik's cube
- spinner ring
- chewellery
- tangle toys.

Products for sensory needs include:

- seamless socks and tights
- compression sheets
- bed tent or pod
- room spray
- sensory toolbox
- sensory first aid kit
- aromatherapy roll ons
- flavourless toothpaste
- weighted blanket
- long cuddle toy
- galaxy light
- bubble tube lamp with fish.

Products for vestibular movement include:

- wobble chair
- hammock or swing
- trampoline.

Index